Szenasy,
Design Advocate

D0109711

Szenasy, Design Advocate

Writings and Talks by Metropolis Magazine Editor Susan S. Szenasy

Edited by Ann S. Hudner
and Akiko Busch
Contributing Editor, Angela Riechers

Metropolis Books

Contents

Perspectives

**"My father taught me to fly.
He taught me to fly
intellectually and emotionally."
Susan S. Szenasy**

Acknowledgments,
Ann S. Hudner and Akiko Busch

As we explored the writings of Susan S. Szenasy, we began to recognize the enormous network of individuals, organizations, and institutions that have influenced her throughout her career. First and foremost is Horace Havemeyer III, the founder and publisher of *Metropolis* magazine, who has given Susan a unique platform from which to challenge and advocate for ethics within architecture and design. His presence and partnership with her for nearly three decades have produced an invaluable and indelible contribution to the archives of contemporary design history. None of this could have been possible without the support of and collaborations with the *Metropolis* staff, writers, and other colleagues both past and present. The magazine's unique approach and steadfast commitment to exploring all areas of design have played a pivotal role in the development of Susan's voice as a design advocate.

It is also important to recognize the many professional organizations, schools, and manufacturers that, over the years, have given Susan opportunities to participate in conferences, class critiques, and industry panel discussions.

Special thanks to Paula Scher, partner at Pentagram, and designer Jeff Close for their capacity to visualize the diversity of voices and ideas gathered here. Diana Murphy, co-publisher of Metropolis Books, has provided expert care and guidance in bringing this project to fruition. Angela Riechers's keen interviewing skills have elicited the perspectives presented here alongside Susan's writings and talks. We are most appreciative to editor Anne Thompson for her sharp eye, and to Oliver Printing and Cascades Fine Papers Group for working with us to print this book sustainably. We are immensely thankful as well to the architects, designers, educators, and other industry professionals who have lent their voices to this collection. Most important, our deepest gratitude goes to Susan for her willingness to participate in this project, allowing us to explore her writings and present a retrospective of her opinions and perspectives from the past four decades.

Preface, Ann S. Hudner

When I first met Susan, in 1995, I had just been hired by Rhode Island School of Design to increase the college's visibility within the national media. I called Susan to request a meeting, and, to my surprise, she said yes. This was my first venture into New York to meet with journalists in architecture and design. I was both excited and nervous, not knowing what to expect. I came prepared, carrying a portfolio of press releases representing various story ideas and projects for her consideration.

As I entered Susan's office, the first thing I noticed were the floor-to-ceiling stacks of books, folders, magazines. She invited me to sit, and, as I did, I noticed a very large cardboard box next to her desk, filled with sheets of paper. I asked, "What's in the box?" To which she replied with a deadpan expression, "Press releases." I honestly can't remember anything else that was discussed beyond that point. What I do know is that I never again pitched a story to Susan. What developed instead was an ongoing dialogue that continues to this day.

The subject of voice—how one develops a perspective, a professional character, and an ethical position across a broad range of topics to enter a collective conversation—has intrigued me since that initial meeting with Susan. I have come to deeply respect her ability to engage complex contemporary issues. Through a voice that blends confidence and humility, she demonstrates clarity of purpose, consistency, relevancy, and a knowledge base fed from an endless curiosity and openness to new ideas.

Her ongoing commitment to informed dialogue has influenced thousands of design professionals, architects, journalists, retailers, manufacturers, legislators, educators, and students. Our intention here is to present Susan's voice, exploring her writings in the pages of *Metropolis* magazine and beyond, and to offer perspectives from people with whom she has engaged over the last 35 years. This selection of writings comes from a range of sources. From editorials published in *Metropolis*—which reveal honest, thought-provoking, and, at times, challenging opinions— to excerpts from early articles, to public presentations such as lectures and commencement speeches, the scope of this compilation documents the evolution of Susan's voice.

As we gathered these various components, a wonderful rhythm began to emerge, revealing the organic development of a social activist. Key world events—for example, the passage of the Americans with Disabilities Act and the 9/11 terrorist attack in New York City—as well as significant moments in architecture and design—such as the demolition of Paul Rudolph's Riverview High School in Sarasota, Florida, and in Susan's own career, including her development of a design-ethics course at Parsons The New School for Design—clearly ignited her advocacy.

To refer to Susan as a critical thinker is to present just one part of the equation. Her ability to anchor her inquisitive nature and her reflective reasoning in a foundational belief in human and civil rights established her as a pioneer in the advocacy of sustainable design. Though her subject range is expansive, her message has been consistent—and often years ahead of the conversation. The first appearance of her critical voice, in 1978, was an editorial on increasing consumerism. And over the years, that voice has continued to address emerging social and cultural issues in terms of design, from social equity to the environment.

Susan's position as editor in chief of *Metropolis*, a highly regarded and influential design magazine, for the past 29 years has given her a platform from which to articulate and expand her viewpoints. Her tireless capacity to travel and to explore new ideas and innovative topics has provided countless opportunities for her to have a deep immersion in the architecture and design dialogue.

To understand the breadth of Susan's impact, we have spoken with a number of individuals whose lives have intersected with Susan's. Some have contributed to Susan's understanding of architecture and design and its social, cultural, environmental, and economic implications. Others have been directly influenced by Susan's advocacy and receptivity to an informed, diverse, and inclusive perspective—and have been challenged by her example. Their perspectives are included in this book as well.

This retrospective of Susan's writings from the past 35 years, and the changing dialogues in design and culture that these pieces represent, has countless entry points. Most exciting to me is the knowledge that Susan's advocacy, and the larger conversation of which it is a part, will both continue.

Foreword, John Hockenberry

One of the first pieces I wrote for *Metropolis* magazine was about the redesign of my kitchen in Massachusetts. My wife and I had a great architect, Jane Langmuir, and I said that I would do one of these typical makeover stories. But it would be angled as a universal-design project, because it was about designing a kitchen for two active adults, one in a wheelchair and one not, who collaborate very closely in the preparation of meals for, at that time, four kids.

Excerpt, interview with Angela Riechers, 2013

That was the beginning of my writing on universal design from a design perspective as opposed to my more disability-activist perspective. That perspective predated *Metropolis* magazine, going back to disability activism from the seventies and eighties and the frustrations of living in America. Then in 1990, the Americans with Disabilities Act got passed, and there was this huge pushback during the Clinton era from those who saw some kind of leftist plot to bankrupt small business. So I would give speeches in support of the ADA, but it was really *Metropolis* that established the idea that universal design can be a discipline—an orientation to, in a sense, life itself. You basically look at a space and consider its usability. You suspend any sense you may have of the rules of the road and imagine in the widest possible way how that space could and might be used. And you make sure that your design doesn't erect obstacles for one group of people at the expense of another.

Architects really understand better now that people can sense it when a building has been constructed with this holistic orientation. The irony is that really traditional architects spend an enormous amount of time fitting their concept to the specs required by disability codes, which involve all kinds of entrances and clever little ramps put over here or hidden little items over here. And what that ends up doing is hiding from people the sense that a building has any holistic orientation whatsoever. Whereas when someone designs with this holistic perspective from the beginning, people get it when they walk in. They feel viscerally that the space is usable by everyone, and this feels modern to them. People intuitively understand these inherent democracies and the value this approach conveys. And I think there is an increasing number of buildings that achieve this.

So I think of Susan as a kind of angelic presence in the cathedral of *Metropolis* magazine, which I see as an intersection of the design world and the architecture world. And in a time when magazines are either irrelevant or bankrupt, *Metropolis* continues to be this intersection. And that's very much a function of Susan's vision. She is the first person to frown at something that's just pretty. You're in the room, and somebody unveils something that's glass and gorgeous and high tech, and the entire room will gasp and applaud, and Susan will be going, "Oh, give me a break."

I mean, she just has this, "We've seen this little circus act before. What have you got? I mean, what do you really have? What do you want to achieve?" If what you want to achieve is to get a bunch of, typically, white males standing in a room after having had a nice banquet of some sort, and some wine, that's a low bar. But if you want to do something that's going to say, in a sustained way, that this building has thought about its existence—not only in the moment that it opened but 50 years from now—then you're in a zone that Susan finds interesting. Her dismissal, at times, of the glitz and glamour of architecture is just a very simple case of her not seeing anything meaningful. It's as though she thinks, "If you're going to do something like this, it's got to address the planet, everybody who would use it, and the idea that it's a sustainable structure, and not something that's going to dazzle us for a few years and then go away. Why would you do that?"

Now, everyone has embraced these principles of universal design and the various other sorts of ideologies that are forming around design. As someone who cried early about things that we now know are an obvious core set of values for design in architecture, Susan, I think, shows some restraint in resisting the urge to say, "I told you so." Instead, she's channeling her efforts toward making the debate or the discussion around sustainability and green and universal design more constructive, and challenging people to take it further. To me, that approach, in many ways, is the definition of a morally driven, sustainable movement.

Once I was in L.A. at a conference at the Art Center College of Design. It was in this outlandish airplane wind-tunnel building that was built by a defense contractor. So in this architectural monstrosity, we would have a discussion about design and architecture. Susan was presenting that year, and I was to introduce her. I was behind on a deadline for *Metropolis,* and I realized sort of belatedly that, oh, my God, she's presenting and she knows I'm so late on this article.

In my introduction, I decided to get a little personal and talked for a while about *Metropolis* as this intersection of things and ideas. You know, there are those New York magazine types who joke about *Metropolis* as though each issue is its last, that it's got to be going out of business tomorrow, without any visible means of support from the glitzy media world. So I was relating some of those kinds of stories.

I got to the end of the whole thing and said, "I have to say, among the things I'm most proud of is that I regularly write for *Metropolis.*" And because I was feeling so guilty about this article, there was something about the sort of emotional cadence in that last line that caused me to almost choke up a little bit. I clearly conveyed that I was proud, and it was all fine—it was just pretty powerful on stage. People were clapping, and Susan comes on stage and says, "Thank you, John. And we'll be looking for that article that you owe us. And you'll send that right along won't you?" She has this utterly benign face of delight, kind of like Julia Child, and so I smiled and that was that. And I think I had the piece to them before I left Los Angeles. I did it that night in my room.

Susan Szenasy: A Life in Design,
Akiko Busch

When Susan Szenasy taught The Ethics of Design, a senior seminar at Parsons The New School for Design, she framed the course around five iconic figures: William Morris, an advocate for the importance of craft and the human touch in an industrialized world; Henry Dreyfuss, whose shaping of American products proved that function and beauty could coalesce in everything from telephones to tractors; and Charles and Ray Eames, whose mission involved delivering, in their words, "the most of the best to the greatest number of people for the least." As to the fifth, students were asked to choose a current design practitioner and the concerns shaping his or her decisions, whether about the global market-place, sustainability, or barrier-free design.

A similar convergence of principled perspectives that leaves room for independent conjecture has characterized Susan's 45-year career. As a writer, editor, teacher, moderator, and, since 1986, editor in chief of *Metropolis* magazine, she has gathered established and emergent voices in contemporary architecture and design. In the pages of the magazine, as well as in classrooms, lecture halls, conferences, films, and symposia, she has expressed a commitment to the confluence of advocacy and ethics. Above all, she has made the case for obligation, responsibility, and standards of conduct in the practice of design.

Susan's view of design as a humanistic endeavor has deep roots. She grew up with her parents and sister in postwar Hungary in Spöte, a small village near the Austrian border. The state had confiscated all private property, including her grandmother's farm, and bombs had cratered the landscape. "By 1944, when I was born, everything was lost. Whatever material good was left at all was hidden underground. My grandmother would dig holes and put clothing and jewelry in them, and whatever else she thought was of value."

But if the countryside had been reduced to rubble, the community of family and neighbors was less impoverished. "I remember the taste of the cherries ripe off the trees," she recalls, "the taste of the eggs that you had just picked from the nest, those wonderful hearty soups with great bread baked by the peasant woman next door, and the taste of the chicken I had helped my mother kill. The realities of life and death were so closely intertwined." In the evenings, the family read aloud—Hungarian translations of classics such as *David Copperfield* and *Uncle Tom's Cabin*. "My mother had this amazingly beautiful voice, and she would read to us every night. There were these collective libraries around the village as well, where everybody gave books to each other, so everybody could read. So I was struck by this, fascinated to hear how things happened, how people behaved, and how you can understand the world through a story."

Books were not the only place in which the human imagination flourished, and stories were not limited to the printed page. Consider an item of clothing she wore at that time. "American soldiers were diving into the airfield outside my grandmother's inn, and their parachutes would get left there. So the villagers would pick them up in the field. And I still remember the kind of beautiful, nubby silk they were made of then, and then we dyed it, red or orange, and it had puffy sleeves and little ruffles around the neck, and my sister and I wore these little parachute dresses. But they explained what it was to us. They explained what a parachute was. We always got the full story."

Because her father had been unwilling to join the Communist Party, he had been relieved of his profession as a pilot and took a job as an office worker at an airplane factory. But when his name appeared—erroneously—in the local newspaper on a list of instigators of the 1956 revolution, it was time for the family to leave. "When that became a matter of public record, you knew what was going to be the next thing: they would find him and put him on trial, or they would kill him," Susan remembers. The decision was made to leave that night. "I like to say it was *The Sound of Music* without the music."

With only a change of underwear and toothbrushes packed in her father's briefcase, the family took cover under a tarp in the back of a neighbor's truck as he drove them to the Austrian border. Through the help of a Presbyterian minister, the family found its way to the United States via Austria, Germany, and a series of U.S. military bases. "My father respected American industrial production and technology and what America had created through these after the war," Susan says. "So along with the idea of a free society and nobody dictating to you what to believe in—all of that made the decision for my father, for us to come to the U.S."

Where, she says, they were a poster family for political refugees. "We were extremely lucky, because we were nice looking—a tall, good-looking adult man and a little, blue-eyed, blonde woman, and two adorable daughters. We were healthy. Everything was going our way. But if there had been some blemish—TB or whatever else—this would have held us back. We were the choice family." The Szenasys were sponsored by the First Presbyterian Church in New Brunswick, New Jersey. Because of his limited English, her father worked as a janitor ("I would clean toilets if I could live in America," he had told his family in earlier days) before establishing a successful roofing and renovation business. Her mother worked in a clothing factory.

New Brunswick in the late fifties was a gracious town with spacious streets, two-family houses with wide front porches, and a bustling downtown. With a park, school, library, and grocery store all within walking distance, the Szenasys' neighborhood was a blueprint for accommodation and human scale in urban design—and a lasting design lesson. If the refugee experience confers upon its constituents a broad perspective on ideas of home, community, and inclusiveness, it would not be a stretch to suggest that the passage from Spöte instilled in Susan a deep understanding of what enables human beings to derive their sense of belonging.

After high school, Susan attended Rutgers University, receiving a master's in modern European history. But it was the study of architecture and artifacts that especially engaged her and eventually drew her to a job at *Interiors* in 1968. "It was one of these magical places for me," she says. "Olga Gueft, the magazine's editor, was herself a Russian immigrant and viewed design as an economic construct. When she talked about the business of design, she understood the history of design and she understood the technology. She taught me that design became important because of the larger cultural context, which included the social involvement, the ecological involvement, and the technical involvement."

Certainly, Susan was attentive to that sense of context when, in 1978, she became editor of *Residential Interiors,* the sibling publication of *Interiors.* As an 11-year-old refugee, she had kept a journal, a verbal and visual document of her family's passage from Hungary to New Jersey. "Because they knew that I was drawing, somebody in the displaced persons' camp had given me an orange covered notebook and a box of colored pencils. So I would always write down what I saw, whether it was the mountains in Salzburg, the apple I ate, a storefront, the first really good pair of shoes I owned, or whatever it was. That little book did more than anything else to bring it all together. But I had not thought then that was what my life would be about."

That small, illustrated notebook was an early tutorial in the power of human narrative and how information can be coalesced via words and images into a rich, revealing document. Now, 20 years later, she was able to apply that lesson more broadly. Editorial content at a magazine approached design as something more than an aesthetic practice. And it did not address home furnishings simply as product. Rather, objects, such as a Chinese peasant stove, were considered for their history and their richness of craft and tradition. And feature stories might examine how the shadowy vaulted ceiling of a Tunisian palace created a sense of a sanctuary, or how architect Luis Barragán used color as a structural device.

Susan viewed the pages of *Residential Interiors* as "having room to play, to think, to reach out, to bring in something that might be unusual and interesting and memorable." Her educational training as a historian drove her to examine design through the lens of the past, whether it be Frank Lloyd Wright interiors or French Rococo furnishings. No less important were emerging innovations in lighting, materials, and sourcing energy. "Through my dad," she recalls, "I was always interested in new technologies. We were a family that watched every space launch. We would watch every shot to the moon. I started growing up here when the American space program began, and it was incredibly optimistic."

"I always thought that a magazine was like a really smart friend," she later observed. "It's not a smartness meant to intimidate you, but to inform, entertain, educate, to create a dialogue, a conversation that has many parts." And part of that conversation, increasingly, was Susan's emerging critical voice. A 1978 editorial questioned emerging trends of consumer excess as reflected in the extravagant scale of home furnishings. "Is this a game of intimidation?" she asked of huge beds wired for stereo, plush pit arrangements, and gigantic finials.

Susan's voice was also often braided with a personalized storyline. She structured her book *The Home* (1985) as a chronicle through domestic space, considering "how you arrive at a certain place, what it felt like to go through the house, room by room, exploring the particulars of each entrance, each hallway, what the doorways announce and how it focuses you into a room." A gold painting above a set of cement steps draws a visitor up the stairway, a hallway lined with books slows the passage through a house, the scent of honeysuckle drifts in through a window. "It is through movement that we get to know the world around us," she wrote.

With the incipient voice of a combined storyteller, critic, and advocate, Susan began to receive invitations for speaking engagements. "I was the child who grew up not speaking English," she recalls. "The most dreadful thing for me was to be in front of the class of perfect English speakers, and even years later, I was petrified of public speaking. But I began to understand how to do this: In order to be heard, you have to be able to say something. And you have to research it and be prepared. And then it started happening for me."

In 1985, Susan was approached by Horace Havemeyer III, the publisher of *Metropolis* magazine, which he had launched in 1981 with editor Sharon Lee Ryder, in part to answer the question: why do buildings and objects look the way they do? From the start, the magazine had set out to explore the designed world, from plates to parks, from cars to cities, and to articulate its discoveries in language that was direct, accessible, informed, and largely free of professional argot. As critical as the point of view of the architect or designer was that of the user. The magazine's oversized tabloid format allowed for a rich and dynamic visual layout of text, photographs, and graphics.

The premise of the magazine was that design is a two-way mirror that reflects and influences culture, and when Susan was offered the editorship, she didn't hesitate. "*Metropolis* was always an incredible idea to me," she explains. "[It was a place where] you could focus on the most complex human endeavor on earth and then drill down into each small detail. It offered the freedom to really explore design, culture, talent, people, creativity, materials, policy, everything."

In trying to articulate the voice of the magazine, she says, "It is smart. It is jargon free, it can be read by anyone. It has a really strong narrative; it is strong journalistically. It can have opinions in the right place, but the opinions have to be supported. It has a little bit of edge. And it has copy that you want to read, that captures you." All of which added up to an inclusiveness and the conviction that a single voice can be enriched by others. To celebrate its fifth anniversary, in 1986, *Metropolis* produced an issue that bypassed "those who build the city, an architecture and design magazine's natural readers, and went directly to those who either benefit or suffer from the built environment." Among the rich dialogue of urban voices: columnist Anna Quindlan, writer Sydney Zion, New York City parks commissioner Henry Stern, actor Peter Boynton, cosmetics czar Estee Lauder, and restaurateur George Lang.

Subsequent themes came to include the changing terrain of the American office, the maturing suburbs, Times Square, ladies' rooms, landfills and garbage, multiculturalism, healthcare, and the global marketplace. In the nineties, *Metropolis* took on universal design, greenmarkets, security systems, the urban waterfront, nature and medicine, and Ben Katchor's comics. Among the writers for the magazine were Paul Goldberger, Peter Hall, John Hockenberry, Karrie Jacobs, James Kunstler, Hugo Lindgren, Tom Vanderbilt, and Véronique Vienne—all voices that would resonate, if they did not already, across the landscape of American culture and letters.

And while *Metropolis* had been launched as an urban, New York–centric publication, it now extended its view to a broader geography and readership. "I found I was reading a lot of Italian magazines, as well as a lot about German design," Susan recalls. "I mean, the first green or sustainable buildings in the U.S. were horrible, Rube Goldberg designs. But the Germans had figured out how to make laws so that everybody [in offices] had daylight, for example, so design had to follow that. And we also found that German toasters and refrigerators were made for disassembly, because they didn't want them in their garbage dumps."

While acknowledging that design had become an enterprise best viewed globally, Susan remained committed to learning how innovative practices could flourish, especially in terms of the American franchise—how American democratic thinking was a natural foundation for the possibility of design as an agent for social change. Equipped with that alliance of pragmatism and hope often so intrinsic to the immigrant experience, she was attuned especially to how architecture and design might be used to secure the American promise; and also to those ways in which the promise can be broken. Nowhere were such lessons clearer than in the implementation of the Americans with Disabilities Act (ADA), signed into legislation by President Bush in 1990.

"I felt that as an immigrant, as someone who really believes in the system, that civil rights was a uniquely American issue," she explains. "When I was growing up, civil-rights legislation was being passed. This was Johnson's Great Society, and these were incredibly optimistic ways of looking at human beings. We could be better. We could do things better. We could be more accepting of each other; we could live better together. When the ADA was passed, I was incredibly excited, because I thought this was going to be a breakthrough, like the civil-rights acts were." The magazine's 1992 special issue on the subject looked at barrier-free living through the design of housing, the office, furniture, transportation, and a host of new products, materials, and technologies.

The reality, though, was that the profession greeted the ADA as simply another series of regulatory measures written to hinder architects and designers from doing their jobs. Attending an American Institute of Architects meeting convened to address the law's application, Susan found nothing but "lawyers and second-rate architects talking about how to comply and how to circumvent." It was a lesson in how design can be murdered by compliance and in how well intentioned legislation could be transformed into a massive bureaucratic tangle that would, in the end, backfire. "I was shocked," she states. "I had grown up thinking that design and architecture were humanist activities, and believing that these people creating our environments were much more forgiving, much more interested in the human condition than I learned that night."

Susan's commitment to the principles of human conduct and social obligation met a greater challenge after September 11, 2001. In the days following the terrorist attacks in New York, she and architect Beverly Willis formed the civic group Rebuild Downtown Our Town (R.Dot), a coalition of professionals in architecture, development, law, real estate, and urban planning; its mission was to influence rebuilding in a way that might restore a sense of street life, integrate the arts community, and address the needs of residents and business owners in a sustainable and lively urban environment. Committed to the idea that civic participation was key to rebuilding an area that extended well beyond the 16-acre site of the fallen towers, R.Dot set out to listen to the voices of Lower Manhattan, including those of businesspeople, artists, residents, and community advocates.

In the end, the Lower Manhattan Development Corporation and lease-holders dismissed a proposition from R.Dot and other civic groups that aimed to restore economic vitality by nurturing a vibrant street life; their commitment was to office space rather than more diverse neighborhood interests. That said, R.Dot's alliance with other renewal agencies demon-strated that catastrophe can initiate collective action, bringing stakehold-ers together to listen, take stock, and share concerns; and that the advo-cate's voice, strengthened in meeting challenge, can acquire a greater power and resonance when it speaks in concordance with others.

Susan's unwavering commitment to informed dialogue continues to recognize the power of voice—its capacity for persuasion, information, education, inspiration, challenge, and reflection. She still guides the mag-azine as deputy publisher/editor in chief, while lecturing, conducting symposia, directing films, and managing the magazine's Web site and conferences; these days, she spends about 50 percent of her time travel-ing. "We begin to use wisdom and logic to create change," Susan stated recently, echoing a sentiment she expressed three decades earlier, when she recognized that "to be heard you have to be able to say something."

Since 1985, *Metropolis* has embraced new technologies to augment older methods, using digital and paper layouts, electronic and pencil editing, and daily tweets as well as copy that takes weeks to compose and finesse. But ask Susan what has changed the most, and her answer has to do with neither the acceleration nor the reach offered by these new modes of communication. It has to do with connectivity. "I don't give talks anymore," she says. "I cross-pollinate." It's a two-way conversation. A dialogue.

Conventional wisdom suggests that digital technology has conferred upon us design literacy. But such literacy tends to be narrowly defined, often little more than familiarity or, more likely, infatuation with the latest apps, mobile phones, or reading devices. Meanwhile, the opportunities for human-centered design—for public spaces, affordable housing, effi-cient transportation, or sensible packaging—remain vast and unrequited; as the world's population soars to over 7 billion, sustainability remains the wheelhouse for human enterprise of any manner. In a 2012 editorial, Susan referred to the invisible links that connect us with each other, with ideas, and with services, whether through smartphone technology, digital studios, open-source wikis, or social networks. "As new patterns form in transportation, education, and collaboration," she wrote, "I finally understand the game-changing meaning of the familiar but narrowly interpreted phrase 'World Wide Web' to be an intense and fruitful connection between information, places, and people."

While the conviction about such enduring and powerful connections may have its origins in a village in Hungary half a century ago—in an analog world where the exchange of bread and books sustained a war-torn community and where the human imagination flourished—its relevance and value in today's digital world is undiminished.

Ethical Design Education: Confessions of a Sixties Idealist, Susan S. Szenasy

"Sustainability is not my issue," protests a senior at Parsons The New School for Design. She's presenting her term paper on a designer and maker of lamps. Two others in the class, also product-design majors, are appalled by this statement; so am I. We've just spent a semester returning, again and again, to discussions of our degrading natural environment and the need for everyone to figure out how to use this knowledge to design more sensitively.

Essay from Steven Heller and Véronique Vienne, eds., *Citizen Designer: Perspectives on Design Responsibility,* 2003

It is 2002, and we're a group of 28 fledgling professionals, pursuing courses of study in architecture; interior, product, and graphic design; fashion; and photography. I'm number 29, their teacher and a design-magazine editor. Having observed every kind of designer at work for several decades, I know that the creative professions make a huge difference in the ways we live. I see designers as active participants in the decisions businesses make about the land they occupy and the resources they use, the technologies they rely on, and the ideas they communicate.

Every Tuesday afternoon, we gather in a windowless room in a hulking New School building on New York's Fifth Avenue—the kind of soulless, mechanically aired space we've all grown to tolerate—for a course titled The Ethics of Design. I have been teaching this senior seminar, part of Parsons's liberal-arts offerings, since 1997, when the school first asked me to develop it. The discussion is all about responsibility: to the planet, to the regions we live in, to the community, to the profession, to the client, and to the self. I interpret ethics to mean that we have a moral duty, an obligation to our fellow humans and to other living creatures. And that obligation calls on us to be prudent stewards of the natural environment that supports and sustains our lives. Sustaining the environment, in turn, is our highest priority as thinking, verbal, tool-using creatures blessed with free will; and yes, we have a choice. In my view, it's ethical to choose fresh water, clean air, nutritious food—the bounties our home planet provides for us—and safeguard these for future generations.

We begin each September by watching *Mindwalk,* a 1991 film that argues for abandoning the Cartesian, mechanistic, linear thinking that lit up the road to industrialization and made the modern world possible. Now, if we are to survive, we need to switch to an ecological systems thinking, which considers interconnectedness and relationships. This is the crux of the 110-minute conversation between a politician, a poet, and a physicist—a brilliant script based on the thinking of physicist Fritjof Capra. There's no sex, no drugs, no rock and roll, nothing but talk about life, all kinds of life, and glorious views of Mont-Saint-Michel, the tiny island built up during the Middle Ages in France's Gulf of Saint-Malo, set to the music of Philip Glass.

When they watch the film, the students see a gigantic metal mechanism in an ancient tower and hear the physicist say that the microchip has taken the place of the clockwork. This is a dramatic visual and verbal reminder of how invisible technology is replacing much of the bulkily visible. What's called for, says the scientist, is a drastic change in the way we see the world: no longer as a machine with replaceable parts, but as a system of relationships modeled on nature's own systems.

And so we build on this thought throughout our four months together, probing how designers can become active participants in the great system of living organisms that dwell on our fragile, blue green planet. We try, as the physicist urges us to, to figure out how we might live and work inside a "web of relationships" and connect to the "web of life."

The first to resist ecological thinking this particular semester are the fashion students. They're skeptical, even cynical. Their lament: The big companies are in control. There's nothing any one designer can do. We're all slaves of seasonal trends and fickle consumers; we're creatures of a throwaway culture. Why should we care about being sensitive to the environment when nobody wants us to be? The world is a polluted, mean, ugly place ruled by greed and ego. To be part of the fashion industry, to make a living in it, we need to figure out how to make money, how to become stars.

I, the sixties idealist who wholeheartedly believes we can turn that ugly world into something more beautiful, try to keep my cool, though I hear my voice turn shrill. I bring up examples from Paul Hawken's 1993 book, *The Ecology of Commerce*. (I've stopped assigning it. Experience tells me that only a few students would actually read any part of it, so why waste all that paper?) I call their attention to large, multinational businesses, such as Ikea, that are making changes in the way they procure and use materials and distribute their furniture, all to reflect their own, and presumably their customers', growing interest in the environment. I mention postconsumer materials now on the market, like the luxurious fleece we wear as parkas and use as blankets, made from recycled soda bottles. Yes, but look at us, we're slaves to mindless acquisition. You're dreaming a naïve dream, Susan, argue the students.

We press on and read William Morris on the "morality of materials," on the importance of craft and the human touch in an industrialized world, on the social responsibility of designers. We learn about his interest in and advocacy of such varied but related areas of aesthetic expression as historic restoration, furniture and furnishings, wallpapers and textiles, polemical writings, and book publishing. Through this eccentric nineteenth-century genius we are introduced to the designer as an advocate, a revolutionary who looks back to medieval times to reclaim human creativity. His life and work teach us that a strong and brave designer can take on powerful socioeconomic forces, like Morris took on the Industrial Revolution, and have influence far beyond his own times.

We read Walter Gropius on his struggles to establish the Bauhaus, a breakthrough art school in a provincial town in war-ravaged Germany. We learn about the dire economic conditions that plagued the early years of his school, and how Gropius overcame these limitations by sheer will and conviction while collaborating with like-minded people. Though his ideas helped bring our world into modern times, we also learn that, initially, the Bauhaus was shaped by Morris's example: his deep understanding of craft materials and methods. We discuss how a great hardship, like the post–World War I collapse of social and economic values, can propel creative thinking and awaken social responsibility among form-givers. We talk about the need for material invention in such times. And we realize that design, as Gropius saw it (and Morris before him), has a significant contribution to make in the reshaping of institutions, as well as our lives. The word "responsibility" runs through our discussions.

We watch A Story of Healing, a short film that follows American surgeons and nurses in Vietnam doing reconstructive facial surgery on children. Working under primitive conditions, these highly skilled professionals bring all their technical knowledge and love of humanity to the task. It's a heartbreaking and an exhilarating 33 minutes that leads to two hours of spirited conversation on professional behavior: it's important, at times, to step out of our comfort zone. For the medical team, that means leaving behind the fancy, well run, high-tech hospitals they work in every day. What does it mean for designers? we wonder.

The nurses and surgeons set up shop in a small, provincial hospital, some spending their vacation time. They talk, between the many procedures they perform, about finding satisfaction in the work. No one mentions money or wealth or prestige. Their faces beam as they come to realize, one after another, "This is why I went into medicine in the first place." They all talk about the joys and surprises of helping those in need, being part of a dynamic team, testing their skills and imaginations at every turn, and learning that even though people's circumstances and cultures are different, they value the same things. Their experience teaches us that acting on our obligation to our human family can result in rewards far beyond our expectations.

Then, sometime around midterm, a fashion student mentions that an instructor gleefully showed off a forbidden cache of monkey fur in class. The room blows up. The kids are outraged. The architects, interior designers, and the product and graphic designers face the fashion designers, arguing the immorality and illegality of hunting monkeys for their fur. The thought of killing primates purely for their coats so some fashionista can parade around in them offends all of us, including the fashion designers.

One architecture student starts talking about hearts of palm. Apparently, she says, whole groves of a kind of palm tree are cut down and wasted so that some gourmand can buy a precious little snack in a can. Monkey fur and hearts of palm. Everyone agrees, eventually, that we can do without these ill-gotten luxuries. I ask: what else can we do without?

But the bigger question now, for everyone in the room, is how to think about the materials we use and what designers must teach themselves about these materials. One industrial design student explains that we have to look at the full life-cycle costs of materials, from resource harvesting to processing to manufacturing to distribution to use and recycling or, better yet, work to engineer materials for nontoxic degradation. It took monkey fur and hearts of palm to grasp the complex system lurking behind every material choice designers make, from the paper we print on, to the clothing we wear, to the furniture we sit on, to the buildings we live and work in, to the appliances we use.

In 2001, our second class of the fall season happened to have been scheduled for September 11 and so, of course, did not happen. The semester was shortened by the attacks on the World Trade Center. For a while, the New School buildings served as staging areas for some emergency services. Several students came closer to the carnage than anyone should. Our academic world became more real as we talked about America's arrogant and profligate energy use, which was dramatically embedded in the Twin Towers, now turned to one big toxic pile of dust. The rubble was burning not far from where we sat. Those who will give forms to our physical environment—my 28 hopes for the future of a new design ethic—had a hard time ignoring this fact of their lives. The collapse shows, among other things, that our current American lifestyle is unsustainable.

But what can we do? ask the students. Henry Dreyfuss provides a helping hand from beyond the grave. He got involved. We discuss Dreyfuss's dogged concerns about how people use things, what we need to lead useful and happy lives, how we see the world around us, how our unique body measurements and movements determine our relationship to tools and rooms and other things. He reminds us that there is considerate, sympathetic thought behind every great object.

Dreyfuss learned to type before he designed a typewriter, he drove a tractor before he designed one, he hung around department stores before he would design a shop. It's inspiring to talk about this "man in the brown suit," as the conservatively dressed, Depression-era industrial designer came to be known. He connected with humanity. That's what a responsible designer does. This gift for making connections becomes the glue that holds us together after our world is torn apart on that sunny September day.

Also providing inspiration are Charles and Ray Eames. We read about their irrepressible, all-American, midcentury-vintage enthusiasm for both the designed and the natural environment. We wonder: what would they do with the information we now have about the life cycles of materials? They would use it to great effect, we surmise. This was, after all, the couple who explored interconnectivity in a most memorable way. In their now classic film *Powers of Ten,* the Eameses showed the many scales that make up our knowledge and experience of the world, zooming from the molecular to the cosmic and points in between. I ask, how about reexamining these scales of existence to help us think about our resources and ourselves? and prod the students to imagine how they would see the world with the Eameses' adventurous, educated, and playful eyes.

Standing on the shoulders of these design giants, who have laid the foundations for responsible behavior, we get ready to explore the ethics of today's designers. To that end, students have each chosen a practitioner whom they'll interview, preferably in person. This exchange becomes the subject of their presentations and final papers. Incidentally, the fashion designers end up choosing small shop owners, independent shoemakers, up-and-coming dressmakers—more in line with William Morris's thinking than Ralph Lauren's—creative and principled peopled struggling to find their own way.

What of the student who professed to be untouched by sustainability? Though her presentation shows a shocking insensitivity to the subject, her paper does not. As I read it, I'm gratified to learn that the lamp maker she interviewed uses recycled materials and searches out nontoxic processes. Perhaps her disclaimer was a moment of youthful rebellion or an honest confusion about the meaning of a difficult word; sustainability, after all, is hard to wrap your brain around. Perhaps when we understand that good design is responsible design, we will no longer need to rely on clumsy, descriptive words. We'll just call it design—a noble and necessary human activity.

Writings and Talks by
Susan S. Szenasy

Of Our Own Time

Our capacity to hold back our own development seems limitless. We devise ingenious ways to return to a vaguely recalled past, to revive slightly understood styles, to relive times that have only tenuous connections with our own. We allow our minds the creativity to figure out elegant scientific solutions, but seem to put rein on them when we reach our own front doors.

Residential Interiors, March/April 1980

Black Hole, one in the recent rash of space-tech films, is a frightening example. We watch a brilliant, but demented, scientist plot a flawless course through a black hole—the ultimate mystery known to mankind. His spaceship is a marvel of high technology where robots are humanoid; the humans are robotoid. Hidden in this container of twenty-first-century technology, however, is a nineteenth-century dining room. And, to emphasize that he is a "civilized man," the lord of the spaceship wears something that closely resembles the garb of Hapsburg nobility; he serves wine in crystal goblets.

This man has obviously changed the world. Yet he sees his home in a traditional light. His is the knowledge that has built the spaceship, propelled it through gravity, computed its trajectory. Yet his home reflects none of this. Where has his (and our) thinking been short-circuited?

Reassuring answers can be found quickly. Someone may point out that the home environment needs to be very different from the work space. Another holds that fantasy has been always important to residential design. Still another argues that elegance is conveyed by well-known images that have survived the test of time.

But these answers don't suffice anymore. We've gone too far and too fast into a new world of technology. So far, we've responded to this by putting ourselves into an aesthetic holding pattern. As far as our homes are concerned, we are happy to let the past dictate our sense of elegance.

But beautifully designed, smoothly functioning machinery is as much part of our sense of elegance today as goldthread was for the Hapsburgs. "Richness and polish in harmonious simplicity" is certainly a broad enough definition of elegance to encompass the unique creations of our age. Electronic technology is part of our contribution. It influences us at every turn. Yet we are still designing as if the machine did not exist or as if it were an adjunct of a late colonial style.

We swear we don't watch TV. Yet every night, Manhattan's Upper West Side is dotted with thousands of blue lights. (And that is just a small neighborhood survey.) It seems rather foolish to keep wanting to hide an object that has become so prominent in our lives.

Consider, for instance, that today we get much of our information from radio or television. In the near future, we are likely to use the electronic media more extensively and more wisely. As we become familiar with VCRs, home computers, etc., we'll see a broadening of our visual and cognitive horizons.

In the meantime, a growing number of independent programmers are challenging the complacent hegemony of the giant networks. "Slowly, almost surreptitiously, American television is moving forward, beyond the bread-and-butter confines of standard formulae," says John O'Connor, TV critic for the *New York Times.*

That the airwaves have been one of our most abused and misused resources is news to no one. But here, as in other fields, we are reevaluating the wasteful practices of previous times. And everywhere, we are all caught in a cost crunch. Each one of us strives to be a more prudent consumer. Just as we seek to evaluate the kinds of programs we watch, or the types of audio/video equipment that suit our needs, we need to gain in-depth knowledge of the products used to furnish our homes. To that end, *Residential Interiors* inaugurates a series of articles that focus on materials. In this issue, we investigate wool fibers, revealing that microscopic structure is what gives this well-known material its tough performance and lasting beauty. In subsequent issues, we will deal with other quality furnishing materials. Our premise: knowing what you're buying and its long-term cost effectiveness make hefty investments less painful.

The issues challenging us today are difficult and far-reaching, be they concerned with high technology, rising prices, or outmoded design approaches. If we use as much talent and energy in confronting them head-on as we do in obscuring them, we might surprise ourselves. We might even find some answers that are unique to our time and place.

Valedictory

Commitment to an idea or a person can bring the world into clear focus. For me, as for many of you, the subject of design is that focus. It is the most visible human action and reaction to an evolving environment. It places us in history. It tells us about today. It forecasts tomorrow. It is smart and it is stupid. It is real and it is phony. It aids function and it obscures movement.

Residential Interiors, July/August 1980

At its most thrilling, design reveals the workings of an intelligent mind. As such, it is a powerful force for communicating ideas. Good design takes us out of the mundane and brings us to a higher level of understanding. Tragically, it is constantly bombarded by forces alien to its creative nature: budgets, codes, obscure desires, secret longings. But through it all, it keeps surviving and proving that creativity is the breath of life.

This abstract notion is easy to forget in the face of everyday realities. And especially in the home, design seems to be constantly at the mercy of hostile forces. Clients think they should have a "special image." Interior designers respond by "creating fantasy." Who is fooling whom? And why does anyone need to be fooled? In this context, the dialogue about real human needs seldom has a chance to surface.

Commitment to an idea or a person can bring the world into clear focus.

A dean of architecture asserts that there's no need for residential design. His glib dismissal of an entire specialty leaves residential work in the hands of the amateur, the grandstander, the frustrated set decorator, and the commercial specialist whose competent space-planning concepts never quite translate to the more personal environment of the home. No wonder that human needs for beauty, humor, honesty, efficiency, and comfort are obscured.

But the urge to make a home is too important to dismiss so easily. Forward-thinking educators understand this. They advocate, for instance, the use of environmental autobiographies, written recollections that reveal students' hidden feelings about their homes. Thus, the design profession evolves and with it our chance to live better.

"We are at that dramatic moment in our national life wherein we tremble evenly between decay and evolution," said Louis H. Sullivan in 1918. In 1980, the scales are in the same precarious position. Environmental restrictions, material shortages, changes in lifestyles force new confrontations. The home is the container of all these changes.

In this context, the current fad for nostalgia and romance are mere delaying tactics. Recalling the past is a pleasant occupation, but the natural rhythm of life propels us onward. True, the pendulum keeps swinging back and forth, but it is the face of the clock that marks time. And time always moves forward. So must I.

The change I seek will perhaps add a new richness to my life, as has the time I spent editing this magazine. I leave with immense gratitude for the opportunity and a strengthened conviction in my beliefs.

Akiko Busch

I was 25 when I moved to New York. It was 1979, and my first job was at a magazine called *Residential Interiors,* where Susan had been the editor for the past year. The offices were on the thirty-ninth floor of the Astor Plaza building, a mediocre corporate tower in Times Square, beige inside and out. I wrote captions to size, did a spring roundup of wallpaper, and conducted a terrifying interview with Princeton professor Michael Graves. I knew nothing about architecture or design, didn't pretend to, and didn't plan on staying long. I had interviewed at a poetry quarterly housed in a brownstone in Chelsea.

A couple of months after I started to work at the magazine, a box filled with advance copies of the most recent issue was delivered to the office. On its cover was a photograph of a hand-built stove in a Chinese peasant kitchen. Images on the pages inside included a lacquered table, an enameled bowl, light filtering through a decorative window grille, a handmade wooden chair, a pile of twigs next to the stove. The images were rustic, rich in tradition, steeped in history. This was not product, and it was definitely not merchandise. There was "very little to buy, but much to see," the copy stated, explicitly noting that design was about more than commerce.

Although it wasn't exactly news that interior design could involve the way light falls into a room or a chair is positioned on the floor or a decorative bowl is placed on a table, how these things might occur in a primitive Chinese cabin was not the usual fare in the pages of such magazines. But diplomatic recognition between the People's Republic and the United States had occurred only months before, and, suddenly, the doors to these rooms were opened to American readers. In those four pages were snapshots of how East and West, past and present, tradition and modernity, craft and industry converged in the small cottages of rural China. The study of design has been engaging, human, and alive to me since that day.

The job at the quarterly never came through. And it was so long ago that I no longer remember what I was looking for there anyway. Perhaps it was some tutorial in how human thought and experience could be distilled into a handful of words. Or those ways in which color, shape, and light can coalesce into meaning. Or how people inhabit the space around them. I can't recall. It doesn't matter. I ended up finding out how those things happened in the pages of a home-design magazine.

Adjustable Desks and Storage

The desk used to be a surface for writing and a box for storing documents. Now it has become a surface that supports machines that can store documents in some mysterious space that some of us can't fathom. It has become a scaffold, a construction of post and beam and slab and container. Its designers talk about "wire management" as they envision an enormous electronic coil through a vast hive of "data processing stations."

The talk about the people who operate the machines and use the desk is as abstract as the work they're required to perform. They are "operators," "word processors," and "users" who are under the constant scrutiny of "human factors researchers" whose findings, in turn, help create "environments" that produce "worker efficiencies," which, until now, have not been measured to anyone's satisfaction. This, then, is the case of the missing person. The poet in us, the dreamer, the very essence of us, seems to have been left out of the tabulations.

But there is a somewhat hopeful side to this dismal accounting. The hope lies in the maze of component parts, modules, and standardized elements to which furniture has been reduced. Like the brick that holds in its simple form the promise of a home, so the new furniture's building blocks can be assembled to fit a person's needs. In order to make that happen, everyone concerned needs to participate. The process is a fragile one. It may come apart at any of its many joints. It requires no less of every person—from the one who designs the product to the one who uses it—than to understand his or her place in a rapidly changing world.

Instead of devising products for a pale, statistical ghost who makes X number of moves in space Y to complete task Z, some designers are envisioning their work being used by the people they know. An image of Mother at the CRT or Dad in the boardroom or a buddy in the lunchroom can invest a designer's work with personal meaning. Such involved thinking has been known to produce things that are clearly understood by many people, who, after all, are somebody's mother, father, as well as friend, in addition to being blips in a chart.

The very presence of products that have that mysteriously personal appeal to large numbers of people is an encouragement. It signifies the existence of industrial designers who like people; manufacturers who can see their customers as more than mere consumers at the end of the assembly line; sales people who can demonstrate the possibilities designed into the product; interior designers who take interest in their real clients—the people who will use the office; and the workers themselves, who can talk with honesty and clarity about what they aspire to and need for the accomplishment of their jobs.

Such ideal worlds, by their own definition, understate the realities of office life, with its complex power struggles and fossilized organization charts. But they also confirm the fact that a whole new range of products can exist and may even help ease some of those tensions, if used with intelligence and imagination.

The new desk—or "systems furniture," as it is often called—accepts human variety as a fact of life. Unlike the old steel desk, with its fixed-in-place files, that required the worker to adapt to it, the new desk can be made-to-order for the person who uses it. It can be adapted to people as different in their work habits as those who scatter papers around them, or those who line things up neatly, or those who confer regularly, or those who use office machines extensively.

Most systems are built on hollow metal beams and posts that channel the wiring from computers, desk lamps, telephones, typewriters, pencil sharpeners, or any other gadgets that are about to show up in the office. This structural system—often called by such organic-sounding names as spine or arterial passageway—receives tabletops of various sizes and shapes, some of which can be adjusted in height; file cabinets of varied capacities; niches and nodes of many functions.

The new desk, with its ability to extend the work area, has contributed to the rethinking of office storage solutions, as have the proliferation of a new generation of accessories that accompany electronic equipment, such as printouts, magnetic tapes, floppy disks, and platters.

The result is a filing cabinet that has become a "storage system." It can build whole walls of storage or stand as a room divider, with access from both sides. It can roll around the floor or hang from underneath the desk or from a divider panel. The variety of exterior shapes and colors is matched by the flexibility of its interior dividers, racks, hooks, rods, sleeves, and drawers.

While they were being reworked to accommodate the changing technology of the office, the desk and the filing cabinet have also become "humanized." This chilling little word is often used to describe the warming and softening of colors, the rounding of edges, and texturings like tambour doors, all of which make the new furniture easy to look at and pleasant to the human touch.

Arriving Home

The choice of where we live in the late twentieth century is determined by many factors, including the neighborhood's safety and negotiability by every member of the family, be they young or old; the building's energy efficiencies; its closeness to work, school, day care, shopping, and entertainment; and its ability to adapt as people change through time, because moving on and "trading up" to a more suitable home have become a speculator's paradise but a homeowner's financial nightmare.

Chapter from *The Home: Exciting New Designs for Today's Lifestyle,* 1985

Only a small fraction of housing is newly built, and often it is necessary to reuse and restore existing buildings as apartments and condominiums, or to tune up detached houses and the neighborhoods in which they stand. Both the home and its grounds, as well as their greater surroundings, need to function for people whose needs have changed. The family group of the 1950s and 1960s that centered around the mother's unpaid labor is now a minority. Today the home also has to fit the complicated work and social lives of single parents and their children; couples, each of whom considers career and home life important; and single persons whose ages, incomes, and occupations run the gamut of the modern population profiles.

Although the computer promises to make the home an island of efficiency, it can also isolate us from one another. On the basis of social needs, many people are thinking of ways to reintegrate communities into human-scale groupings where neighbors work together to bring about occasions and services for the benefit of everyone.

The modern "village" is usually a developer's scheme of quaintly styled condos and detached houses, where the "community" swimming pool or golf course brings people together. Nearby support services are also required for families, so that parents don't have to drive extra miles to pick up children, food, and dry cleaning after they've extricated themselves from gridlocked traffic.

Motorways supplemented by paths, rest stops, commons, and play areas with benches expand the concept of home life to include the neighborhood. When coming home is a pleasurable experience, less time is needed to unwind, and more energy can be given to shared activities or to pursuing personal interests.

Whether we travel homeward to an urban maze, a suburban sprawl, or a rural scattering, we look for markers to tell us how close we are to the one place where we can safely unbuckle. When familiar landmarks—an evocative sculpture or fountain, a grove of willows, or a gable peeking through the foliage—greet us, the pleasure of coming upon their mysterious shadows, changing colors, and refreshing scents and sounds lifts the spirit.

Similarly, an attractive architectural detail that becomes a touchable familiar as we enter the front door welcomes us home. And when an object is designed with sensitivity to the light changes that time brings and with an understanding that a thing may be immensely satisfying both at a distance and close up, then a simple detail can be a source of many different experiences.

A fanlight over the door may glow from inside at dusk, dapple the interior hall on a Sunday morning, or filter the milky mist of midafternoon. Attention to small details like these makes memorable homes out of houses. For even as the fanlight functions to make the hallway safe and bright, it adds unexpected dimensions to the experience of moving about. It's also a sign of human habitation and caring, akin to the impulse that built the fountain, preserved the willows, and lavished attention on the gables that enriched our homecoming.

Because signs of personal expression are missing from most modern buildings, many people choose to restore and renew old, solidly built structures. Made with large windows—or offering the potential for these, as well as for skylights, atria, and clerestories—they have been built with lasting and attractive materials, embellished with details that show a belief in symbol and craftsmanship. Now they accommodate home living as cavernous interiors divided up to fit the smaller-scale domestic life, displacing the large-scale industrial production of the past. The pattern has become familiar: shortly after the evening news reports on the closing of a candy factory, as hundreds of the newly unemployed file out toward an uncertain future, a newspaper story tells of the building's conversion into luxury condos.

As a result, today we live in watch factories, firehouses, stables, schools, churches, stores, grain silos, and corncribs. For the past decade, these conversions have played havoc with one of the most often cited rules of design: form follows function. It seems that function may not necessarily coincide with intentions of a building's or a product's designers. As successful adaptations of buildings tend to point out, a design is most meaningful and lasting when it accommodates possibilities far beyond its original intent.

In sections of cities where real estate values make renovation and restoration imperative, town houses are being turned back into the plush single-family homes they were designed to be at the turn of the century. Many choice pieces of Victorian architecture are also being converted into elegant small condominiums, in the process revealing the richly carved and polished woods, the ornamental plasterwork, the beveled glass, and the marble tiles that were once used to great advantage by the building trades, only to be covered by the detritus of nearly a century of living.

The mammoth apartment hotel, another turn-of-the-century creature created for the wealthy, who had minimal interest in housekeeping and enjoyed room service from the building's own restaurants, is making a comeback. Even as the old buildings, which had become rather frayed with age, are converted into the next crop of valuable cooperative apartments, a new generation of luxury high-rise marketers sells condominium spaces the maintenance fees of which include hotel services geared to the wealthy professional couple, neither of whom wants to program the microwave.

Outside the central city, once a sea of single-family detached houses, the American landscape is changing noticeably. Now clusters of condominiums are being built to resemble giant châteaux, farmhouses, or haciendas, depending on a style's suitability to the climate and local building traditions. This trend of being "true to one's own region" is giving builders high marks for awareness mainly because their predecessors, dominated by the grid and encouraged by government policies of cheap energy, completely ignored local conditions. Indeed, the new clusters can save energy all around if the siting is able to capitalize on the special qualities of local sunshine, breezes, plantings, and materials in addition to being close to jobs, schools, and services.

However energy efficient cluster housing may be, like other forms of housing, it costs an immense amount of human energy to acquire and maintain. Today, in the mid-1980s, an "incubator" condominium in California—a 340-square-foot box for living—is being sold for $50,000 in the hopes, as one developer puts it, of getting people "in on the merry-go-round we call home ownership." In New York, the $500,000 "dockominium" is now the choice development scheme for hitherto-neglected waterfront properties.

Because we tend to view our homes as one more commodity, made to be used for a while, then replaced by another, we accept the available offerings with relatively little thought. The hard questions about how we want to live are often answered by decorative clutter. Or they may be answered not at all by ourselves but by market researchers and media advisers to builders, charged to attract buyers with romantic names for buildings and streets, embellished facades and lobbies, clever mechanical controls, and, now, celebrity tennis tournaments arranged to put the "fun" into searching for a home.

Increasingly, we search for alternatives. In Maine, for instance, architects can build a house in the woods for the price of a California incubator. Weather tight and solar heated, such houses are thoughtful responses to concerns about nature and its resources and how people want to live with both. In fact, many of the most interesting houses are built by architects who give their clients a sense of being in control of their immediate environments. There's genuine interest in making houses less technology dependent. For those who live there, this can mean a life of added chores, like sowing morning glory seeds beneath the trellis that shades the south-facing windows, which will welcome the heat and light during the bare winter months but need to be protected from heat gain in the summer; maneuvering openings to catch the breezes, block the glare, and keep the heat from escaping; and stoking the wood burner to take the chill off.

What may appear to be merely a new interest in historical styles is often a serious study in making good houses. After decades of ignoring the lessons of the past, it turns out the Roman villa, with its atria, grilles, colonnades, and solid masonry construction, is a natural building type for warm climates. The nineteenth-century New England seaside house, with its many breeze-catching windows and small rooms piled on several floors, is perfectly adapted for the long summers of childhood. Another nineteenth-century invention, the California balloon frame, can have an outside appearance of a constructivist metal sculpture with a homey inside, animated by its many different light sources.

There is, however, scant historical evidence on how to reconcile house, person, and car. Our main mode of transport lives inside the house as we do. It gets a big door, fitting its power, size, and importance. We—though powerful, large, and important in our imaginations—enter our section of the house through a small door that lands us in the kitchen, the family room, or, perhaps, through some freakish twist of the floor plan, the spare bedroom.

The front door, like the erstwhile front parlor, seems to be an endangered species. But the acts of separating public and private behavior, the need to receive guests with some ceremony, the wish to welcome them to our special place demand that we continue the tradition of the front door. It's here that we begin to distinguish ourselves as people who are proud, intelligent, mysterious, artful, puritanical, practical, bland, or any other image we choose to adopt.

The Magic Door

When I was a young girl in rural Hungary, I used to read about doors that opened as if by magic. Later, I found out what the magic was about. It was someone's imagination that opened those fairy tale doors. Still later, I began to notice that some things around me had the same wondrous qualities, which keeps those magic doors returning to my memory.

Editor's Note, *Metropolis,* April 1986

Intrigued by the infinite possibilities for combining imagination with memory, I was delighted to find people who shared my enthusiasm. They were designers and architects, almost every one of them. They talked about the things that we all do, things like eating, reading, and walking, but they approached our everyday movements in a special way: as design problems. This was like stumbling into a secret society whose aim was to remake the world. And I could take an advance peek at the plans. I was, frankly, awed.

But time and living have taught me a thing or two. Now, my fascination with the process that creates spoons or houses or communities is tempered with an awareness of human frailty and folly. As a result, I can identify some of the sources of my frustrations that come with living in this wonderful and wearing city. Much of our current discomfort comes from the designed environment. It need not be this way.

Observe one morning your fellow passengers on any of the newer local buses. More than half will ignore the Metropolitan Transit Authority's instructions about how to make a graceful exit. People of all sizes and ages push through the back doors, with great exertions to spine and arm. Not a good way to start a day that is likely to bring other, small design failures like glare on the computer console.

Why, then, aren't bus riders making use of considerate technology, devised to eliminate unnecessary physical exertion? The door, after all, opens like Sesame when it's gently pressed on the right spot. The MTA identifies it as a "Safety Exit Door." Farther down, at foot level, on this machine for leaving are two small acetate labels, each printed with bright yellow letters that read, "Air assist door." Then again, "Door opens automatically when: 1. Green light is on; 2. Tape is touched."

And so we've been told, three times no less, the obvious. We're standing in front of a door. But where is the "tape"? For most of us, that's the sticky film that holds the wrappings on gifts.

On some buses, alert riders have located two thin, yellow plastic bands centered at the top of the door. This must be the "tape." So someone with a black laundry-marker has printed on it, "press to open." Surely this could have been part of the original design of the buses. Instead, there were too many instructions.

It's all in the details, as a very famous architect warned. And when the details are neglected, design gets a bad name and so does the creative spirit. The same persons who were clever enough to devise the magic door should also know something about the way the rest of us are likely to use it.

I cannot give up on the magic door.

I cannot give up on the magic door. One, long-remembered example of it I bring here from a small town. Other, subsequent glimpses of its new forms I spot daily while riding through this chaotic but somehow workable city. Both serve to remind me that human imagination is everywhere. When this is expressed in the work of intelligent, sensitive, sensible, and playful designers, everyone benefits.

We believe this, each of us in our own, unique way. That's why we think that we can make *Metropolis* the most exciting, accessible, and of course, wonderful magazine about design and architecture that you are likely to find anywhere.

Ralph Caplan

It seems to me that her seriousness changed the magazine substantially.

The Zen of Shopping

To semiologist Roland Barthes, the function of the Japanese package was "not to protect in space but to postpone in time." That hardly appears an apt description for clothing stores commonly associated with instant gratification. Yet the analogy of the package and the shop is a safe one. Postponing a purchase is a comfortable possibility in a low-pressure shop that seems designed to encourage contemplation. Such a serene space, set in a nervous city, can linger in the memory like an ancestral shrine, to be revisited religiously.

Excerpt, *Metropolis,* October 1986

Not surprisingly, the Japanese have become the most successful purveyors of emptiness. This may be seen in the remarkably restrained retailing spaces that are American outposts for Japanese fashion empires with French names. These shops offer total integration, not only of materials but also of the sexes. Here, both women and men feel at ease and often look good in similar clothing. Others shops, those designed by Americans for American merchants, still separate the sexes. But often the interior design succeeds in integrating the old with the new, the lasting with the ephemeral, in spacious settings that have reminded one writer of "shogun concrete."

The Japanese ability to integrate conservative social patterns with sophisticated technology is a compelling model for American architects and designers looking for ways out of a maze of historical styles. This time, they're learning from Japan. As Martin Friedman, director of Minneapolis's Walker Art Center (where *Tokyo Form and Spirit,* a traveling show coming to New York in December, originated), wrote, "Despite trappings of modernity, the past is not only alive there, it is a shaping force in the Japanese contemporary culture." Some highly visible and memorable shops around town remind New Yorkers of that attractive possibility.

In these shops, altarlike slabs of granite, stone, marble, wood, steel, and concrete isolate a special piece of clothing in an artful display. Clearly, an attempt has been made to show an everyday object as a highly valued, rare item, in the same way that art is shown in a gallery or museum. With the elimination of multiples — there is one, one-of-a-kind shirt instead of 30 in many colors and sizes — the customer is assured of the possibility for unique self-expression through dressing. This artful expression of the self is attached to a larger price tag.

Ideas of how to combine the expensive pieces into something fresh and new are provided at the occasional interruptions to the space, often on large slabs. Here, an attractive ensemble is stretched out as an offering in a temple. But the offering is merely a prelude to the larger ceremony. The clothes come alive, they move and drape on the attractive bodies of youthful sales people who come and go in outfits they've gleaned from the racks, where only one of each style hangs.

The glamour of celebrity adds to the excitement of shopping when the omnipresent television screen, located at some site crucial to the shopper's decision making, catches the customer's attention. This might be at the mysterious entrance, where the timid are separated from the adventurous who dare to push through the doors. Or the screen might be near the "cash wrap desk," as the merchandising trade calls the old cash register that has metamorphosed into a small, silent computer. At such points of potential hesitation, the artful video reinforces each decision. It presents a perfection of fantasy as a joyous procession of reedlike models with magazine-cover faces.

Coincidentally, the video images of clothes in action also help the space planners' intentions for keeping props to a minimum. There's no need here for bulky mannequins to show coordination. That space can be left empty to create distances between products and people. The shop's resulting openness calls attention to permanent, templelike surfaces that surround everything.

Giving a sacred aura to a container of worldly activity is not foreign to American memory. This integration of seemingly contradictory aspects of life was already brewing here in the seventeenth century. In the Midwest and New England, the Shakers built ascetic and luminous rooms to house their daily lives. Their harmonious artifacts are products of a simple, all-embracing belief in "hands to works and hearts to God," as was foretold by the sect's founder, Mother Ann Lee.

In less than a hundred years, in the midst of nineteenth-century material excesses, the East Coast transcendentalists wrote and lectured extensively on spirituality, detachment, and self-control. Although more verbose than the Far Eastern philosophers who inspired them (a Zen master can express a thought in a brief haiku, a Japanese poem that is always 17 syllables), Americans once more gave their voices to eternal yearnings for something beyond the material.

The hundred-year cycle of American spirituality renewed itself in the 1960s counterculture. A whole generation looked for ways to connect the many scattered concerns of modern life. Although specialization and standardization produced a life of material abundance, that life of many parts was increasingly difficult to comprehend. Once more the East, with its philosophy of integration, was a source of inspiration. Popular teachers like Alan Watts assured their audiences of an eternal life that is an "on/off pulsation." Like the transcendentalists a century before him, Watts put the individual in charge of understanding the world. It is up to men, he wrote in 1966, to transform "this immense electrical pulsation into light and color, shape and sound, large and small, hard and heavy, long and short. In knowing the world, we humanize it."

During the same turbulent decade, Barthes, whose work subsequently induced a generation of American architects and designers to consider the products of their work as "instruments of meaning," was also drawn to the East. After a trip to Japan, he began to decipher some of the signs of that culture. He observed in *Empire of Signs* that "all of Zen" is concerned with ways to "halt language, to jam that kind of internal radiophony continually sending in us, even in our sleep." The way of Zen, he discovered was "to empty out, to stupefy, to dry up the soul's incoercible babble"—the unstated aim, in fact, of these shops. Twenty years after those words were written, people living in computer cultures stressed with information overload are beginning to understand the importance of emptying out.

Jack Lenor Larsen

I am a magazine person, giving up on newspapers and television to read as many as 100 journals in a single week. I learned early on that editors, far more than designers, are in the know, on top of things, and the first to experience the new and—often—the true and worthy. I have also known many of the great editors during my long time in the business, and Susan differs from many in the breadth of her interest. She explains not just what but who. She digs deeper: Who? Why? What are the applications? What is the impact on the environment? On happiness?

Capturing Light

It's nearly noon on December 21, 1986. The breakfast room at the tip of the galley kitchen on the third floor of Liberty Terrace, where model apartments are being shown to condominium shoppers, is unbearably hot. This tiny inferno adds a false note to the sales manager's letter that invites prospective owners to "come home to generous light-filled rooms."

Excerpt,
Metropolis,
March 1987

Located on the windswept esplanade of Battery Park City on the shore of the Hudson River in Lower Manhattan, Liberty Terrace offers one of the island city's few waterfront locations, as well as an opulent amenity package. The unexpected surprise is the stifling winter midday heat, when the steel gray waters outside send freezing winds around the boomerang-shaped building. On that winter day—the shortest day of the year—the low-lying sun poured its light and heat through the "expansive double glazed sliding insulated windows," as the sales brochure describes the building's apertures in their undecorated state. In fact, the winter sun has been in direct contact with the southwest-facing room from around 11 in the morning and it would remain there until four in the afternoon. That day, the sun turned the room an orange red by 4:30, its last spectacular light shimmering on the Hudson River and tinting the nearby Statue of Liberty's cool green gown with a flaming russet.

But this winter drama only begins to foretell the potential agony of the coming summer. In that season of long days, when the sun is high in the sky as it moves westward, it will bombard the room most of the day and into the early evening with its warm-hued, hot-tempered light. Respite from the glaring heat will not come until eight in the evening, when the sun begins to set over the New Jersey flatlands across the river.

Liberty Terrace's other views bring less discomfort and for some, perhaps, less drama. Just after sunrise, the north windows—which spread their even, cool light inside throughout the day—will admit sunshine to the room's west wall in the summertime. This direct hit will last until about nine in the morning, feeding resident plants and breakfasters, alike. From that time onward, the north light will remain consistent—as steady as natural light can be, always at the mercy of high, errant clouds and shifting films of pollution closer to the ground.

The windows facing east provide sunlight when people need it most in a northern city. In winter, when nights are long and cold, the morning sun comes as a reminder of the rekindled fires. In the summer, the east light is the coolest in temperature, though it's known for the rosy dawns it visits on the city's many reflective surfaces.

Light captured from the four cardinal directions—south, west, north, and east—make Manhattan's interiors unique places to live. This is so even for apartments on landlocked streets. (The latter is the rule in the island city: proximity to water, as at Liberty Terrace and other new and planned buildings at Battery Park, is the exception. This new development, named for that park, is celebrated for its pioneering plan, underwritten by public and private financial sources, for rescuing part of New York's neglected waterfront.)

Whether they're near the shoreline or at midblock, most interiors in the Borough of Manhattan benefit from the city's northern location, its compass orientation, its street plan, its surround of reflective waters, as well as its many reflective rooftops and facades of glass, steel, masonry, and other building materials in close proximity to one another. Most significant, the streets' grid layout above Houston Street, in conjunction with the slight twist of the island (Manhattan's north direction is nearly 30 degrees to the west of its north and south avenues), works to create many different lighting effects in seemingly uniform dwelling units.

"The nature of the city, its length, determined the way the early commissioners laid out the grid of Manhattan in 1811," explains Jim Morgan, a New York architect who spent the late 1970s working on passive solar projects. (He and many others took advantage of the Carter Administration's energy policies, which between 1977 and 1981, under the Department of Energy (DOE) provided incentives for the research of low-tech, inexpensive ways to trap and use sunshine to create pleasant and affordable interiors. That government support has dried up.)

As Morgan comments on Manhattan's unique mix of nature and human intervention, "Fate was such that the sunrises bring the early morning light even into our north and south streets. And this is the best kind of light, especially in the summer when the mornings are still cool."

Though the city's buildings benefit from their locations' serendipitous light conditions, they are shaped more by the planning grid than by any consideration of the natural environment. This bias toward geometry stretches buildings both skyward and close to the edge of property lines, so as to wring maximum profits from the island's minimal landmass.

But it's only after a building is up that most people notice the drastic changes in the quality of light in their neighborhoods and inside their apartments. Some tall buildings, however, add to the amount of light in a neighborhood instead of subtracting from it. Lighting designer Peter Barna offers a hypothetical example of an apartment on the seventh floor that faces a 14-story building: The lower apartment will receive sun inside during the summertime. This happens because the light waves that land on the facade of the taller building bounce down and across the street and into the facing interiors.

Architect Morgan, who currently resides on the Upper West Side, points out that light also can bounce from a lower building into a higher one. "I live on the tenth floor to the south of buildings that are five-stories high. There's a lot of light bouncing off those roofs and landing on my ceiling."

In uncovering the many facets of city lighting, Morgan also considers the issue of how a building's color contributes to its neighborhood's daytime illumination. "I used to sniff," he remembers, "the way most architects do, at the white-brick apartment buildings. It's true they aren't beautiful, but they certainly throw a lot of light around the street and into adjacent apartments." As a case in point, Morgan brings up Wright's Guggenheim Museum on Fifth Avenue. "Just north of the museum there's a really forgettable white-brick building. But I bet if you were to study it, you'd find that there's a lot of back light bouncing from the apartment house onto the Guggenheim's skylight dome during the day."

Architect Brent M. Porter, who studies such things, brings up another historically significant location in town. "Fifth Avenue, especially between Forty-second and Fifty-ninth streets, is a unique area because of its predominance of limestone. The natural reflection of these buildings is a wonderful treasure for New York City. They can teach us a great deal about how buildings can create an overall ambience of light." It turns out, then, that some buildings are good neighbors while others are not. "The Citicorp Center's smooth aluminum and glass walls, for instance, create a lot of glare in the surrounding shops along Lexington Avenue," observes Porter.

Most observers agree that some of the best city neighbors (buildings that also contain some memorable naturally lit rooms) were designed before the sun took a secondary position to the incandescent bulb. Renovators of late-nineteenth- and early-twentieth-century factories, row houses, and apartments take delight in their high, amply proportioned windows set into thick walls. These window niches were often designed with enough interior space for folding up the interior wooden shutters on overcast days. Brought up to current standards (one layer of glass in ill-fitting wooden frames is replaced with two or three layers of glass set in insulated metal frames), the revived windows begin to combine an intuitive use of sunlight with high-tech design.

When assessing the window as a light source, a good rule of thumb— known to urban builders like those of seventeenth-century Amsterdam, who cut tall openings into the fronts of their narrow row houses—is suggested by lighting designer Barna. "Light tends to penetrate into a space about twice the height of the window." Specifically, he says, an eight-foot-high window will admit light 16 feet into the room. But because it is diffused by the various interior surfaces, the entering light grows duskier as it moves deeper into the room. So in order to trap the maximum amount of daylight, special attention must be given to the area immediately under the window (the first three or four feet are crucial).

"The floor is the primary surface where the light falls," Barna notes. If a lot of light comes into the room (especially through unobstructed windows with southern and western exposures), "a dark floor is terrific," contends Morgan. But in a naturally darker room, "it's smart to keep the floor a light color so that the entering light can bounce deep inside," he adds. This effect occurs because the sunlight always comes from above and lands first on the floor. When the floor is a light color, much of the light falling on it bounces, like an uncontrolled ball on a squash court, up to the ceiling. If the ceiling is white or pastel it, in turn, acts as a source of reflected light in the room.

"It's possible to create a space that is higher than the entering light," Barna says. "That may seem like a contradiction in terms, but it has to do with the whiteness of the surfaces and their reflective qualities." Light inside a room (or on a city block), then, is a summation of all the reflections there. This physical fact is surely responsible for a familiar story told among architectural journalists. Morgan, a writer as well as an architect, recalls talk about Richard Meier's Douglas House, on Lake Michigan. "It's that white house that climbs the hill: it's a beautiful sculpture. But usable art is not also considerate design. Apparently, the woman who lives there conducted an entire interview wearing her sunglasses," says Morgan.

He concedes that "Meier's work is wonderful. But he's ignoring the power of nature when he refuses to put any kind of shading on his windows. I would want the window treatment to give the room's users maximum opportunity for adjusting the light that enters their home." Morgan's plea for adjustability also applies to external shutters and awnings for southern and western exposures, but these time-tested devices rarely occur on urban buildings.

Perhaps it's time—in light of all that has been learned about historical precedents in buildings and new ways to measure and record information—to combine history with technology into designs that pay attention to the sun. "You only have to go up to the top of a tall building in downtown Manhattan and look northward to see that by a fluke of the early planner's imagination, the city has a tremendous frontier of south-facing facades," Porter observes. Historically, Americans have never before resisted the challenge of a new frontier.

Sylvia Plachy

Starting in 1982, I had a weekly photographic column in the *Village Voice* called "Sylvia Plachy's Unguided Tour," and after about eight years, the paper discontinued it. At that time, I already worked for *Metropolis*. Susan had hired me to do some photographs, and whenever I was on assignment for the magazine, I would stop off and talk to her. I don't know how she knew, but when Susan became aware I wasn't doing "Unguided Tour" anymore, she called me up and suggested I do a monthly piece for her. She thought that instead of only taking the pictures, I should also write something to go along with them, to make a two-page photo essay having to do with design and the city. I didn't want to write! But Susan wanted the column to have a voice, not just the images. I decided to come up with a concept that would loosely fit the idea of design. Sometimes the column wasn't so much about design as it was about life. It was a kind of free association with the world and what it looks like. When *Metropolis* did an issue on furniture, my column would be called "Sit," and then it was about sitting and chairs and all the various ways of sitting and what it meant to me. I was given over to an incredibly good, smart editor named Marisa Bartolucci, who showed me how my writing could get better and better; she made me sound completely brilliant. Susan and I would work on my column together—I would go to her office and bounce ideas off her, and my columns eventually became a book, *Signs and Relics,* published in 2000. Working with her changed me—she actually made me dare to be a writer.

Chaises Longues

Youthful, good-looking, well-dressed men and women seem to be doing something called "numbers crunching." These new American heroes of the TV commercials have arrived in the office before dawn and are often there after the maintenance crew has left. The subliminal message of this commercial slice of life is that the highly competitive international marketplace demands, indeed rewards, people who dedicate their lives to their work.

Excerpt, *Metropolis,* May 1987

Such intense work requires an intense support system. In the late 1980s, this support system is a small but powerful computer (the product sold in the advertisements) and a comfortable office that is an elegant room, furnished with considerable thought to function and efficiency and a nod to the ideal of "humanism." Such an office contains at least one ergonomic chair, an innovative piece of furniture that can be recognized by its slim, tightly upholstered, contoured shell that is set to rock, roll, swivel, and vibrate over a sturdy nontip base. There is also a cushioned club chair and an expensive couch—signs of luxury that encircle a sleek coffee table where people socialize, briefly, between bouts with their computers.

Though the living-room setting expresses the social side of doing business, it doesn't really reflect the real needs of the office's occupant. A famous case in point is the story of Hollywood director Billy Wilder, who didn't want the stigma of having a "casting couch" in his office but needed a place to stretch out in private and, at times, take a quick nap between scenes. Wilder's friend Charles Eames came up with a solution in 1960 when he designed an ascetic-looking long chair (some like to call it by its more familiar French name, chaise longue). With its waferlike leather cushions on a slim steel frame, the chair was made to lift the head, stretch the back, raise the knees, and keep the feet level with the heart. (Since the late nineteenth century that position has been advocated by various physicians and furniture manufacturers as a healthy way to relax the tense body.)

When Eames suggested the long chair for Wilder's office, he was at the forefront of a trend toward domesticating the corporate high-rise. A quarter century later, executive's offices often look like gentlemen's libraries or suburban living rooms. Dining tables are being used as desks and folding chairs are provided for visitors.

Aside from its homey associations, furniture also solves a chronic space problem. With skyrocketing rents (some New York offices pay $40 a square foot), each piece of furniture needs to do double duty. So the dining table hosts conferences in addition to being a work surface, and when the meeting expands, more folding chairs are brought out of the closet.

Some new designs are reminiscent of the late-eighteenth-century daybed, also known as the recamier. Named for Madame Juliette Recamier, who was painted by Jacques-Louis David as she lounged in her French Directoire salon, the daybed (an innovation of the time) has continued to intrigue furniture designers for nearly two centuries.

The recamier's stiff, somewhat self-conscious line gave way to a more exuberant container for the reclining body in late-nineteenth-century America when an upholstered, metal-framed folding chair, widely known as the "invalid chair" became the rage. Though it folded flat into a bed, the chair's back had several intermediate positions and its leg rest could be raised or lowered likewise.

The reclining figure also inspired some of the most memorable early-modern designs. During the late 1920s and throughout the 1930s, the long chair was rendered as a slim-profile form in resilient steel or laminated wood, tightly upholstered with leather, pony skin, or a thin membrane of sturdy fabric webbing. Each designer seemed to be asking the chair's user to think about his or her own intention before sitting down.

Le Corbusier, for instance, played with the notion of adjustability; his long chair can be shifted to raise the head for reading or the feet for idle relaxation. Alvar Aalto assumed that lounging meant snoozing or daydreaming, so he put the body in a floating position. Marcel Breuer, too, had his fun-loving moment with the long chair when he designed one in 1930 to roll around on bicycle wheels. Five years later, Breuer was rethinking lounging; this time, instead of preoccupation, he was concerned with occupation. So he made a long chair for the active person who prefers to sit relatively upright, supported firmly at the back, with knees raised just enough to turn the lap into a convenient support for books and papers.

The long-chair designs of Le Corbusier, Aalto, and Breuer, as well as the elegant designs of other European avant-garde modernists such as Ludwig Mies van der Rohe, René Herbst, and Bruno Mathsson, were considered luxury items and sold to progressive, well-to-do households with libraries and swimming pools. The same pieces, revived during the past decade or so, have been introduced to a wider, though still upper-class audience. Hardly anyone talks about selling or buying a long chair for the office, except when the office is in someone's home.

In the private environment of the home office, people seldom ask themselves if their behavior is "businesslike." A posture that might be frowned upon as "lying down on the job" in an office, where many eyes watch and thereby control each person's actions, is perfectly acceptable at home. And so reading a long document, working on a computer, and even writing a report on a yellow pad are activities that can be moved from the desk to a chair that keeps the body in an alert but relaxed position.

Thomas Jefferson worked in this manner at Monticello. Author of the Declaration of Independence, planner of the University of Virginia, and architect of his own mansion, Jefferson also knew something about designing furniture. He combined a comfortable but rather stiff club chair with a footstool, a table, and candles to make a compact workplace for himself. Arguably the genteel life on an eighteenth-century tidewater plantation cannot be compared with the fast-forward habits of postindustrial urbanites. But Jefferson's enlightened ideas about sitting and working, like his ideas about life, liberty, and the pursuit of happiness, continue to occupy people's minds.

Electronic Clutter

In 1984, Islip, New York, passed a tough noise code. The ruling came in response to an outpouring of emotions from the suburban community. The residents, expecting to live in peace and quiet, were increasingly disturbed by frequent flights into a once-sleepy airport on Long Island. Back in 1981, only 163,000 passengers passed through MacArthur Airport, owned and operated by the town of Islip. By 1986, there were 1 million people landing and leaving there. MacArthur had become a container for spillover traffic from New York's major airlines. (At La Guardia alone there were 22 million passengers last year.)

Excerpt, *Metropolis,* October 1987

Some 18 planes take off every minute across the United States, observed a panelist on a recent PBS broadcast of *Washington Week in Review.* He went on to describe the airline industry's uneasy relationship with the public: while people complain of crowding and failing services and talk more than before of their fears of flying, they take advantage of bargain fares and special deals encouraged by airline deregulation. The result of this increased activity is an overstressed system long overdue for expansion. No new airports have been built since 1974, the TV panelist added.

Plans for new developments are met by NIMBYism. "Not in my backyard," say the townspeople to garbage dumps, power stations, and airports. Instead of expansion, they're asking for solutions to some serious problems caused by existing systems. Water and air pollution are high on the list. Noise pollution too, as the Islip case shows, is an active public issue.

Noise is a strangely elusive pollutant. It can't be seen. It can't kill anyone. (Though every summer there's news of several people shooting or knifing one another over a too-loud radio.) In addition, each person hears things somewhat differently than another. An individual's expectations, activities, moods, and health often determine whether he or she identifies a sound as pleasant or irritating. For instance, the pyrotechnics over Central Park punctuating the New York Philharmonic's performance of Tchaikovsky's *1812 Overture* is exhilarating to a person who sits in a garden chair while cool night breezes ruffle leaves and banners around the park's Great Lawn. That same person, living in a high-rise with windows open to the park, can find the explosions highly disturbing as she's about to fall asleep after a long and wearing summer's day. Because sound is so subjectively interpreted, it's difficult for a community to agree on what part of it is a nuisance and should be outlawed.

Noise creeps up on people. All of a sudden there are a thousand designed objects that beep, talk, squeak, crackle, pop, click, grind, whoosh, murmur, and rumble, in addition to the familiar scream of sirens, screech of subway cars, and boom of helicopters and airplanes. What's more, some recent innovations seem designed to add to the electronic clutter.

The new fare boxes on New York City buses beep each time a payment is dropped in. Since the digital readout has already shown the driver what's in the box, why the beep? It's for the passengers, "welcoming you aboard," the MTA brochure explains of the modernization. What the hundreds of high-frequency sounds are about to do to the driver's already foul moods seems to be a forgotten issue. (In frustration, some bus drivers disconnect another bell, this one designed to signal a requested stop. Conditioned to expect an audible response to most actions, city bus riders grow noticeably agitated when they can't hear a bell or a buzz. Frantically, they press tapes, tug cords, and shout to be let off the bus. Only a few riders seem to notice the silent signal flashing overhead, a simple white-on-red light of recognition.)

Another people conveyer, the elevator, is designed with a new set of sounds. Though its rapid movement is barely marked by its discreet whoosh, the new elevator often chimes and simultaneously sends a verbal message on arrival at each floor. The redundancy of sounds is a well-intentioned design feature; it has been included to help hearing- and sight-impaired passengers. (However, the message of the socially conscious design was lost on one tense rider who, in response to the voice and bell, began to speculate about the identity of the ubiquitous electronic female. Her elevator voice, he said, sounded like the same woman who's constantly warning him to make a move in computer bridge.)

The many signals are part of a noise buildup that begins early in the morning. The Robot Coupe is making carrot juice. The Braun is pulverizing the coffee beans. The Conair is blowing wet hair into submission. And through the sounds of many small appliances doing their chores, Tina Turner with her ex, Ike, can be heard singing about a big wheel turning. It's not yet 9 a.m.

Sealed inside a glass box that hums with its own mechanical system, the urban office worker has just escaped from the sounds of construction, ambulances, police cars, fire trucks, garbage and sweeper trucks, car horns, and the roar of a thousand engines. And that only begins to describe the way to work above ground. Underneath the city, crowds press into subway cars that roar through antiquated tunnels in hellish dissonance. In the humming office, laser writers squeak, computer keyboards click, and commands on operating the copying machine are issued by a mechanical male voice. Phones warble, chime, buzz, and ring ceaselessly.

By day's end, the city dweller (the suburbanite, too, as the Islip case shows) is exposed to thousands of unwanted sounds. Those who go out to dinner scream across a wall of noise at one another in restaurants praised for their clever design and elegant food. At home, the upstairs neighbor's stereo plays for hours into the night, its bass vibrating through the floorboards. From next door, the soundtrack of *Miami Vice* and then amplified gunfire from *Crime Story* ricochet across the walls. Sleep comes from total exhaustion around midnight; it's broken into at 3 a.m. On summer mornings, a rooftop air-conditioner, installed with minimal insulation during a recent spurt of renovations, switches into higher gear and lets out a shriek, followed by 20 minutes of heavy rumble. From that moment on, the machine shrieks and rumbles nearly every hour.

"Earplugs. Get yourself a pair of earplugs," the sympathetic listener says to the frustrated noise victim. "Turn on your air conditioner," advises another. But the tiny, low-tech solution to what feels like a huge high-tech problem seems laughable. And the suggestion of fighting noise with noise seems downright antisocial; it merely adds to the general commotion that has created the discomfort in the first place.

As more people retreat behind the foam of earplugs or music from headsets and seal themselves inside vehicles, their many individual antinoise decisions amplify the din they've created in an unexpected way: in a community of the hearing impaired (though the handicap, in most cases, is a simulated one), it becomes necessary to increase the intensity of warning sounds of emergency vehicles. These essential community services must signal their need to move fast, without endangering life, on congested streets. So the brass bell of the pre–World War II New York City fire truck was converted to a loud siren, which became too weak after 20 years so the scream had to be made even louder, then louder still.

Clearly, noise pollution is in a growth pattern. Its complexity increases when noise is identified as a health hazard. Since the late 1960s, evidence has been mounting on noise's contribution to (even if it's not pinpointed as a direct cause of) some typically modern maladies. High blood pressure, heart disease, and ulcers are linked to it. Hearing loss and shortened attention spans are attributed to it.

The distracted citizens of Islip began concentrating on their own noise problem and set up a 24-hour hotline. Complaints decreased dramatically when the town's noise code was enforced: at MacArthur Airport, construction was ordered to stop on a runway and the airlines were asked to use quieter engines. Though the Islip ruling didn't identify noise as a design issue, it does send an implicit message to designers of public facilities and industrial products. People are looking for relief from noise produced by the designed conveniences they want to have.

Hilary Jay

The task for design writers is to convince people that they live in a designed world and that everything can be improved or changed for the better. And careful listening is part of this ancient, human-centered approach to design.

Music for One

Miniaturization is hardly a new concept when it comes to finding novel ways of disseminating information, be it the audible or visual kind. Before books became the personal portables of a new age, monks in medieval monasteries painted small intricate portraits of people, places, flora, and fauna to accompany learned Latin texts. By 1586, there was a word to describe what the monks were doing; they were making miniatures. In 1946, a hard, modern edge was given to the soft, old word, which became the active verb "to miniaturize." It described an increasing concern by industry to reduce the size of practically anything, in an effort to make products more personal and appealing to affluent consumers.

Excerpt, *Metropolis,* November 1987

By 1956, Dieter Rams had designed the Phonosuper, a phonograph and radio combined into a 22-inch-long box, manufactured in West Germany by Braun. Three years later, Rams and Braun had a pocket-size version on the market. Though the nine-inch-long phonograph/radio required large pockets, its weight was decreased by Rams's substituting plastic for the wood housing of earlier models.

At about the same time, John C. Koss, who was operating a TV-rental business in Milwaukee, began looking for a gimmick that would make a compact phonograph different from its competitors. He found it in a military surplus store. Koss and his partner, Martin Lange, hooked up a B-29-bomber headphone to a record player: they got predictably feeble results. Made to block out noise from airplane engines while transmitting the human voice, the military headphones were uncomfortable (they clamped tightly to the head); they were clearly unsuited for transmitting the new stereophonic sounds produced in recording studios for the hi-fi sets of the Eisenhower years. Only a major reworking of the headphones' electronic interiors would begin to produce the crisp highs, rich midranges, and deep bass sounds that have since come to be associated with music recorded in studios and performed in acoustically sophisticated concert halls.

Although by 1968 Koss was selling $1.8-million worth of headphones for use with home stereos, as a 1981 issue of *Success* magazine reported, it took another 10 years and a new wave of miniaturization to make private music listening a public fad. In 1979, Sony introduced its Walkman radio. What distinguished this Japanese portable (a five-and-a-quarter-inch tall, anodized-aluminum unit) from its contemporaries was its headphone attachment. From these tiny nodes came sounds of previously unheard of richness and clarity. The little round sponges between the transducer (a device that converts electrical power to acoustic power) and the entrance to the ear worked like the more bulky cups of the old military headphones. They kept music in and noise out. But the miniaturized versions, intended for private use in public places, had to admit essential noises like sirens and car horns for personal safety.

Sound waves bombarding the eardrums directly, without meeting with soft surfaces to dissipate them and hard surfaces to echo them, became a new sensation to millions who purchased the affordable portables. Until then, only a few special persons and a limited number of home-stereo headset users could hear a "soloist in the middle of the head," as the surreal experience came to be called.

Embraced for the convenient way they provided "music on the go," the miniaturized products also produced some subtle changes in human behavior. They challenged notions of privacy. Once associated with physical seclusion, privacy could be created with the aid of an electronic device that could transport minds to another place without relocating bodies. The same device could tame sharp urban noises while vibrating in the head with tunes no one else could hear. (The public, however, is increasingly an unwitting participant in private moments as tinny scrapings leak from too-loud headphones.)

"When you are using open-air headphones in a noisy environment, there is a natural tendency to turn up the volume enough to drown out the background noise," E. Brad Meyer writes in *Stereo Review* magazine. In describing tests he did with various headphones in noisy and quiet places, Meyer recalls, "The music did not seem particularly loud with the background noise on, and to hear the soft parts I would have to turn up the gain another 10dB (decibels) or so. But against a background of silence, it was almost painful." To prevent exposures to sounds that could cause pain and even hearing damage, some manufacturers of portable listening devices have added warning signals that flash on or interrupt the music when it gets louder than 90 decibels.

In addition to their potential for causing hearing damage, headphones are also criticized for their limitations in providing a total body experience some associate with auditory sensations. By concentrating the music inside the head, these well-directed devices bypass the viscera, that soft part of the human anatomy that vibrates with low-frequency noise and contributes to the physical pleasure of feeling musical sounds.

Karrie Jacobs

What I remember from that period in the eighties is that I had a lot of things on my mind that I wanted to write about, and people kept saying, "No, this isn't a story." The queerest example was this garbage crisis—some barge going up and down the East Coast. They couldn't find a place to deposit its trash. In my mind, there was a connection between packaging and the quantity of garbage, which now seems obvious but wasn't something anyone was talking about at the time. I remember pitching the idea here and there, surely to the *Village Voice,* maybe to a business magazine I was writing for at the time. And so I came to Susan with this list of articles that everyone had been rejecting, and she was just, "Oh yeah, this sounds great, yes, yes, please write this."

That receptivity to ideas was amazing. So it was paradise for a while, because I could write these endlessly long articles. I have no idea how I wrote them. They were over 3,000 words, probably more like 5,000 or more, written initially on typewriters because we hadn't switched to computers yet. There was one about the culture of convenience. There was one about corporate logos and what the increasingly abstract logos said about the nature of corporations. There was another about the design of mannequins. There was all this stuff that I was interested in, and nobody had ever let me off leash on before. But Susan was always, "This is very interesting, this is fascinating."

In her edits, she would use Post-it notes, commenting on everything, like, "Oh yes, this makes me think of such and such." It took me a while to figure out that she didn't mean I was supposed to include information about such and such. She was just having a dialogue with me. She's very maternal about ideas. She's always interested, and so ideas that other editors reject are the ones she adopts to nurture and grow.

It's a funny thing, but her genuine interest in everything is really a very important and lovable quality. No matter how abstract my ideas were, she encouraged me to pursue them. She just pushed me forward and told me to keep refining, keep working. She was the first person I met professionally in New York who said yes to pretty much everything I wanted to do.

Making Home Work

"I find myself feeling guilty if I'm not working," Dick Wolf, co-executive producer of *Miami Vice* told writer Tony Schwartz in a *Vanity Fair* article last year. Wolf is not alone. Millions, 24.9 million Americans to be exact, took work home in 1988. Of these "homeworkers"—a market researcher's term that fuses the opposing notions of home (leisure, privacy, family, retreat from jobs) and work (fast pace, office politics, a community of strangers, money making)—6 million worked at home full time. With a 22 percent increase from the year before, the full-timers account for the fastest growth among all those who work at home. These numbers were compiled by Link Resources, a New York City–based research and consulting firm that began documenting home work in 1986. Before then, communications-equipment manufacturers and vendors could only guess at what everyone suspected was a growing trend and a lucrative market for the many scaled-down and "user-friendly" electronic devices for sending, receiving, recording, and processing information.

On his way home, Mark Ethridge, the managing editor of the *Charlotte Observer*, can't unwind in his car as he once expected to. During the half-hour drive from the office, Ethridge thinks of "more things I should have done back at the office. So when I get home I'll often say to my daughter, 'Just a minute, Emily. I've gotta go to the computer and send a few messages to people.' And unfortunately, these people have computers in their homes, too, and they answer my messages. And then suddenly, I look up at the clock and it's time for the kids to go to bed, and I've missed being with them altogether," he told Schwartz in *Vanity Fair*.

Call them workaholic or careerist, dedicated or driven, self-absorbed or ambitious, these men and women (Link's 1988 figures show a 50-50 division between the sexes) spend more time with their cellular phones, fax machines, computers, printers, and stock-quote machines than they do with microwave ovens, blenders, washers, and other labor-saving devices designed to do the work of the household. Newspapers report that traditional housework is now the specialty of strangers who come to prepare meals, pick up laundry, do the ironing, and bring up baby. "In Boston, you can hire someone to walk your dog, shop for presents, and send cards," Maureen Dezell wrote in the *Boston Phoenix* in 1987.

How are such significant social changes altering the design of the house? Are interior spaces designated for the comings and goings of messengers, consultants, and domestic-maintenance workers? Are rooms planned to separate work life from family life or to integrate the two lives into one seamless whole? Do the contours of household furnishings show that the residents may want to relax while they're working?

Excerpt, *Metropolis*, March 1989

There are some small signs of change. For instance, one of *Builder* magazine's 1987 Builder's Choice Grand Awards went to a university faculty-housing project in Santa Barbara, California. Planned and designed by the IBI Group, architects in Newport Beach, California, the two-story, Mediterranean-style clusters of attached houses, with floor areas of 1,800 to 2,000 square feet, have studies opening to each unit's central courtyard. Along with a large kitchen, an extra bedroom, and a den, the study or library may be the beginning of a home office. But such traditional planning solutions to a newfangled problem don't do far enough, warns Julie Eizenberg, another architect from California.

"The standard housing provided by developers is still stressing the house as a separate place from work. But an increasing number of people we know work at home," says Eizenberg, half of the young couple that founded Koning Eizenberg Architecture in Santa Monica. "For these home buyers or renters, one suitable building type seems to me to be the urban loft," she adds, "but loft space in Los Angeles is growing scarce." At the same time, "loft sensibility" is no longer restricted to the artistic professions that set the trend for converting industrial buildings into live-work studios.

One alternative to the urban loft is the "suburban loft," according to the architects. Koning and Eizenberg have built two adjacent houses in the Hollywood Hills for clients they've identified as either a single person or a childless couple, all with intense work habits and an interest in keeping up with the downtown cultural scene. They choose the Hollywood location for its closeness to Los Angeles, its access to the freeway, and the availability of land for a garden. In this densely built suburb, the architects stacked rooms three stories high instead of spreading them out horizontally. They also provided a separate office with its own entrance from the street.

Koning and Eizenberg's Hollywood houses contain lives that might have been profiled by the researchers at Link. "One house is occupied by a couple in the movie business. Both of them work at home," Eizenberg explains. "The woman's office is downstairs, because she has contact with the public. The man works upstairs, in a sort of attic space next to the bedroom, on his computer. The house next door is rented by an architect who works full time in a large office elsewhere. For him, the home office is as much a guest room as it is a workplace." Eizenberg suspects that the architect chose the house less for its office space than for its aesthetic.

And the aesthetic is clearly industrial. Metal-mesh window guards, exposed concrete block, and pressed glass decorate the stark stucco buildings and distinguish them from their hacienda-like conservative neighbors.

What also sets these houses apart is their interior organization. Large square rooms piled on top of one another become increasingly more private as the residents ascend the stairs. The most public space in each home, the office, occupies the first floor over the garage. It is reached from the street and the front door and is kept separate from the rest of the house by a stairway door.

The work space looks out on the street, allowing for its occupant to keep an eye on the neighborhood. "There must be eyes upon the street, eyes belonging to those we might call the natural protectors of the street," Jane Jacobs wrote of urban neighborhood safety in her 1961 book, *The Death and Life of Great American Cities.* Her admonitions also apply to the suburban neighborhoods where the number of people working at home has increased traffic of delivery trucks and cars. Jacobs went on to say, "The buildings on the street equipped to handle strangers and to in- sure the safety of both residents and strangers must be oriented to the street. They cannot turn their backs or blank sides on it and leave it blind."

Residents' eyes connecting with their neighborhood also concern Anthony Pleskow and Mark Shapiro. The two young architects designed a separate office building to be located off the main entrance and on the street front of a reclusive-looking suburban house in which the residents' private lives take place behind a densely constructed facade. (As of now, the project remains a theoretical one, but it has had some public exposure and critical acclaim.) To Pleskow and Shapiro, the home office building with the residence in back is an idea that could be mass-produced by a suburban developer.

The architects imagine each little office (little, because it only needs to hold the compact electronic tools that hook up to a mainframe) occu- pied by a lone person who sees others working in their own home offices. "You look up from your work and can't help but know your neighbors or at least see them," Pleskow says. Even if eye contact never goes beyond nodding acquaintance, it can add to people's sense of belonging to a larger group pursuing similar interests. And any possibility for connecting people to one another is worth exploring, says Pleskow, who in his 26 years has watched as television, then cable television, VCRs, and com- puters worked their progressive isolation on people who "just sit in front of their TVs and never talk anymore. They don't even watch the same show anymore." Pleskow wants architecture to "force some kind of interaction" between people living in their "isolated cells."

But integrationists like Pleskow work in a society with some deeply ingrained attitudes toward individualism. "The New American Dream: Working on Your Own" was a trend identified by *Home Office Comput- ing* magazine in its September 1988 anniversary issue. Editor Claudia

Cohl paid "tribute to the people who dare to be one of a kind" and dedicated the issue to all those who now occupy home offices, run their own businesses, telecommunicate, or bring corporate work home. A significant shift in people's acceptance of home computers—first as plaything, then as work tool—is reflected in the magazine's two title changes in five years. Started as *Family Computing*, the magazine first expanded to *Family & Home Office Computing*. Then, in the summer of 1988, with a 350,000 "targeted home office" circulation, it became *Home Office Computing* and identified an $89-billion market for its advertisers of electronic hardware and software.

Cohl's editorial talks about "people with guts who are willing to gamble for themselves." It's next to an ad for Sharp products. "The home office comes of age with Sharp," claims the ad and quotes the same figures used in the magazine's promotional materials and its editorial pages. "Each machine is simple enough for you to install," the Sharp ad says. "These small, portable, lightweight products (fax machines, copiers, electronic memory typewriters, calculators, and laptop computers) are also integrated in function, to take up a minimum of space." Indeed, the six pictures in the ad show six extremely compact, cozy, and endearing home offices.

A slim glass table fits into what looks like a corner of a bedroom, along with a typist's chair and a shelf unit on wheels; the desk portion of a white, built-in kitchen cabinet is next to a black stove and a red metal chair; an old-fashioned desk and wall unit are shown with an old wicker chair in a wood-paneled den. Further into the magazine's pages, in the main editorial well, are the real people. Their offices resemble the ones in the Sharp ad: Alsy Graham is an accountant in Shawnee Mission, Kansas...Brian Bauer is a mail-order consultant in Somerville, Massachusetts...and Ash Jain is a computer-industry analyst in Irvine, California. They're all smiling.

Happy people living in farmhouses or on boats "interface" with their computers without any signs of the alienation and loneliness observed by Pleskow and predicted by social historians. There are tantalizing things about the personal freedoms they've come to associate with working at home. One Texas man told *Home Office Computing,* "You can cater to your own idiosyncrasies. You can play your favorite music, at any volume, and wear Bermuda shorts if you want." Another said, "You are your own clock; you set your own time and your own rules." The dressing-down-for-success advocate is photographed wearing a shirt and a tie, a crumpled pair of chinos, and scuffed loafers as he lounges on a bright yellow raft afloat on blue water; on his lap he holds a computer, in his hand a cellular phone. The man with the flexible time schedule has two consoles, a keyboard, and various small beige boxes scattered about; he's perched on a backless bentwood stool with knee rests. Are these happy home-workers comfortable?

They certainly look less tense and regimented than office workers doing the same kinds of jobs on similar equipment. There isn't a fluorescent tube in sight. Sunlight is everywhere. It shimmers through sheer curtains and dapples tawny wood floors, bringing to mind a cozy retreat, a soft refuge from the hard world of work. Signs of domestic comfort, as described by architect Witold Rybczynski in his book *Home,* surround the new work tools: "Convenience (a handy table), efficiency (a modulated light source), domesticity (a cup of tea), physical ease (deep chairs and cushions), and privacy (reading a book, having a talk). All these characteristics together contribute to the atmosphere of interior calm and that is part of comfort," Rybczynski writes.

Deep chairs and cushions are great for catching up on reading during work hours or stretching out to relieve cramped muscles. But the stiff wood and metal chairs and the cheap typist chairs that usually show up in ads for consumer electronics or are featured in decorating magazines and in pictures of real home offices are guaranteed to cause discomfort for people working on computers. The computer demands long stretches of concentrated attention.

The computer, in fact, has changed the ways and means of working. Shoshana Zuboff details this transformation in her 1988 book, *In the Age of the Smart Machine.* She writes of people who once ran a paper-manufacturing plant from the floor, then from computers in a separate room: "The main effort has shifted to what they could do with their minds, but it was difficult to fully comprehend that one could be working while sitting still." One of these workers was prompted to ask himself, "What is work now anyway?" Then he defined it: "It seems to me that our work has really changed and our work is now a lot of sitting, and watching, and thinking. You try to anticipate problems and concentrate on the process, even if you're having a conversation. Your mind never leaves the information."

Often "you find yourself on the edge of your seat," observes Bridget N. O'Connor, an assistant professor of business education at New York University and coauthor of a new book, *Automating the Office,* which she wrote on her home computer. O'Connor's business course introduces students to ergonomics—how people in offices use their bodies and computers and furniture to get the work done. She translates some of that information to the home office.

Office workers sit on chairs designed for the abstractions of their job titles assigned to them by interior designers; executive, managerial, secretarial, and word-processing chairs reflect the hierarchy of organizations. But home workers are free to choose chairs that fit them properly. While architects and interior designers have access to showrooms where they can choose from hundreds of chairs and work surfaces designed especially for the working body, ordinary people's choices are limited. Most furniture stores and galleries continue to cater to home fashions and not home work.

"Increasingly people call up and say, 'I want to buy a chair for my husband or wife who is working at home,'" says William Stumpf, the designer of successful office chairs manufactured by Herman Miller. Stumpf's chairs have an organic, inviting look ("like climbing into your grandmother's lap," he says).

In studying the working body for his chair designs, Stumpf likes to look at photographs of writers such as E .B. White in their homes. The photos prompt him to think about the designs of houses that receive work comfortably while accommodating everyday living gracefully. What Stumpf calls a "presentation house," a house built for show, status, and style, seems to him ill-suited to receive the new work patterns. He'd like to see the idea of a "studio house," a house built for "working at home in a healthy way," take hold. "To me, all this talk about the house of the future is not so much a technological issue as a change in emphasis from the presentation house to the studio house," Stumpf says. What is his model for this studio house? Particularly appealing to Stumpf are the houses of artists, artisans, and farmers, in which the residents are surrounded by their work.

Architect Turner Brooks has designed some successful studio houses. Brooks's natural integration of work and family may have been inspired by the Vermont farm country where he built his first houses. He thinks it comes from his love of "little factory towns where the workers' houses were near the factory and the church. There's something embracing about combining those two aspects of life."

Not so long ago, men talked about "holding down a job." Now their sons and daughters are searching for "satisfying work" and ways to integrate it with their private lives. They're asking, as Brooks does, how to combine work with home and "make the experience of both the house and the workplace richer and more exciting?"

Inclusive Design:
A New Challenge

The dot patterns you see on our cover this month and the ones that identify the various departments in the magazine (slugs, as these graphic devices are unflatteringly called) dramatize how far we are from universally accessible design in 1992. The most our flat dots can do is to remind the sighted that another alphabet, composed of patterns of raised dots, is used by the blind. But while braille exists in the world of the sighted, it may as well be a foreign language, an undecipherable code. We, the sighted, don't need to learn it (unless an accident forces us to); we don't need to concern ourselves about it or, for that matter, about the people who use it. Or so we used to think.

"Notes from Metropolis," Susan S. Szenasy and Horace Havemeyer III, November 1992

We reasoned that, in examining our attitudes toward access and physical barriers, we would discover why we keep making public spaces, workplaces, homes, and objects that exclude a large segment of our population. We think such soul-searching is essential to the survival of our democratic society.

Modern design history is filled with examples that can inspire today's universal designer. The important works of the moderns are there for all to study—not simply for their style, but for their innate sense of humanity and, yes, their social mission. Look, for instance, at Le Corbusier's 1929 Villa Savoie in Poissy-sur-Seine, France, and how he resolved the house's internal circulation with an artful system of ramps. What kid wouldn't love such a house? What old man wouldn't welcome the gentle incline of the ramps? And what cleaning person wouldn't appreciate the vacuum cleaner's easy roll down them?

Or study Alvar Aalto, the modern Finnish architect whose students recall his urgings to imagine their girlfriends standing in the window when they designed a house. Aalto's beautiful lever handles, his sensitively angled sinks and faucets, and his many other designs can provoke thoughts of a world that is better, more inclusive, than the one we've made for ourselves.

Patricia Moore, an industrial designer and gerontologist in Arizona, says she thinks a lot about her grandfather when she designs products that older people can use comfortably. And Bill Moggridge, a San Francisco industrial designer known for his high-tech work, has a granny. We all might be better people if we thought more about Granny, if we considered the needs of a little child, a pregnant woman, a teen with a broken ankle, a paraplegic in a wheel chair, a deaf or mute or blind person, or anyone else we know who doesn't belong to the fully abled, vigorous group for which virtually everything is designed today.

Patricia Moore

Universality in design—providing a means by which all people can achieve and maintain the quality of life that they deserve and desire—didn't resonate with the mainstream creative community until recently, because the consumers requiring attention were erroneously thought to be in need of medical interventions, not design systems. When Susan joined *Metropolis* magazine, her capacity for understanding and promoting inclusive design solutions for a person's entire lifespan, regardless of level of health or wealth, was a game changer. She has always been a significant proponent for design as the great equalizer, encouraging designers to embrace their role in the provision of compensatory places and products that promote autonomy and independence. While there have been significant improvements in the application of universal design principles over the last few decades, we are still essentially at the starting gate and there is much work yet to be done.

A Call for Design Activism

When I began to think about talking to this distinguished group, I went digging through the piles of magazines that have collected themselves in an obstacle course on my office floor. I was looking for recent copies of the publications that address the subject of interior design seriously and comprehensively. Not the many new consumer titles that now deal with design—interiors often being their primary focus—but the titles that can claim to understand the profession from within: the journals of the trade. I put them—*Interiors, Interior Design, Interiors & Sources,* among others less well known—next to my ergonomic chair, starting, as I like to do with any new project, a pile of focused information I can dig into. I was looking for the profession's image of itself. How it sees its processes, its products, its struggles in the world, its issues, its ideals, its shamans, and its devils.

Delivered at the annual meeting of the International Interior Design Association (IIDA) College of Fellows, Chicago, June 18, 2001

Then, I got a phone call from one of the editors of *Interiors* saying that the magazine had just shut down. For me, this news was a heartbreaker. I cut my teeth on *Interiors.* I learned design journalism there. I also learned about the richness, the beauty, the economic and cultural necessity of interior design. I got to know the field first by covering the market and discovering new products for all kinds of furnishing projects. Later, I got to meet the designers who used these products. What struck me was their broad and generous view of the world. They knew art, they loved architecture, they chose objects with care, they bought great books, they talked about theater and film, they traveled extensively and purposefully, they wore great watches, they became my ideal designer.

I was also disturbed by the demise of *Interiors* for a more professional reason. A field, any field, is as rich and as lively as the dialog it generates. And we at *Metropolis,* who observe and report on all of design, we are at our best when there's access to solid material from each of the professions. We're always looking for primary material—the inside stuff—that only the trade knows about itself and is willing to discuss among its peers. When one more voice of design is stilled, we, all of us, are diminished somewhat.

It was at *Interiors,* before the magazine began to lose its way, that I found my passion for design during the 1970s. It was also the place where I discovered the deep and dirty little secret that haunts much of design-trade-magazine writing to this day. The stories are written from pictures. This approach may explain the lifeless copy, the vapid and skimpy text adjacent to the gorgeous images. Very early on, I began to wonder how you can write about something you haven't experienced. The quality of light, the colors, the textures, the space, the people in it—all need to be perceived by a writer who tries to describe a room. After all, rooms are meant to be lived in, worked in; it's there where we spend most of our lives. Because of this intense involvement with our immediate surroundings, our rooms deserve to be treated with according intensity of thought and purpose. The rooms you design are much more complex in their meaning and use—much more resonant—than some clever composition pulled together for the camera of some latter-day Jaime Ardiles-Arce. Our rooms and our furnishings, be they private or public, may be our most important personal and cultural artifacts next to our clothes.

Then, I started to notice that you, too, found superficial coverage of your field empty and maybe even dangerous. That the publishing model set up to cover your area of expertise was becoming tired and needed to be rethought as the world around you changed. When the IIDA began to put out those information-rich copies of *Perspective,* I thought, great, the trade journals will surely reflect this new understanding interior designers are reaching for. So what happened? You got Addison DeWitt on the back page of *Interior Design* bitching about something or another. And you got *Interiors* doing movie reviews set in such miniscule type that the magazine should come with a magnifying glass.

Here you were struggling with huge issues like environmental sustainability, integrating technology, understanding the rapidly shifting business world you operate in—and you got pictures along with some rare and clever copy about the foibles of your profession. Where were the floor plans, the axos, the detail drawings, or any other informational graphics to help you understand what was in those pictures? But more than that, where were hard-core analyses of the chemical soup you were brewing— with all the best intentions, I'm sure—in those sealed environments still being provided by architects and their builders? Where were the debates about the changing nature of work and how people behave in their places of work and, more important, how these behaviors relate to your own work? And where were all those much-needed lifecycle cost evaluations of the products you used? In other words, where were the stories in your trade publications that helped you do your jobs, which have the potential for making the rest of us comfortable or miserable.

A growing number of those stories have started showing up in *Interiors & Sources,* in the magazine, on their Web site, and at their conferences. But your major design publication, the one that continues to get your fealty, the one that rules this trade show we're attending, has been mostly silent on those issues. I went through the NeoCon issue of *Interior Design,* after Addison DeWitt had vacated the premises, and found only one mention of the environment in 368 pages; that mention was an ad bought by Interface, a letter to the industry from CEO Ray Anderson announcing his successor.

If the demise of *Interiors* broke my heart, this current issue of *Interior Design* made me afraid for you and, by association, those of us who come in contact with your work. Granted, I caught the magazine between editors, and it's unkind to be critical when a competitor is down. But I'm talking about years of developing a publishing model, not just the current issue. And the appointment of a marketer as editor should also give you pause. There are, after all, real, tried-and-true reasons for separating church from state, in our case, editorial from marketing. There's a natural friction between these two very different arms of publishing. There's editorial integrity and independence and there's marketing savvy and pizzazz. While the two must always strive to coexist, they should never cross into each other's sacred territories. Unbiased, well-documented, critical writing is what your profession desperately needs—not more marketing hype. Heaven knows you're already inundated with that kind of happy talk. Though this edgy conflict between editorial and marketing is an historic one, today it's being blurred by magalogs, zines, and Web sites where there seems to be no knowing what you're being sold and why. There are more opportunities to muddy the waters of information—and, in the process, cheat you, the seeker of useful facts and thought-provoking ideas.

As you know, most design magazines are going through a shift dictated by a roster of economic, social, technical, and cultural indicators. There are, for instance, growing signs that people are more aware than ever before of their home and work environments and how these express them, as well as serve them. Many of us know from firsthand experience that baby boomers are inheriting their parents' savings. And prognosticators tell us that those 80 million fiftysomethings are more likely to use their inheritances to change their lifestyles, as well as adapt their homes to be more accessible or start new careers. If you watch network TV, you might surmise that Americans are mostly presbyopic, arthritic, dentally challenged, techno-savvy, ecosensitive, wealthy, mature folk who look great and are determined to move fast and run fun businesses. That, as well as the new generation of well-heeled and well-educated young entrepreneurs and managers, foretells a growing need for design services of all kinds, including interior design of all kinds.

Are you ready to serve a wired population that is concerned about the environment?

It has become a well-known fact that a growing number of people are fundamentally worried about the degradation of our natural world. The man and woman on the street have experienced polluted air, compromised air quality in offices, impure water, as well as E. coli–infected vegetables and fatally diseased meats. At the Metropolis West Conference in San Francisco, these popular concerns were interpreted by an investment councilor as reflecting potential buying patterns. It is now understood, a Solomon Smith Barney spokeswoman told us, that 75 percent of American consumers believe that buying green products is a good way to help the environment. She added that 58 percent would like to buy as many green products as possible, but that 73 percent believe they don't know enough to identify a green product. Do you know enough? Now, think of the interior designer as the Colossus of Consumers. You buy chairs 500 at a time, while the rest of us mortals buy two or four or six or eight at a time, and probably thrice in a lifetime, if that often. With your kind of buying power, you can literally remake the consumer society we live in.

But I worry about you. Mostly, I worry because as an editor I judge the vitality and effectiveness of each profession by the sophistication of the literature that serves it and surrounds it. And as I see it, among all the design professions—including graphics and product design—interior design has not been able to develop the habit of encouraging critical writing, the kind of informed dialogue that has helped the other designers see themselves better, more realistically. Just look at the shelves of architecture books. Among the vanity picture books you'll find plenty of others that make you think about the built world. And even though the worldview of architects is in transition, and architecture itself is fighting its own alienation from society, architects have a tradition of critical thinking which will surely help them get safely through this current confusion.

I also worry that your educational system is not as rigorous, as broad ranging as it needs to be in these challenging times, which demand more of you than you ever imagined when you entered design school. Let me tell you of a recent experience that made me think of this. I was part of the panel of judges that gave the SOM Foundation travel fellowship this year in interior design. We came up with two finalists, one with a smashing presentation of some warmed-over ideas gleaned from Rem Koolhaas, Herzog & DeMeuron, and other star architects. Our other choice had submitted a rather tentative presentation of a poetic idea inspired by Pablo Neruda. When we interviewed these two young women, we found out that the sophisticated, computer-savvy presentation was the work of an architecture student. It showed skill in rendering, in spatial configuration, in understanding interior-exterior relationships, as well as a connection to the entertainment culture of our time. This student had had a sum total of nearly eight years' training in two Ivy League architecture schools. The poetic, amateurish entry was by an interior design student in her senior year at a state college. These two will probably compete for the same entry-level job. Which one would you hire? We went for the poetry, with the hope that travel and experience will broaden this young designer's skills and outlook. Perhaps our choice also expressed an exhaustion with sleekness, thus the appeal of the unfinished, the unformed, the raw potential. But the reality remains that the architecture student got a better, more thorough, more solidly grounded education.

I stand outside all the design professions. I am simply an observer. And when I see interdisciplinary squabbling, it makes me sad—sad for the combatants and sad for the rest of society, because your attention is being diverted from the larger, more critical issues of our times. I would suggest, as some of you do, too, that you drop your territorial combat with the architects and join forces with them instead. We need places and rooms where we can live healthy lives, do productive work, play, and refresh our bodies and spirits. You have the basic training to give us what we need. And I know you're working to update your already impressive skills and extend your knowledge. While you are doing this, you also need to pay renewed attention to your already well-known ability to collaborate. I say this, because the problems we face are much too complex to be handled by any one profession. It has become patently clear that in the struggle to achieve sustainable design, all designers, as well as your advisors from other professions, must join together and share information on every aspect of the natural and the designed environment. Society needs your skills. And if you don't live up to design's high calling, our legislators will force you to.

Think of the ADA. I thought when Congress passed the Americans with Disabilities Act in 1990 that it was recognized how dismally designers in every known specialty have failed in serving the needs of all of the public. Urban planners showed little understanding of how people with reduced abilities can get around safely; architects forgot that people are blind or have difficulty walking or ambulate in wheelchairs and could not negotiate conventional entrances to buildings; industrial designers ignored the possibility that their grandmother might have trouble opening a can of peas with a stylish can opener; graphic designers simply flaunted every law of basic communication and used either supremely understated or extremely overstated type treatments at the expense of information sharing; and interior designers specified chairs no pregnant woman could get out of and used shiny surfaces that would disorient their grandfathers. So, as I see it, a law was passed to make our world kinder and gentler because designers weren't doing it. Remember it was George Bush Senior's VP, Dan Quayle, who championed the ADA, which forced designers to think about complex human needs, at all stages and ages of life. While a lot of architecture and design firms saw it as another nuisance regulation, I saw it as a flawed but great piece of civil-rights legislation. What is more American, after all, than access to the good life for every-one, regardless of ability or disability?

You have the potential, in collaboration with the other design profes-sions, to come together and create an immensely powerful lobby group for environmental change. It might be instructive to add up your income clout, that is, to document how much of our material resources all the design professions are responsible for putting into production, in terms of natural capital as well as financial capital—a Gross Designed Product, or GDP, as I like to call it. You will be surprised how powerful you are—together. Then, use these figures, along with your considerable powers of persuasion, to convince those in political power to change the way they write laws that regulate how we use and allocate our resources.

You already have a well-honed relationship with your suppliers. You can build on that relationship and create a much more positive role for yourselves. You can become even more valued collaborators to manufac-turers than you already are. They, like you, are looking for materials and processes that help us live lightly on the land. Your job can no longer be interpreted as a super-salesperson of high-priced products. You have an expertise and a growing body of knowledge to share with them—as with others in your profession. Yes, it's time to release all that proprietary re-search embedded in each of your offices—your edge is your design, not the data you hoard. As leaders of a powerful association, you can decide to become the central library or bank of shared information, connected by AIA, IDSA, ASID, AIGA, BIFMA, IFMA, etc., and a growing number of environmental and technical groups.

This world of design collaboration can happen in many ways. You may want to think about creating an information bank into which each and every designer can make regular deposits and is welcomed to make withdrawals as needed. You, as well as all your sister and brother orga-nizations, already have the electronic infrastructure in place; your Web sites are rich in information. So, who will make the first move to bring all of design together?

I suggest the role of conciliator should fall on you, the interior designer. I say this because you already deal with the output of all that the other design professions create. You see how it all fits, or more likely, doesn't fit in the rooms you design. Your mission, should you choose to accept it, could lead to a new, more inclusive definition of design that takes respon-sibility for creating a cleaner, healthier, better world for everyone.

Our Missing Symbol

It's one of those clear, late summer days in Manhattan when the sky shimmers: a day like the one that turned into 9/11. But today, a gray cloud hangs over the southern tip of Sixth Avenue—the vapor left behind by the twin towers of the World Trade Center. TV newscasters say that the cloud is part steam, radiating still, after five days, from the hyperheated steel beams of the buildings' fallen skeletons.

My journal is filling up with strange facts. It reads like the banal entries I made with each death in my family. In those moments of personal loss, I turn into an objective recorder of time, place, and event. That same feeling of desolation and helplessness hangs over me now; but this time, it's tinged with an inexplicable optimism. When I look away from where the twin towers once were, I keep seeing them in my mind's eye. They were, as so many other buildings could be, great and powerful symbols of their time. In their aggressive and bombastic forms—which would not submit to being tempered even by such details as Italian Gothic arches— they represented a heightened version of "heroic capitalism," as Kenneth Clark once described the modern boxes of glass and steel of Sixth Avenue.

We know now that these dramatic symbols of American optimism, wealth, technology, and, yes, hubris, were what doomed them. But I want to think about their incredibly positive legacy for architecture and the urban form.

They were, after all, buildings that thoroughly expressed the ethos of late-twentieth-century America, in all its many mercantile complexities. And when architecture does that, it takes on a special meaning for the society it serves.

Millions of others were taken in by the towers' magnificence. For most parts of the city, as well as from the surrounding suburbs and highways, they became a beacon of the metropolis I fell in love with. Though architecture critics hated them—complaining of their monstrous size and how they threw the once romantic skyline off balance—most of us on the street marveled at these colossal structures.

When I found out that their architect, Minoru Yamasaki (who built the towers in 1972–73 with Emery Roth & Sons), was afraid of heights, the buildings took on another, more emotional dimension. As it turns out, their elongated form and unorthodox design (their steel skeleton was external rather than the more common internal skeleton, thus avoiding disruptive supporting columns) seemed as much a personal triumph over fear as it was a professional triumph over the expected. And after the towers survived the 1993 bombing, I had complete faith in their ability to stand up to any trauma, as apparently, did many of those who went down with them. I believed, like Yamaski, that they would withstand a collision by a jet plane (as he's been quoted saying).

On that horrible Tuesday morning, as we watched from the corner of Sixth Avenue and Twenty-third Street, the north tower's top burned, but the building itself seemed solid. Then, shortly thereafter, we ran over to Fifth Avenue and watched the south tower engulfed in smoke. I was panicked but hopeful. The towers would be damaged, and the inferno raging therein would kill hundreds, but the buildings would stand up to the assault. Or so I blindly repeated to everyone who would listen. Then, in a moment, they were gone; and apparently so were thousands of people. With them went everything we valued in late-twentieth-century America, except for our hopeful nature and our community spirit. Suddenly, the sleek images of a week ago seem irrelevant and out of place. On Times Square, where the hyperkinetic NASDAQ sign is replaced by listings of emergency numbers and Motorola's gigantic cell flashes the numbers of blood banks, the theatrical angst of Gap models looks ridiculous.

There is real anguish everywhere. It's in all those small, handmade posters of the "missing" taped to phone booths, bus stops, and shop windows. Union and Washington squares are filled with expressions of sorrow, put there as shrines, art works, memorials. The faces of those with lost friends and relatives are pained beyond belief; the rest of us have that blank, empty look. We reflect the emptiness that I see at the southern end of Sixth Avenue.

Many are asking if a new, perhaps more humane, ethos will be born of this catastrophe. Pundits and priests tell us that our undying capacity for hope and abiding love of community will surely sustain us. And some of us feel, somewhere deep inside, that this new and strong culture has the promise to create memorable architecture and a revitalized urban form that will express who we have become. The twin towers of the World Trade Center have set up that expectation for us. When I close my eyes, I can still see them gleaming in the morning sun.

Finding Our Voice
After the Attacks

October 4, 2001, New York City: "It's coming down! Get away from it!" "Notes from Metropolis," December 2001 a man screams on Citywide 1, the local cable channel capturing rescue workers' calls for help on September 11. Another terrified voice hollers, "We've had another tower collapse!" Someone else: "We have officers trapped!" Three weeks after the world witnessed the destruction of the World Trade Center, these conversations are being made public. We can now relive the horror of that day through the recorded anguish of human voices. Who, among them, is still alive?

This morning as I listen, sobbing, to strangers sending out their pathetic distress signals, I feel connected to them. Recalling what we witnessed that day, I find their desperation real and forever haunting. Now, in addition to its enormous scale and mechanical drama, the collapse also has a voice—strong and brave and precise. And so the inevitable questions arise: How do we, the survivors and bystanders, honor those cries? How do we find our own voices and give them meaning?

It's been hard not to feel mute and defeated and insignificant living inside the whirlwind of rumors, facts, and events that tear through the city each day. Bomb scares. Sirens. Avarice. Impatience. Even before "the missing" were pronounced "the dead," a TV reporter talked about the $100 billion needed to bring New York back.

On October 2, Gridsite.com reports what sounds like a done deal between Silverstein Properties (the leaseholder of the twin towers and other real estate at the World Trade Center) and the local architecture firms Skidmore, Owings & Merrill and Cooper Robertson Architects. Larry Silverstein promises us "something of spectacular beauty—something that again will become the icon of New York and serve as the economic generator of activity of the financial district and [honor] the lives lost and the courage of those who came to help." Although Silverstein's desire to rebuild is admirable, his haste is not. It has become impossible to conduct business as usual, especially in urban redevelopment. The world now has a connection to that site. It has acquired a kind of spiritual eminent domain in which every New Yorker—if not every U.S. citizen and person everywhere—feels a profound connection to its future.

On the same day, crammed into the small, hot conference room at the Guggenheim SoHo, 30 of us struggle to find our collective voice. We're all die-hard New Yorkers: business people, architects, designers, citizens. Among us are representatives from the Manhattan Borough President's Office, Community Boards 1 and 2, the Partnership for New York City, the Alliance for Downtown New York, the Lower Manhattan Cultural Council, the New York League of Conservation Voters, the Earth Pledge Foundation, the Municipal Art Society, the New York Hall of Science, the American Institute of Architects, the Guggenheim Foundation, the Architecture Research Institute, and *Metropolis* magazine. We eventually decide to call ourselves the Twenty-First-Century Building and Action Coalition.

Different disciplines and skills, we tell ourselves, are needed to figure out what shape the twenty-first-century city might take. We're asking questions. We're not ready to make proposals. We hope to draw up a list of ideas about human needs. We're certain that these needs are different today than when the towers were built 30 years ago. So we ask: How do people live and work? How has our new relationship with technology changed the daily patterns of urban life? How do we integrate sustainability, history, and technology into our new city forms? Can we have a city less dependent on cars? How can art, memory, spirituality, health, and education get a hearing in the rush to reinvigorate the economy? How do our voices get heard?

We work to hear each other over the jackhammers outside. Annoying though this familiar noise is, someone from downtown says she's nostalgic for it and wishes it was still part of her now bombed-out neighborhood. One gentle voice starts defining what I see as our new direction. It belongs to a young man, an architect. Rafael Pelli, of Cesar Pelli & Associates, the firm that designed the World Financial Center, believes that today we have the technology to make buildings much more energy efficient than they are. We need to start looking at the city not as individual buildings but as a collection of "buildings that are consumers of air, water, and power," he says. "Everyone in New York understands how a street has to work, how public spaces have to work." But it's harder to understand sustainable design, which is pretty much, Pelli adds, "still in formation, like a research project." What developer, we wonder, has patience to experiment when "economic generators" are called for? And yet what developer can afford to ignore the environmental consequences of its real estate projects?

Though puzzled and somewhat dismayed, we make plans and set the date for our next meeting. We know that if we are to become effective advocates for an environmentally sensitive and humane city, we must find our own strong and brave and precise voice. That brutal pile of rubble, that obscene hole in the ground, and that lingering cloud of smoke urge us to try. It's the least we can do for those thousands whose lives we watched turn to dust.

Beverly Willis

Susan and I had set up a lunch date for September 12, 2001. The day before, Sue called me and said, "I think we need to cancel our luncheon because of 9/11." I said, "No, we shouldn't! It's imperative that we get together to discuss what we're going to do about it." Everybody in New York City—all the attorneys, accountants, managers—were coming together in their own professions and disciplines to contribute to rebuilding Lower Manhattan. We all needed to figure out what to do to keep New York functioning with this tremendous wound in the city fabric.

Susan and I started e-mailing people we knew, asking if they wanted to contribute their time to our effort. The immediate response was overwhelmingly positive; we wound up with 500 volunteers. We divided them up into separate committees based on their areas of expertise, and we all got down to work.

Susan and I formed a nonprofit agency called Rebuild Downtown Our Town, R.Dot for short, focused on the entire city zone below Canal Street. It was clear that state and local government people were going to deal with the 16 acres immediately surrounding the disaster site, but we knew it was important to look at everything around it as well. Over a three-year period, we put out five papers and five booklets, including the first white paper that dealt with how to get things working again in Lower Manhattan. We covered transportation, retail stores, housing—the main sections of the physical environment that needed to be redone or replaced.

Because the downtown electrical grid was so damaged in the terrorist attack, the city ran power to affected areas via what we called extension cords. It was unbelievable to walk around the streets and see these huge high-voltage cables plugged into buildings everywhere. The equipment was so heavy that it not only crushed the surface of the streets, it destroyed the utility infrastructure underneath as well. So, ultimately, everything under the streets in Lower Manhattan had to be replaced, simply because of the need to get that heavy equipment into that area. And, of course, that's the oldest part of town, with the smallest streets in the city.

We started R.Dot quickly and for a while we were the only action in town. All the other existing civic organizations, being large, moved slowly. They were required to follow certain steps and procedures, which we didn't have to do. Our working process functioned very smoothly. I accepted the management responsibilities and wrote up first drafts of the documents. Then I'd turn them over to Susan, who did all the editing. Graphic designer Roland Gebhardt created and prepared the documents for publication. I wound up taking our plans around to most of the local government representatives, while Susan took them around the country and talked about them on her trips. We held media conferences attended by international press. Susan has the most incredible capacity for work, getting off the airplane and heading straight into group meetings where she's either a speaker or a moderator. I do not know anybody in the field who does what she does. Our efforts made a great impact during a time when everyone wanted to help restore normal conditions in Lower Manhattan, but no one was quite sure what to do or how to get started.

Back to the Drawing Board

The six plans proposed for rebuilding the World Trade Center site in Lower Manhattan go on display tomorrow in Federal Hall at Wall and Nassau streets. In this historic place, where George Washington took the oath as our first president, visitors can study the proposals drawn up by the Lower Manhattan Development Corporation and the Port Authority of New York and New Jersey. Both these organizations—having been treated to worldwide editorial derision since the plans became available last week, plus a day of public contempt (live at the Javits Center) on the weekend—have decided to rethink their efforts. It isn't hard to see why.

Opinion editorial, *The New York Times*, July 23, 2002

Each of the six schemes is dominated by an office park that could be anywhere—tall buildings arrayed in either L or U shapes. Each plan has similarly massive retail spaces, calling to mind the suburban shopping malls along any highway service road. And each scheme offers up some space for a memorial to the victims of September 11. The word "memorial" is on all the plans, showing that the planners see the need to remember our day of great loss and destruction. Or perhaps they're putting this word out front because all their plans are dedicated mainly to the financial obligations of the current leaseholders for 11 million square feet of office space, 600,000 square feet of retail space and a 600,000-square-foot hotel.

Those who visit Federal Hall or log on to www.renewnyc.org will get an opportunity to study the plans in some detail, including bird's-eye views of Lower Manhattan spinning around. It's easy to be seduced by the technology. But you'll get over it quickly, as did the more than 4,000 people, mostly area residents and workers, who attended the town hall meeting at the Javits Center on Saturday. We were seated 10 to a table, forming a skeptical and wary crowd. Those in charge assured us they wanted our feedback. That's what the wireless keypads were for. By the end of the long day, there were signs that the "decision makers," as the men in charge of rebuilding were called, realized that the original program needed some reassessment. Probably the two most common comments were "timid" and "boring."

For those of us who believe in the power of informed planning and inspired architecture, what we saw was especially disturbing. Is it possible that our city's robust architecture offices—the firms who worked on the plans were Beyer Blinder Belle, Architects and Planners; Peterson/Littenberg Architects; Skidmore, Owings & Merrill; and Cooper, Robertson & Partners—can only come up with such anemic proposals?

Ever since I first saw the plans at the Lower Manhattan Development Corporation office last week, and again as I walked away from the Javits Center on Saturday, one thought kept going through my head. It had to do with ethical professional behavior, with how architects and planners view their obligations and responsibilities. The Lower Manhattan and Port Authority planners understood their obligation in the narrow sense: to serve their clients, forgetting their larger obligation to the people of New York. While they made much of designing for the millions who are expected to visit the memorial, they neglected the men, women, and children who live and work and go to school and play in the area now and will do so in the future.

Most significantly, the planners left out residential buildings from the site. Housing, the lifeblood of any city neighborhood, was not requested by the clients. But these planners and architects are professionals who understand the facts of urban existence very well. They're learned people who know that it is the many individuals, going about their daily lives, that animate the streets and create the vitality that cities such as New York exude. By keeping a narrow focus, they designed a place that would almost have to seem desolate.

Ultimately, would their clients be happy with such sterility? Will such a space attract the tenants they want? Will there be enough jobs to fill all those millions of square feet as computerization continues to change the places and the ways of work?

Thinking about these six tentative plans and the surprisingly loud and consistent cries of disappointment that greeted them, I wondered if we have lost our knack for bringing together big bucks with big ideas. In earlier generations, planners had the gumption and the vision to build grand and memorable public projects like the Brooklyn Bridge, the Lincoln Tunnel, and Rockefeller Center. Are we at the end of our creative run? Have we reached a moment when we are capable of designing only bland office parks and lightly nostalgic shopping malls? If so, we better snap out of it and fast. We can start in Lower Manhattan.

New Yorkers expect a twenty-first-century city to rise from the ashes of the twin towers and connect with the historic city. We need a "high-tech Machu Picchu," someone said at our table in the Javits Center.

Our culture has so many talented architects and planners, both within the large, established companies and at younger firms. When will we start asking them to help us imagine our future? We need designs that will truly revive and support our economy and satisfy our dreams for a world-class metropolis. These architects and designers need planners who are skilled at analyzing demographic and economic trends and who can use this information to create a realistic blueprint on which to build.

There are many ways to honor those who turned to dust, and those who were forever scarred, on that horrible day last September. While we must build a memorial for them—and a burial ground for those whose remains were never found —the most respectful memorial to the future our lost New Yorkers might have had will be a beautiful new city rising from that 16-acre hole in the ground. This architectural masterpiece will become the hopeful place that people are so desperately asking for, a place worthy of being a pilgrimage site.

Inclusion

There's only one man in a wheelchair inside the cavernous Schimmel Auditorium at Manhattan's Pace University and he's behind the last row of seats. He's attending a public hearing along with 700 other New Yorkers on an evening in May. We've gathered at the invitation of the Lower Manhattan Development Corporation (LMDC), who wants to hear (or so it tells us) what we think about the future of the World Trade Center site. "Notes from Metropolis," August/September 2002

After the opening niceties from the mostly white, middle-aged men seated on the stage—"We're embarking on a remarkable journey together," intones Daniel Doctoroff, New York City's deputy mayor for economic development and rebuilding—the crowd, kept in line by an expert facilitator, opens up. The first barrage of comments is a call for independence for the disabled and a need to include this often neglected constituency in the LMDC's transportation committee. The city and the building we're in, notes the speaker, "is difficult enough to navigate on two good legs," adding that nowhere in any future development plans is there a mention of universal design principles.

Universal design has been the law of the land since 1990, when the Americans with Disabilities Act (ADA) was passed by Congress to protect the civil rights of millions whose daily lives are frustrated by their environment. Setting out to right the wrongs perpetrated on the public by designers, architects, and their clients, the ADA has spawned some clumsy adaptations to buildings. Sometimes when I see those awkward ramps and clunky railings and gratuitous signs in braille in places that no blind person will ever find, I think the design community is protesting government's tyranny over their freedom of creative expression. It's hard to argue with such protestations, especially since the ADA administrators seem to show no inclination toward artistic interpretation.

Instead of pointing fingers, however, it might be more productive to remember that creative freedom comes with responsibility. The designer is ultimately responsible to the greater public—to that wonderfully complex entity of unique individuals who call themselves Americans. And while the audience that night was certainly more inclusive than the LMDC—Chinatown, for instance, was represented by garment workers, union members, and other men and women all speaking through an interpreter—the setting, the public transportation, and the streets that brought them there all deprived those with disabilities from being heard.

I thought of this exclusion that evening as I ran up the stairs to the mezzanine. The steps themselves would have been impossible to negotiate by someone walking with a cane, but the design of the auditorium presented even bigger problems. Upon entering, I recoiled from the steep incline of the floor. The idea of walking—or plunging!—down those steps sent me back downstairs, where it seemed less vertiginous. Who but the fearless student population could feel comfortable in a room so aggressively insensitive to the needs of anyone over 21?

Was this exclusionary design recognized as an object lesson by the LMDC? Facing TV film crews, flashing cameras, and relentless criticism, some members on stage looked stunned, others seemed bored (one was apparently asleep). Will these political appointees think of the public—all of the public—when they make plans to rebuild downtown?

Real issues like how to build the twenty-first-century city and make it accessible, environmentally sensitive, poetic, inspiring, secure (for users as well as for their protectors, like firefighters and police) were on the public's agenda that night. But three days later, our newspaper of record reported something else about the long and colorful evening. "At Hearing, A Resolve to Rebuild Twin Towers," read the New York Times headline. Though that idea was met with thunderous applause, so were many other ideas that were more constructive. Such hasty and inaccurate reporting makes me pause. I can't help but wonder how we can hope for a serious public dialogue on real issues if our most influential paper doesn't recognize them.

But the idea of inclusion dominated the evening, as everyone who was there knows. And it must inform any rebuilding plan. The silent hole in the ground—now that the noisy recovery and cleanup effort is over—compels us to remember the acts of humanity performed on that heartbreaking day. We heard of strangers guiding blind men to safety and others who carried a woman in a wheelchair down hundreds of steps without even knowing her name. Let those actions inform and inspire the great ideas that will shape the twenty-first century.

After the Fall

My mailbox is known for being the most overburdened one in our office; "Notes from Metropolis," October 2002 some days, it looks like a file folder on steroids. So, in late July, no one noticed the most recent flurry of papers, a deluge of proposals for rebuilding the World Trade Center site. This postal frenzy—my electronic mailbox grew just as crowded—was in response to a July 23 op-ed piece that I wrote for the *New York Times*. Its editor encouraged me to voice my dismay over the six lackluster plans released a week earlier by the Lower Manhattan Development Corporation and the Port Authority of New York and New Jersey (LMDC/PA). The public revolt against those plans has become a legend by now, but at the time, my outrage was still news.

After the *Times* hit the newsstands and the proposals started to arrive, a disturbing question kept vibrating in my brain: are designers ready for the coming public debate on issues that touch our lives? As the twenty-first century takes ever more global contours and new technological, environmental, and behavioral issues present themselves in rapid succession, we look for enlightenment from those among us who possess specialized knowledge. Architects and planners, for instance, can help us understand new urban forms. They know how buildings relate to the natural environment and to the public; how transportation systems can benefit a region; how technology can be used to create safe places; and a myriad of other quality-of-life issues. But if the content of my mailbox is any indication, our designers may not be prepared to enter the new public dialogue.

Proposals came to me from architects, artists, scholars, and environmentalists, a book publisher, and ordinary citizens. The architects, as expected, drew their ideas as seductive forms. And while each one was more sensitive to people's needs than the LMDC/PA's simplistic commercial-development proposals were, all had one shocking feature in common. None of the architects seemed to remember that the basis of design—any design—is solid research and analysis. This leads me to ask why so many designers are willing to create forms without a plan. Is this urge to draw stronger than the need to understand? Or is drawing confused with understanding? Are we pushing designers—as the LMDC/PA's designers seem to have been pushed—to give form prematurely?

The basis of a plan that serves the ultimate client—the people who use it—is thorough research and analysis. This may be intuitive, observational, experiential, or statistical research, or better yet, all four. If there was ever an argument for such an approach, it was those six dreary LMDC/PA plans. Their inadequacy—and the inadequacy of the firms that drew them up—was blasted worldwide by the media. While the civic groups that formed after 9/11 were feeding the LMDC useful information on everything from mixed-use to sustainability to multicentered cities to transportation hubs and managed streets, all this input was ignored by the planners. Instead, they concentrated on the client's need for square footage. But it became very clear, very quickly, that such simple statistics are not sufficient to understand the complexities of developing 16 acres of empty space bordered by existing neighborhoods and the scene of a national tragedy.

What cheered me up finally was reading the issue you hold in your hands. It reaffirms my long-held belief that designers and planners can accommodate public need while serving client greed. They show us that it's possible to make mixed-use central to humane urban development, as Portland, Oregon, did by building residences above its public library. That it's desirable for generations to mix, as they so creatively do in an Oklahoma elder-care facility. And that truly good things can happen when designers like IDEO use intuitive and observational research to create new programs for hospitals, thereby changing a moribund health-care system.

So while the contents of my mailboxes may have depressed me, reading this issue encouraged me to believe in the power of design and designers. And so I ask, What wonderful things could happen in New York City if some of these talented people were called in to examine the existing conditions at the tip of our photogenic—but distressed—island city? They were drawn here before 9/11 by our movie-star skyline, by our lively streets, by our many excellent cultural institutions. And, after last September, people everywhere became New Yorkers. The designers among them want to help us become the great twenty-first-century metropolis we deserve to be. Let's ask for help.

A Question of Civil Rights

On a bright, crisp mid-December morning, Cesar Pelli's recently restored Winter Garden glimmered with holiday lights strung above the palm trees. The crystalline pavilion was filling up with members of the press bearing bulky coats, cameras, notebooks, computers, and cell phones. The best seats in the house were reserved for the business, arts, and public-service sectors, their representatives all busy working the room. As we waited for the presentation to begin, I watched the workers from the World Financial Center gather on the surrounding balconies. I wondered what they would think of this event, clearly choreographed as a public-relations moment, not a public dialogue seeking real input.

After all, the new designs about to be revealed for the World Trade Center site would have the most profound meaning to the people who work and live in the area. Any design, the thought kept buzzing in my head, must be first and foremost about the people who use it. These particular people know their urban environment in intimately horrifying ways. They walk by the pit every day, watch as more restaurants and shops get padlocked, negotiate hard-to-pass streets, dodge traffic, and risk their lives crossing Route 9A (quaintly called West Street) — and through it all, they simply try to live with what happened there on 9/11.

I kept glancing in their direction as architect Daniel Libeskind began with his trip down into the pit and talked of "listening to its voice," which at once shocked and inspired him. What survived the collapse — the great slurry walls that hold back the Hudson's waters — is at the core of his design. His words were filled with sympathy for people, an understanding of their sorrows and hopes and memories, a sensitivity to how New Yorkers use their city's streets, parks, and skyscrapers. Here was a theoretician who could have spoken in the obscure tongues of his peers, but the tragedy of the place and its potential rebuilding brought him down to earth, took him deep inside, and then sent him soaring into the sky with glass-and-steel behemoths.

When Lord Norman Foster spoke, we heard a voice made strong by a deep understanding of how the natural world can coexist with our high-tech inventions and how green design can sustain all kinds of life on the street, below the ground, and in the sky. Foster, who has become a recognized master of green architecture in his native England and elsewhere, offered two towers — "the tallest, greenest, strongest" structures — that would touch each other in the sky but not touch the footprints of the twin towers that were there before. His gardens in the clouds looked workable and showed an imagination rarely seen in green design here.

As morning became afternoon, the differences between Lord Foster and our homegrown talent — including the Meier-Eisenman-Holl-Gwathmey and the SOM teams — were depressingly revealed. Our men were capable only of timid nods to sustainable architecture; roof gardens and PV cells are nice details, but they need to be part of a whole system of thinking for an environmentally challenged twenty-first century.

The Lower Manhattan Development Corporation (the agency charged with rebuilding the site) did seem to play the role of informed client: its development program made mention of green design. But the agency also overwhelmed its architects with square footage. The LMDC's original program, publicly derided when the first six plans came out last summer, was still in place (and somehow grew bigger), clearly dismissing the public's misgivings about size and scope and approach, even as the agency promised to listen to us.

Roof gardens and PV cells are nice details, but they need to be part of a whole system of thinking for an environmentally challenged twenty-first century.

Here were some sexy new designs for 10 million square feet of offices, 1 million for retail, a quarter of a million for a hotel—and still no residential development within the 16 acres (though some of the proposed skyscrapers suggested this possibility). What we saw were star architects acting as salespeople for developers. These wonderfully creative minds were giving us advertisements for a muscle-bound, unsustainable development.

How did all this play on the balcony? Do the folks from the neighborhood make the link between their dying streets and the polluted air they breathe, and the possibility of fixing these ills through design? Do the designers themselves make that link? How will we know the answers to such questions if we don't talk about design and architecture in a real public forum? Do we even know how to have a public forum?

Lower Manhattan can be the place that brings architecture into public service. But this won't happen if we insist on treating architecture as advertisement.

Roger Mandle

Susan always tried to look beyond the story for a real truth. She brought a level of maturity and sophistication to the magazine, plus an edge of professional curiosity. Her own perceptions are strongly influenced by her interest in art in general; she's not just about design and manufacturing, or design and business, or design and trendy stuff. She's one of the most grounded people I know in her approach to her commentary on design. Reading her editorials, I felt that there was somebody there with great substance, always trying to look beyond the story for a real truth.

Susan came to RISD a number of times to attend various events at our invitation or to cover issues out of her own curiosity. Her approach to design education went beyond her first impressions—she dug deep to find the answers to fundamental questions. Some people frankly accuse her of being tough. Well, too bad. She is a force to be reckoned with.

Interior Designers:
Your Image Isn't Working for You

On June 18, 2001—in those more innocent days before 9/11—I addressed the IIDA College of Fellows. I started that talk with a look at the publications that served or are focused on the profession and reported on the many new consumer titles and TV shows that dealt with home design and decoration. Looking through all these outlets of interior design information, I was trying to find the public image of the profession—and maybe more important—the profession's image of itself. I was trying to see how you talk about your processes, the products you spec, your struggles, your issues, your ideals, your idols, your shamans, and your devils. But first let me tell you why I have this abiding interest in you. I learned to be a design journalist at *Interiors* magazine first by covering the market—going to showrooms and trade shows—to discover new products. For instance, I would collect samples of the most important and innovative fabrics, bring them back to the office, iron them, and then photograph them for extensive reports. I wanted to break news, not just repeat press releases and use PR shots of products.

Keynote address delivered at the third annual conference of the International Interior Designers Association (IIDA), Mexico City, October 9–11, 2003

Later, I graduated to features on maintenance, fiber content, manufacturing, and such—all stories that I found by locating experts, listening to designers' concerns, and trying to figure out how to provide useful information to the field's practitioners. As I got to know more and more interior designers, I found them inspiring, personally and professionally. *Interiors,* particularly my editor in chief Olga Gueft, taught me about the cultural and economic necessity of interior design. I learned that this complex and necessary business was about process, product, invention, psychology, and materials—but most of all, that it was a profession that had immediate and direct impact on people's lives. I noticed that there were some interior designers who shined when it came to color and light. Others had an uncanny sense of space and were able to create a memorable sense of place.

My own idols were the ones who could do all of these things beautifully. But whatever their skills, the interior designers I got to know all had a generous curiosity about the world. They knew art and told me about artists I should know. They loved architecture and told me of their visits to the great and powerful places of our rich world. They knew everything about objects—who made them, what they signified, what historic period they represented, and why this was important to know for a rich and rewarding life.

My interior designers discovered great books, and we would pore over beautiful photos together. They loved film and knew the best set designs; they examined theater sets for their light, space, and drama.

They traveled extensively and purposefully and always knew about an exquisite small hotel, a restaurant whose decor was as delicious as the food, or a street of small and beautiful shops.

I felt that such people needed solid information they could use. Of course it had to be accompanied by beauty, but that could not be all there was. When you wrote for such perceptive people, you had to describe qualities that were only possible to describe if you had been there.

You all know the theory that we learn more and understand places, ideas, and people much more deeply through our whole physical being rather than just through one of our senses. This is called body memory. So writing about design requires the writer to have occupied the space, touched the shiny and textured surfaces, dimmed and blasted the lights, and watched how the sunlight travels through the space through time. Writing, like designing and living, is an incredibly rich human experience. Anything that is less than this is an insult to the human condition.

So, once again, as I did two years ago, I decided to look at the magazines that serve or represent interior designers. What I found was very pretty, but also terribly depressing. Let me go with you through the recent issues of several magazines that concentrate on interior design. I leave *Metropolis* out, because we cover all of design in a cultural context; we believe in interdisciplinary design and cover interiors as part of the larger designed environment. In *Architectural Digest,* modern houses— the kind of houses that brim with design ideas about making great spaces—are mostly marginalized. They're presented in the front of the book, between the ads, on single pages showing rather small pictures, so as not to compete with the ads. For instance, there's architect Tom Wiscombe's concept house, which is brimming with ideas about generous spaces, depicted through small and darkish computer renderings.

The big splash pictures and spreads are spent on the familiar, on styles and approaches that every good interior designer has already learned in school. There is the obligatory rough, country-mansion look (the one I looked at belonged to the actor Dennis Quaid). There's the decorator modern look, showcasing pricey art collections in beige rooms with overstuffed couches. There's the manorial Chippendale townhouse, and at least one overstuffed seaside estate for one princess or another. There's a sprawling New York apartment the size of Versailles, in a city where respected professionals live in 400-square-foot studios; this New York sprawl belongs to TV celebrity Starr Jones—at least we get the rare African-American user of interior design services. Not one single floor plan anywhere. What's next to what, how you get from one room to the next, and how you capitalize on views and deemphasize bad features are all left out in these fests of material acquisition.

This is interior design to a large group of readers aspiring to wealth and fame. You hire an interior designer/decorator to help you purchase the goods, then use him or her to push these goods around to make pleasing vignettes you can show off in a glossy magazine. This is not home. This is decorator show-house design.

I go on to *Elle Decor*. There's at least some affordable consumption here, but readers whose median income is $125,000 can hardly afford that $20,000 antique mahogany dining table and equally pricey silk wall covering. No matter: let these readers dream of things of high monetary value! As we leaf through the front of *Elle Decor*, we find out "What's Hot." That means you covet the Armani Casa tea set in this issue, but it will have cooled down considerably by the next issue, where you will see — and covet — the newest hot tea set. This drive to acquire, this insistence on maintaining your display shelf's "hot" status, may be the reason for all those sheetrock and vinyl McMansions sprouting all over the United States, Canada, Australia, and points between. You have to have room for the stuff that's no longer hot, for that stuff that you've really grown to love but don't want your friends to know you're hanging onto, as the objects are so hopelessly passé.

The one honest thing about *Elle Decor* is that it shows social acceptance: gay men now regularly appear in the homes they have designed for themselves. One small step for mankind. But those McMansion owners by the millions, those aspiring homemakers: are they encouraged to work with interior designers, beyond consulting with them on what to buy? I haven't found such advice in these magazines.

Now for your professional bible, *Interior Design*. Much energy, time, and money are spent on setting up knockout, fantasy product shots. These photos certainly teach manufacturers about romancing the chair, the table, and the lamp. But manufacturers know better: most ads are clear, good, simple product shots that show you a reasonable facsimile of what you'll specify. This confusion of the active professional interior designer with a bored fashion-magazine reader is offensive to me.

Now, don't misunderstand what I'm saying: I love those backlit, theatrical, mysterious club chairs that look as if they were just off the runway and landed in *Vogue,* and that you must have NOW. But you're probably buying 200 of them for a health-care facility and you want to know how they're made, how well they can be maintained, how well they support debilitated patients, and how well they comfort emotionally wrought families. Fashion is the last thing on your mind. So why does your professional magazine think it is the first and only thing?

I look for floor plans to understand how all those gorgeous rooms work and relate to one another. In the last issue of *Interior Design,* I find exactly two. But one is the size of a pair of postage stamps stuck together, with no furniture placement shown; the other is somewhat larger, but not large enough to study how the space really works. Now, the interior designers I know can tell more about a room from a good floor plan than from a hundred glamour shots; in fact, they always go for the plan if they want to explain the space. Hasn't anyone on the staff of your über-professional publication talked to you about this? How do they know what story to tell if they don't understand the backbone of your work?

I wrote down some words from *Interior Design* that tell me about how it understands your work, your influence, and the job that you do. These words are "luxury," "art," "riches," "style," and "chic." There is no mention of words like "sustainability," "green design," "technology," "ergonomics," "universal design," "security," "health," "safety" and "welfare"— the stuff you struggle with all day. After this realization, I stopped looking at how magazines report on interior design. I could not face more of your humiliation. Then, I remembered a recent incident that brought me to an epiphany about interior designers' horribly mistaken public image, which, unfortunately, also has some truth attached to it.

On a gorgeous Sunday in early September, a group of New York IIDA members went out to visit [textile designer and decorator] Jack Lenor Larsen at his LongHouse on Long Island. I was there because Hilda Lonchenotti asked me to do an after-lunch conversation with Jack, who, by the way, is one of the most knowledgeable, artistic, globe-traveling icons of American modern design that we have. I prepared for the conversation by reading Jack's books and inquiring about his most recent interests (gardening and theater); I came armed to interview him with a set of hard-nosed questions and a game of name associations.

After a tour of the magnificent gardens, which are accented by all kinds of progressive artwork and designs, including a real Bucky Fuller dome, we had one of those elegantly casual meals that only a person with Jack's sophistication can serve up. Then, he gave a gracious tour of LongHouse, explaining its Japanese temple antecedents, his favorite Wharton Esherick furniture, and his new fabrics, which covered the sliding doors between the kitchen and breakfast area.

Then, we gathered in the great, sunlit room for our conversation. Many of the interior designers were hanging on every word Jack said; he told—and tells—wonderful, human stories about people, places, and being a designer. When he wanted to end our talk, we went downstairs. I spied in the shade a group sitting around a linen-covered table with glasses of wine, talking loudly about some adventure or another. They did not bother to hear what Jack—who can explain the American century through design—had to say. They came, they ate, they drank, they gawked—and they learned very little (or at least it seemed to me). I know, I know: they've heard Jack before. But maybe not this Jack. And anyway, how do you ignore such an opportunity?

So what do we do about interior designers' rotten image? You can't blame it all on the slackers, society decorators, and status hounds. You have to do something about it NOW! Here's what I suggest we—all of us—think about:

1) Let's identify the heroes of the interior design profession: the American and Mexican men and women who paved the way for you. Let's establish scholarships in their names, fund university seats in their memory, and finance fellowships and necessary research projects in their honor.

I have my own candidates for the heroes of interior design, which should not be some phony Hall of Fame judged from dead pictures and reinforced by the profession as a bunch of superficial party givers. I nominate Olga Gueft as my hero, my mentor on *Interiors,* and the person who was there at the founding of today's profession and professional organizations. Who are your heroes? Let's figure out how to make Ken Burns–ian films about them and let's enlist schools in this endeavor, as there's so much talent in film, graphics, and design history to document, record, analyze, present, and publicize these magnificent founders of your profession. We all need heroes.

2) Let's emphasize scholarship in space-making (which is an incredibly important skill usually misunderstood as mere furniture placement). For materials research, let's set up a collaboration between schools, each of which could undertake a specified part of a larger materials research project. Each school could find materials that could sustain its particular region's growth and reflect its unique aesthetic conditions.

3) As professional organizations, let's support academia's psychosocial research about our technologically harassed society. So, what really is our relationship with technology: not the hype, but the real relationship?

4) Existing research that is embedded in large firms must be shared with up-and-coming companies. If you are a giant, admit to the status and take the responsibility to share your information with the next generation of practitioners. How will you do that? If you are already doing it, tell us about it.

5) Let's stop the squabbling between architects and interior designers, and among different design associations. There's so much to learn and so little time to waste on nonproductive arguments of who's better than whom. Everyone is a potential contributor. What can each organization contribute to better the human condition?

6) Let's figure out, once and for all, a positive and productive relationship between interior designers and their suppliers. You are not salespeople of their products, no matter how many Learjets you take to their corporate headquarters. You contribute to the discipline's knowledge with the knowledge you gather every day in the field.

Manufacturers need this detailed understanding, rather than just your consulting advice on how to make a worktable an inch deeper or shallower. You are the one who knows what, for instance, workers think about their spaces, how they use them, and what they love and hate about them. Use your enormous purchasing power to push your suppliers to create a better, safer, more useful, more relevant, and more sustainable product. When you spec a thousand ergonomic chairs, you must ask if they're designed for disassembly. The makers want your orders; they'll live up to your high standards if you choose to press them on it. And you must choose to press your suppliers to make better products—the safety of our water and air supplies depend on this. I guarantee that if you behave like knowledgeable, responsible professionals who have solid scholarship, your image will follow your great profession. You will be proud to be called an interior designer, and you will get respect.

After all, how can you get respect when you put your flaws out for all the public to see? Here's just one example of how you lose respect every day. It's a small detail, but it's emblematic of your current status as a profession.

That detail is the braille sign on every new hotel door. The sign is a pure and simple compliance with the ADA, the Americans with Disabilities Act. This 1990 civil-rights legislation is about inclusion, about making sure that the 40 million Americans who are physically challenged can go about their lives as the rest of us do. But how useful does a blind person find that potentially helpful braille signage? I know, installing the signage is the law, but you must do much more than comply with the law. Getting a blind person from the front door of the hotel to her room is a complex design challenge, one that you are highly qualified to resolve. Tactile and audio cues embedded in surfaces could make the passage from front door to room interesting for all users. This needs to be figured out. Your profession—in tandem with industrial designers, engineers, and sound designers, and with advice from disabled people—can do it.

Furthermore, the current confusion between public and private space is an interior design problem. I'm talking about the most dramatic change: the unintended consequences of cell phones, which are leading to the erosion of privacy in public spaces. Aside from creating etiquette for cell phone use, there's a space issue here. Just as there are quiet cars on the new Acela trains (designed after the introduction of cell phones), there is a need for spaces in airports, hotel lobbies, and parks that separate cell phone users from those who don't want to hear about some stranger's personal life.

I arrive here from the heartland of America, where some hopeful changes for the future of all design professions are taking place. Iowa State University's design school is instituting new programs that go to the very foundations of design education. From now on, all students entering the school—whether they end up as architects, interior designers, or graphic designers—are taking the same, enriched foundation course. Liberal arts, culture, and science—all disciplines that help us understand the world better—are taught to all students of design. Leave it to solid Midwesterners to figure out the solid foundations for the twenty-first-century design education.

While visiting Iowa, I took part in a new architecture graduate program. Students there come from all disciplines—art history, computer design, and landscape design, to name a few—to learn about architecture in a holistic way. At the time of my visit, the students were working on public baths, covering in depth the history, culture, biology, engineering, physics, social behaviors, materials, and structure; in short, they were looking for a deeper understanding, rather than just expressive form-making.

This approach is worth studying for interior designers, too. You contribute a huge portion to what I like to call the GDP: the Gross Designed Product. You must start learning about the health and environmental effects of the materials you specify. When you understand the properties and provenance of your materials, you have the potential to change the marketplace with your high-volume purchases. You have the power and the duty; all you need is the will to support positive change for a sustainable designed environment. I know you can do this, because you asked me here to talk about what's wrong with the profession. You should know that of all the design professions *Metropolis* covers, interior designers are the first ones to ask me to talk about the field's shortcomings. And as you may know, architects are just as much in a crisis mode today as interior designers are.

Fixing your public image is an inside job. You must put your own house in order before you can do it for others. You are the most skilled problem-solvers I know. In everything you do, remember that "international"—one of the key words in your organization—now has a new meaning. It's no longer about International Design and creating sameness everywhere; it's about learning from your international sources who they are, what they do, and how they do it. By doing this, you can do your beautiful and useful work here, in Mexico City, in this magical place where the early morning light is truly heavenly.

Local is no longer provincial. Local is real, it's rich, it's useful—and it's beautiful. Discover it anew, and make the rest of the world want to come into a place that cannot be found anywhere else. Remember what your countrywoman Frida Kahlo said: the intensely local is universal.

Ethics and Sustainability

An enormous smoke cloud is seen hovering over the northeast United States. Its origin: fires burning somewhere in China. The dramatic image—with hundreds of others like it—is posted on the Earth page of NASA's Web site; here satellite cameras record the degradation of our home planet's environment. Such graphic information is now routinely available to anyone with an Internet connection. We can see for ourselves how human actions in one part of the world affect human health in another, distant part.

Delivered at the American Institute of Graphic Arts National Design Conference, Vancouver, October 23–26, 2003

On the day of the smoke cloud, many New Yorkers experienced breathing problems. Most of them probably blamed the difficulties on local pollution caused by automobile and bus exhaust and chemical clouds wafting across the Hudson from New Jersey. But China? That's too far away! Well, as it turns out, you and I share one large breath with all human beings and other creatures living on this earth. We are closer to each other than we ever could have imagined. And now we have the science and the technology to document how interconnected we really are. The smoke cloud over the northeast United States is a powerful graphic communication. The NASA Web site may not be designed to your liking, but it provides information that is very hard to ignore. And this is where ethics enters the picture.

Continuing to act in a way that you know can have harmful consequences is irresponsible, unethical behavior. So you didn't start those fires in China, why should you be held responsible for polluting the environment? But I say that you—collectively, as graphic designers—are starting other fires, metaphorically speaking. You are responsible for helping to create 40 percent of North America's solid waste; paper accounts for 81 million tons of waste annually, according to the Printers' National Environmental Assistance Center. Furthermore, the pulp and paper industry is the third-largest industrial buyer of elemental chlorine. Chlorine is used to whiten paper, a process which is linked to a proven cancer-causing chemical called dioxin.

You know this, because you've been reading a little beige booklet in your conference packets. This booklet—No. 7—is part of the AIGA's Design Business Ethics series and deals extensively with print design and environmental responsibility. It documents current knowledge on the subject and gives useful contact information. It is there for you to use. My health, your health, and your children's health depend on how well you understand the information provided for you by the AIGA in booklet No. 7.

I am a graphic design client and I, along with thousands of other clients, need for you to do the right thing. Here is my story: I am the editor of a design and architecture magazine called *Metropolis*. We print around 60,000 issues 11 times a year at Brown Printing Company, in East Greenville, Pennsylvania. Brown's giant web offset presses, perfect binders, and poly wrappers produce some 500 titles, including elegant fashion catalogs and mass-market news magazines—all of them designed by someone, maybe some of you in this room.

Brown is an efficient, noisy industrial plant with hazardous waste signs posted everywhere. The paper waste, just from our small print-run, is staggering: garbage cans are filled with color proofs during the test runs. As employees of a magazine that has a commitment to covering environmental issues that shape our designed environment, our editors and art directors live with constant guilt. We know that the processes that produce those beautiful color pages are highly toxic and wasteful. We have been assured that our paper comes from managed forests and that waste paper is recycled, but those assurances are not enough for us. We know more can be done, but it seems that we're too small to make a difference. However, if every art director and every editor of every one of those 500 titles at Brown started asking questions about soy inks, recycled papers, safe press-clean-up procedures, chlorine content, and washable stock—the kind of paper that [William McDonough and Michael Braungart's environmental manifesto] Cradle to Cradle is printed on—we might end up with a less toxic product and contribute less to the earth's health problems.

Now, to me, the choice is not to eliminate print because it's dirty, but rather to clean up its production and then use print in ways that only print can provide. For instance, when Paula Scher redesigned Metropolis some four years ago, we decided to print the feature well on a different paper stock from the rest of the magazine—this to provide a distinct, noncommercial zone of uninterrupted reading, an experience signaled by the tactile and visual change in the paper. As we spend more time in the visual world of our computer screens, we search for multisensory experiences in our physical world. Paper technology, or polymer technology like Michael Braungart talks about, can satisfy some of our sensory needs, so we must figure out how to clean up paper technology and make it work better. It is the right thing to do. It is the ethical thing to do.

For a while now, I've been talking about something I call the Gross Designed Product, the GDP, and how it needs to push environmental change. Think about this for a moment: an interior designer will buy 1,200 ergonomic chairs for one job, while you and I may buy 12 chairs in a lifetime. If each interior designer demanded that the chairs he specifies be designed for disassembly, made of nontoxic materials, and their parts not shipped from thousands of miles away where they might be made by semislave labor, the contract furniture industry would have to pay attention. Solid knowledge about your materials and processes can indeed be power—and this power is in the numbers. Put these numbers together and you have an interior design community that can make positive change, at least the way furniture is made. And we're talking about changing one industry at a time.

Interior designers' new buying habits can also change the way industrial designers think about their own work. Charged with making environmentally safe products, industrial designers would no longer be slaves to the annual style change in endless ergonomic chairs with slight differences for each brand. As a result, the designers might even design a whole new set of products that better suit our new ways of working. Some months ago, Santa Fe architect Ed Mazria sent us a paper he wrote, connecting architecture, its processes, and its materials to global warming. We knew this but didn't have the facts to prove it. So, with me searching for the GDP's environmental impact, and all our editors looking for designs that make a positive—and beautiful—contribution to a cleaner environment, Ed's paper hit a nerve. It became the backbone of our October cover story—the cover itself being three rolls of blueprints emitting a huge black cloud of smoke, an image designed by Pentagram's D. J. Stout—with the accusatory cover line "Architects Pollute."

Ed reconfigured the old pie chart that depicts North America's energy use to show that architects put in motion 48 percent of the fossil fuels that cause global warming. I think this may be a conservative estimate when we know what goes into buildings—such as interior furnishings, signage, and electronics—as well as all that paper your profession puts there. So the GDP is probably responsible for producing 80 percent or more of global-warming gases. And make no mistake about it: global warming is here. It's no longer discussed—except, perhaps, by Bush the Younger's administration—as a remote possibility. The climate changes we're experiencing are dramatic, we all know this first hand.

So, is there any good news in all of this? Yes. And it has to do with design. Designers today stand on the brink of being seen by society as essential contributors to its health, safety, and welfare. If you—together with the other design professions—decide to examine the materials and processes endemic to your work, as well as demand that these materials and processes become environmentally safe, you will be the heroes of the twenty-first century. Truly, when you get away from interdisciplinary squabbling and join forces with other design organizations—each organization is now making steps in this direction, by the way—you will have the kind of positive and life-affirming power that [Bauhaus founder and interdisciplinary designer] Walter Gropius couldn't have imagined in his wildest dreams.

Ethical decisions are personal. It is you—each one of us—who has to decide to do the right thing. Today, we ponder the meanings of words like morality, responsibility, obligation, community, social justice, and interconnectedness: words we once knew intimately, then proceeded to forget as we got lost in the pursuit of what we used to call "the good life." We have observed the sorry spectacle of corporate executives in handcuffs, doing the perp walk on the six o'clock news. These ethically flawed CEOs may still have their ill-gotten gains, but they don't have the power that once quickened their heartbeats. And watching them, we began to understand that power without ethical standards can dissipate in a New York minute and cause a great deal of anguish all around.

I am exceedingly hopeful about the future of design, and designers' growing power in society. This hope comes from my students, and students I meet everywhere. The best of them know that they follow in the footsteps of the great, humanist designers of the nineteenth and twentieth centuries. At Parsons, where I have been teaching design history for 12 years, I was asked to develop a course on ethics five years ago. I interpreted this request as a sign of the times, as a rising need for some sort of anchor in a world of great uncertainty, a kind of reassertion of our complex humanity.

We are much more than homo economicus, and we know it. Consumption isn't our only value, and we want to assert our interest in the life of the mind, in culture, art, science, and more. Yes, I thought, this request from Parsons was to be a search for values. I was sufficiently intrigued by it, but also puzzled by how I could pull it off. Do I build ethical arguments on such designer issues as knockoffs or cutting and pasting without giving credit? Though important, these issues seemed paltry next to the big question that, five years ago, was focused on environmental ethics. But that, too, seemed to ghettoize the subject of ethics. Environmentalists by then were a boring lot, often rabid zealots; when they were designers, they often made ugly things and buildings.

Then, I watched the 1991 film *Mindwalk,* based on Fritjof Capra's writings, and realized that we needed to talk about a whole new worldview. I realized we needed to get away from the Cartesian, linear, mechanistic thinking that shaped modern humanity and gave us the Industrial Revolution (and with it, amazing things like central heating and computers, as well as horrible things like overflowing landfills and air pollution). I understood that we needed to start thinking of the world as a system, a cyclical system of interconnections, a web of connections—"the web of life," as Capra says.

We needed a comprehensive ecological worldview. And I also understood that this was a long-term project, not to be mistaken for a marketing trend like one furnishings manufacturer told us. ("Green?" he said. "Yes, well, we did that last year, but we're doing something really exciting this year!") In fact, green was only a part of it, a central part that must deal with environmentally benign materials and processes, restoration, recycling, reclaiming: all the things we have to do to remedy the damage we've done to the natural environment and to ourselves in it. Have you asked yourself why, for instance, is a mass medium like TV running ads for cancer drugs? We must be in the midst of an epidemic. And the general population already knows that there are such things as chemical carcinogens: everyone remembers seeing the movie *Erin Brockovich*.

So as I planned the course, it became clear to me that we needed to talk about the ethical implications of Descartes' cogito ergo sum principle of a man-centered universe and contrast it to a more communal, collaborative approach in which social justice is at least as important as individual well-being. This is where my students and I would find our ethical issues, and along the way also take part in building a new worldview. We don't have a great summing up of this worldview yet—as Descartes' cogito summed up the modern world. We now use awkward and hard-to-grasp words like "sustainability," "ecodesign," "green design," "greenwashing," "biophilia," "biomimicry," "bioinspiration"; we even use "universal access" and "universal design," since social justice is part of this new thinking.

These are early days, but incredibly exciting ones. The last time that humanity was challenged to rethink the world, we came up with the Enlightenment, which served our kind very well up to now. So use whatever words you like, but understand that you are at the center of a revolution where an ethical compass is useful and even essential. This may be a time when intellectual pursuits become as important as financial and entertainment pursuits. For without understanding the new world taking shape around us, we will surely go the way of dinosaurs.

So what can you do to be part of this eco-revolution? I offer a few suggestions. You—designers—should get out of your darkened rooms, with their big, flashy images, and figure out how to talk about design in the sunlight. In fact, just try talking about design once in a while without showing anything. It astounds me how creative people can readily buy into the mind-numbing, homogenizing visuals of corporate blandness.

PowerPoint presentations have killed thinking in the late twentieth century. We're living in new times now. Stop using PowerPoint for everything. Give others credit for being able to follow your argument without the aid of bullet points for every factoid you flash. Spend your time and our precious energy resources on creating truly inventive and persuasive presentations.

Let's cut back the time we spend looking at screens in mechanically cooled rooms that always hum with the powerful machines required to keep them a steady 70 degrees. Let's design rooms that take advantage of the great and beautiful world outside, with its shimmering waters and colorful foliage and cooling breezes.

PowerPoint presentations have killed thinking in the late twentieth century.

This shift of worldviews is a complex and serious business. It needs all kinds of expertise and it needs every one of you, and more. Many of you are already involved in education. Turn your involvement into something significant, relevant, and timely. Develop courses where collaboration, research, social justice, and scientific and cultural understanding are at the heart of the design problems being solved. Make universities — with their unique capacity for research and analysis — into the intellectual leaders of your profession, with you as their collaborator. We know what happens when the design professions — all of them, including architecture and graphic design — lead academia. That's what we have now in some places, and everyone's unhappy.

If you teach at a university where there's a teachers' college, infiltrate that teachers' college with your design ideas by making friends with the professors there. While it's great that some designers do wonderful programs with public schools, these efforts are few and far between. We have an urgency here. It would be more productive to educate the educators. Help them figure out how to add your design methods to a more linear way of learning. This can lead to a better understanding of the designed environment by future grade-school and high-school teachers and their students.

Such an understanding is crucial to a well-informed citizenry. Nowhere was this need for design-informed citizens better demonstrated than during the so-called design debates about the schemes presented for rebuilding the World Trade Center site. Our esteemed architecture critic on our newspaper of record confused a planning and massing document with architecture; the architects — except for Daniel Libeskind — spoke in jargon that even they couldn't penetrate; and the public had no idea what they were looking at and what the design debate was about.

Become citizen designers. When architect Beverly Willis and I launched our civic group, R.Dot, in those heartbreaking days after 9/11, we didn't know we could attract politically savvy designers who'd want to attend regular meetings and work very hard pro bono. As it turns out, a graphic designer, Roland Gebhardt, an industrial designer, Brent

Oppenheimer, and an architect, Ron Schiffman, became the guiding lights behind several of our detailed and comprehensive position papers on managed streets, culture zones, and housing.

Roland and Brent, for instance, used the kind of anthropological and anthropometric studies they learned as industrial designers and office planners to create a whole new system of maps. They called it experience mapping, which is a way to understand what works and what doesn't work in neighborhoods by interviewing residents and visitors about how they use the neighborhoods. Experience maps are great graphic presentations of people's everyday lives. They're much more revealing than cold statistics.

The citizen designer is on the ascendant, especially post 9/11. [Graphic design critic] Steve Heller even named one of his books after him and her. Find collaborators in whatever area of expertise your project requires. Become a design detective, a forensic designer. The path has been cut for you by others: make it wider.

One of those pathfinders is Kirsten Childs, the interior design partner in the Croxton Collaborative, which has become a sought-after green architecture firm. But 15 years ago, Kirsten began looking for the ingredients of the chemical soup she was brewing with the furniture and furnishings she was specifying. So she hired a chemist. Together, they started asking questions about the fibers, fiberboards, finishes, and glues she was putting into offices—usually located in sealed buildings designed to control the temperature. Individual decisions. Personal, ethical choices. That's what Kirsten started out with. Others in her field are following.

She's a good example for you, too. Thousands of these personal choices put together will make our world, as Bush the Elder so memorably hoped, a "kinder, gentler" place. But I'm also with Blanche DuBois on this. We need to start relying more on "the kindness of strangers."

The citizen designer is on the ascendant.

Find collaborators in whatever area of expertise your project requires. Become a design detective, a forensic designer.

Von Robinson

When I was a student at Parsons The New School for Design, I took Susan's course, The Ethics of Design. In a class like this, potentially, someone's going to just lay it all out for you: here's two tablets, the kingdom, the mountain, and that's that. Ethics are ethics, after all. But as long as I've known Susan, she doesn't tell you what to do. She would describe a problem and lay out the options, and we'd realize that we're all running in our own individual tracks. She would ask questions insistently and let you know that how you answered was very critical—and very telling about you. It forced us to examine what we believed in.

She understands sustainability as a living system that's not always made up of linear choices. If someone in class brought up sustainability, she would remind us that there's aesthetic durability, too: if you make a chair out of a material that you think is bad, but you keep that chair for 30 years because it has aesthetic durability—in other words, its design will still look good years into the future—isn't that better than making a chair out of sustainable materials whose design will look dated in two years and then you'll want to buy a new, different chair? Which is the more realistically sustainable approach?

In my work at Steelcase, I think, "How would Susan do it?" Part of the answer is always that she'd do it with principles, she'd do it with passion, and she'd do it with strength. Knowing she's out there is sort of a reality check.

Trapped Inside the Grid

The lights flicker and then they're out; the phones go dead; the fridge stops humming. We gather at the large windows facing Twenty-third Street to check out what's going on. The gym across the way is dark, but traffic moves well and people walk at the usual New York pace. Cell phones appear, but few seem to be connecting. Small groups begin to form on the street below. Someone in the office finds a portable radio; power is out all the way up to Canada. When our eyes meet, we see that fearful look reminiscent of 9/11, and some of us say the word "terrorism." Others counsel calm. We're experiencing "Blackout 2003," as the media would later label the event.

We leave the office and file down the dark staircase. As we set out to walk to our homes, the streets have grown crowded. Radios play in parked cars; we stop and listen as a fire truck speeds by. I think of how everything I do is hooked into the great electric-power grid that just failed. Everything in my apartment downtown—the front-door buzzer, the phone, the radio-alarm clock, even the toilet—is plugged into now-dead outlets.

The huge wrought-iron gate of my building has been propped open. How will I walk up the pitch-black stairs and hallways? A small group with a flashlight comes along and invites me to go with them. There's water left in my boiler, but it won't last long. And there's no way to flush the toilet anyway.

I spend the next morning, a sweltering Friday in August, searching for food and water. There's some cool watermelon and a bottle of water—double the price of what they were yesterday—at a nearby bodega. It's nearly 3 p.m. when I hear the fridge click on. By then, I have gone through all of my catalogues looking for things like an FM radio/flashlight set and candlesticks with diffusers designed for reading—knowing all too well that shopping will not get us out of this fix.

When I turn on the TV, I hear the new mantra adopted by reporters: upgrade the grid, bring it into the twenty-first century. But there's little talk about the possibilities of life off the grid or alternate energy sources or the ways we use the energy we produce. Why does a perfectly good lock-and-key system need to turn into an electric eye? And if it must, why is there no mechanical redundancy designed into these locks? Why are buildings kept so cold during summertime that you can catch a chill just by walking past the front door? Why did I buy the cool-looking radio alarm clock that had its reproachful blank stare on me throughout the blackout? We need to seriously question everyday decisions about how we produce and use energy, when we use it, and what we use it for, just as Santa Fe architect Ed Mazria has done for three decades. Ed is convinced that architects have the skill, humanity, and intelligence to help us out of our current dangerous reliance on the grid and its polluting ways. I know he's right. Countless design decisions have gone into producing our system of energy use, and we must question all of them.

While living through the worst blackout in New York City history, I tried not to move a muscle. I forced myself to think about the house that Ed Mazria built in Santa Fe. I went into fantasy mode: If I were living in such a place, I would not be a soggy victim of the utility company. Instead, errant breezes caught by well-placed windows would cool my skin. My solar-powered fridge would be filled with cool drinks and refreshing fruits.

I envisioned cool autumn days and thought about the upcoming symposiums we've organized with Ed. He is determined that everyone who practices architecture, hires an architect, passes a law, or writes about the built environment confront the problem of global warming. I'm also determined—determined that no one else should ever have to spend a sweltering day trapped inside the grid.

Edward Mazria

I was teaching a little seminar in the office to the younger architects at my firm back in the early 2000s, and in the course of our research, we learned that the building sector was the largest consumer of energy and the largest contributor to greenhouse-gas emissions in the United States. I asked the staff what magazine we should approach to publish the information, and all of them immediately said, "*Metropolis*." I said, "Well, I don't really know anybody there, but I'll give it a try."

When I cold-called *Metropolis*, Susan wasn't in that day. I talked to Martin Pedersen, and in traditional New York fashion he said, "Who are you?" I remember he was busy and trying to get off the phone, and I had to think fast to get him engaged. I said, "Let me ask you one question before you hang up. What's the largest energy consumer in the United States and contributor to greenhouse-gas emissions?" He said, "That's easy, it's the internal combustion engine." I said, "No, it's buildings." And he replied, "Oh, I don't think so." I offered to send him the data and I got a call back a few weeks later. He said, "We checked it out and it seems you're right."

The magazine sent Christopher Hawthorne out to New Mexico to come talk with me and write the piece, "Turning Down the Global Thermostat," which was the cover story for its October 2003 issue. The whole layout was beautifully designed, but the cover was especially provocative. It was an illustration showing three smokestacks made of rolled-up blueprints producing black clouds that partially obscure the *Metropolis* logo, with the line "Architects Pollute." If you understand designers in general, and architects and urban planners in particular, their whole purpose is to create work that enhances peoples' lives, and so to have a cover that says "Architects Pollute" is a stab in the heart. I heard Susan received some flak about that cover for quite a while. Prior to this, the general perception was that in the area of energy consumption and greenhouse-gas emissions, transportation was the main villain and the SUV was the poster child for the worst thing you could do to the environment. The building sector was not even on the radar, let alone seen as the worst offender.

After the article came out, my practice began receiving requests for more information. It seemed there was an infinite number of questions, so we kept digging deeper and deeper into energy and climate-change research. By 2006, we couldn't handle the workload anymore. It literally became half the practice and was taking up too much staff time without generating income. Fortunately, some foundations, including the innovative Rockefeller Brothers Fund, approached us and asked if we would start a nonprofit and staff up to address this issue. That's how Architecture 2030 was founded, and in 2006 we issued the 2030 Challenge to reduce greenhouse emissions from the construction sector to the point where all new buildings and major renovations are carbon neutral by 2030.

It was a big step and not an easy decision after practicing architecture for more than 40 years, but it all started with *Metropolis*. I doubt we would be this far down the road today had the magazine not published the article in such a thought-provoking way, but it certainly was a game changer and a life changer for me. The article actually pushed us to conduct additional research and publish more information. We developed momentum and new strategies and programs to help the design professions accept the challenge and take appropriate action to meet it.

Since then, nearly every day a new book, newspaper article, or magazine feature comes across my desk addressing either sustainable design, zero-energy buildings and developments, or new sustainable cities. What this means is that the transition has traction, and *Metropolis* was the initial catalyst. U.S. greenhouse-gas emissions in the building sector are down 11 percent from 2005 levels, which is a huge drop. Climate change is a new global crisis, and if we can address it so that the impacts are at least manageable, this will be Susan's greatest legacy. She is the consummate professional, publishing work of the highest caliber with incredible integrity. When you combine those qualities, you have someone who is going to make a difference.

Something of Value

In an idyllic all-American town called Lakewood, a retired couple are being interviewed by Mike Wallace on *60 Minutes*. These well-spoken people tell a frightening story of urban planning gone terribly wrong. Their house, now paid for and perfect for what they believed would be their "golden years," has been pronounced "blighted" by the mayor. Wallace is looking for signs of blight, but in this well-kept neighborhood of single-family homes, he can't find the decay that the word implies. Blight in 2003, in small-town Ohio and in many other places across the country, refers to homes that don't have at least three bedrooms, two baths, central air, and an attached two-car garage—our current symbols of upward mobility.

The land in Lakewood on which the couple's house stands, along with 54 other houses, is being claimed by the city under eminent domain, the legal term for the right of the government to take private property for the public good. But use of eminent domain today is not what it was intended for. In the twenty-first century, a city can condemn low-tax-yielding property that gets in the way of high-tax-yielding development. And so this Ohio neighborhood is to hand over its land and all they built on it (at a "fair market price") to a developer of expensive condos that, Mayor Cain claims, will bring in the taxes her town needs.

What strikes me most about this sad story is the unsustainable values it represents. It seems that the technical override of nature (in this case, conditioned air) has a higher value than a less energy-guzzling way of life. Why would houses built with deep, shading porches and well-placed windows that catch breezes from Lake Erie need central air-conditioning? Do Americans really want to spend their nights and weekends as they do their workdays, in artificially cooled rooms? And exactly when does a breeze lose its value?

The architects hired by the Lakewood developers have the moral duty to challenge the city's plans. They need to be advocates for the people, not just for the developers. They know the program that informs the development. They have the training and the ability to offer alternate sites in other, less-contested areas of town that would suit the mayor's needs to raise higher taxes. They know more about sustainable design than they've ever known before; they're probably building to LEED ratings now. But do they have the will and the ethical fortitude to challenge this kind of destructive development in the face of eminent domain?

Jean Gardner

From 2000 until 2003, I co-chaired a task force on sustainability for the Association of Collegiate Schools of Architecture (ASCA), along with Kim Tanzer, then the organization's southeast regional director, and John McRae from RTKL Associates, who represented the Association of International Architects. Kim was very interested in the "whole-building matrix," an educational method I had developed, and said, let's use it for the 2003 ASCA Teachers Seminar conference. The association holds these every year at the Cranbrook Academy of Art to teach the teachers of architecture from more than 250 schools of architecture about new areas important to the discipline. We were going to educate the architecture teachers about sustainability, which was just kind of hovering around and not entirely accepted yet.

I invited Susan to be the keynote speaker, because when she gives a talk, whether it's to a conference or a class, she engages her listeners. If they're students, she'll talk about when she was a student and not present herself as a spokeswoman, which she really is.

The "whole-building matrix" looks not just at whether a building's form follows function, or how it functions socially or its environmental features. It also considers the building's overall quality, material sensations, surprising features, design details, graphic images, function, ecology, aesthetics, criticism, and theory. If you want to know how something works, you look at it all. The conference took place over several days, so we applied this matrix to some of the buildings on the Cranbrook campus—that is, we did a sustainable-design evaluation of buildings designed by very well known architects, including Eero Saarinen. We got such pushback from some of the male teachers of architecture. They screamed at me, "How can you subject these buildings, which are aesthetic, to these other standards?"

My argument is that aesthetics are part of sustainability. We know you have to have this love and this feeling of being drawn in and attracted, which you get from the use of elements in the building that are close to natural systems. If sustainability is limited to a building's performance—to the evaluation of its materials-energy footprint, to the distance materials traveled, or energy consumption—and doesn't deal with the effect the building has on human behavior, that's only half of the ballgame. Sustainability has to engage the human spirit.

So Susan was one of the first to understand that how people use space affects human behavior. And architects who think that way have to be brought into the discussion. Susan and I both always had this inclination. And that is what happened at Cranbrook. We introduced the teachers of architecture who were invested in these iconic buildings to the idea that you would ask, how does someone use it or what is the effect on behavior? Once the client is no longer the person using it, there is a whole other way that we have to think about architecture. You are not working for your own culture anymore. You have to say that my way is not the only way.

That is such an important thing. And I think Susan and I agreed on this without ever having to discuss it.

What Do Ethics
Have to Do with Design?

Why should we cloud our lighthearted discussions on creativity, art, and beauty with something as difficult and even quasi-religious as ethics? Ethics, after all, concerns rights and wrongs, and, in an age when anything goes, why should we burden ourselves with making a distinction between the two?

Apparently, we must: ethics plays out in the media every day, and we can't ignore it. This morning, another gaggle of CEOs appeared in court—this time, the gray-suit-and-red-tie gang from WORLDCOM. Their ethical misstep? The abuse of shareholder trust, leading to the now-familiar financial bankruptcy of many small investors, which happened as a direct result of WORLDCOM management's own moral bankruptcy. Ethics, it seems, has to do with personal decisions—in the case of WORLDCOM, the personal business standards of a few wealthy men wanting to gobble up even more wealth.

When you knowingly do something that's harmful to others—be it running a business, participating in a relationship, or designing a building—you cross the line between ethical and unethical behavior. The operative word here is "knowingly." So if knowledge is power, power must come with responsible behavior.

Now what do architects and designers know? That if they ignore ethics, they create injury to others? For years, the design community has heard and learned about environmental degradation caused by design processes and practices. We know about wasteful packaging, the poisonous contents of electronic gadgets that land in the trash quickly and poison our groundwater, toxic inks and bleaches used in printing everything from brochures to ads, and equally toxic building and furnishing materials. And so we know that many of the things designers specify in huge volumes are harmful to the environment, children, and other living things.

But if this ethics thing was as simple as making our materials and practices environmentally sound—and, of course, that's far from simple— we might have this problem solved in short order, or at least in a decade or two. But it's much bigger than that. The ethical crisis we face today has to do with a worldview that can be traced to Descartes' cogito ergo sum principle of a man-centered universe. This view had worked well for centuries, but now it's in crisis. We know the old systems of industrialism, individualism, and modernism don't work anymore. We know that amnesiac modernists have done—and still are doing—a great deal of harm to our species, from making sick buildings to creating brownfields. We first knew this instinctively, but now science is proving our intuitions correct. As we begin to understand whole systems and the web of connections that produce them, we are learning the importance of connectivity.

Delivered at the Design Exchange's Future: Perfect seminar, Innovative Thinking in Architecture and Design, Toronto, May 25, 2004

As playwright Andrew Ordover tells us, "We carry our ancestors with us. Without [a] sense of rootedness, without [celebrating]…what we have pledged to one another, we forget what our culture has learned… we lose all sense of awe and wonder, and allow life to become mean and hard and thin." Awe and wonder—they aren't luxuries. "Too many children in our culture," continues this young writer, who is also an advocate for arts education in New York City public schools, "are cut off from any sense of wonder, and they come to see themselves as nothing more than sacks of shit and blood, snarls on their faces and fists in the air, with nothing to contribute to the planet but rage and fear."

I don't know about you, but that frightening statement—which is very real to our schoolteachers—should be a call to action to the creative community to help reintegrate our lost children with our great and awesome planet and its fantastic process.

Architecture is one of the propagators of this dislocation. You notice I say "one of," not "the." I no longer believe that any one profession can act alone, or see itself as an über-fixer, when faced with today's complex environmental and philosophical issues. So let's just remember what architecture—with a few commendable exceptions—has done for these children: apparently everything possible to alienate them from earth and sky and the sun that gives us life.

Generations have grown up in mechanically heated and cooled rooms with sealed windows and the constant hum of machinery. Kids often don't see daylight, and when they do, it's on a mean asphalt slab expunged of anything that can move. They go through metal detectors as if they were common criminals and sit in chairs nailed to the floor—all in the name of security. They have no idea where the water they drink comes from, or how scarce it is in some parts of the world, or where it goes when it flushes away their waste. All of this signals a mean and ugly quality of life, regardless of how many DVDs, PDAs, SUVs, and other comforts these kids' families may possess.

What are the stars of architecture—our superheroes—doing about fixing this malaise? They do great form, which lately has begun to feel like empty gestures. Think, for instance, of the most celebrated building of the spring season: Frank Gehry's Walt Disney Concert Hall, in Los Angeles. I was there in April and can report the following: the courtyard, which can be reached through a flight of stairs, keeping the public realm largely private, offers a grand moment in architectural miscalculation. (I don't want to say ignorance or unethical behavior, because I, like many others, find Gehry's forms seductive and hard to attack.)

This miscalculation? A part of Disney Hall that faces the courtyard is clad in a sparkling metal. As the sun hits this section of the building, the glare bounces into the apartments across the street; the people who live there are mad as hell and they're acting out. The remedy—at least in April—was to drape a chunk of gray vinyl over the offending detail. Now, you would think that the designers, engineers, contractors, even the concert hall's managers—all living under Southern California's relentless sun—would have seen this coming. Ignoring what you know about the sun is obviously not a good idea, as it may soon be unheard of to not use the sun's power.

Closer to home, we've been watching the fiasco at the World Trade Center site and it makes me sick. The tragedy that befell us was dramatic and overwhelming; its images are seared onto our retinas. Aside from the destruction of the architecture and its stinking and messy aftermath, it's the people we remember. All those lovingly posted Xeroxes of personal moments in the lives of the lost and the dead! You could see those lovely and handsome young faces—so many of them were so young!—in the midst of a birthday party, on vacation, at work. Their lives had purpose, dimension, and, yes, reality. We were seeing tragedies unfold on those walls, and understood their personal implications. I return to Andrew Ordover: "Tragedy sees each human being as sacred and irreplaceable, and it deals with the consequences of that with relentless honesty." For me, those homemade posters dramatized the tragedy we saw. Ordover takes his lesson from the ancient Greeks when he writes, "Homer details the death of every character that falls. We know the wound, we know the pain, we know the person—his family, his wife, his background. Every death hurts; every death counts. Every death is a real life, lost. Compare the war scene in *The Iliad* to any scene in *Rambo*."

We thought we had witnessed the nobility of human behavior as depicted in *The Iliad* on 9/11 and the weeks after. But what we're getting is *Rambo* architecture: meaningless, cold, calculating, and defensive. It didn't start that way. Daniel Libeskind seemed to understand the tragedy. As far as I know, he was the only architect in the site's design competition who actually went down to the bedrock of ground zero and came up with a plan that seemed to commemorate all those personal losses while celebrating human endurance and ingenuity. The slurry wall—that grand feat of engineering constructed to hold back the Hudson when the Twin Towers were built—is now gone from the master plan. In fact, most of the poetic features Libeskind proposed have evaporated.

The developers may have expunged the poetry, but, for many of us, it's hard to forget those faces in the homemade posters, now themselves gone, victims of wind and rain. I'm not sure if there is room for anything but rentable space down there, although Libeskind did talk about something hopeful and meaningful and lasting, and we are all the better for his having said it. Some architecture insiders called his impassioned speeches corny, politically motivated, embarrassing — sometimes, I thought so, too. But I also feel that he showed architects and designers how to speak the people's language.

People understand relationships, their kids' health, and their own well-being; they want clean water, clean air, and healthy food — the real things in life that design should be servicing. I'd like to ask all designers to think of your wife when you design a chair; think of your husband when you design a coffee pot; think of your mom when you design a house; think of your dad when you design a car. They're all real to you — not some abstract marketing aggregate. And they need you to understand the stages and ages of their lives and their varied and changing capabilities.

My students, many of them, are intuitive environmentalists and natural techies; they are true heirs to the creative professions and humanists who tend to be ethical in their practices. And that's exactly why designers became designers in the first place: to make a better world. Now that our world is in distress, we need you more than ever. It's your chance to become what you always wanted to be — NEEDED.

People understand relationships, their kids' health, and their own well-being; they want clean water, clean air, and healthy food — the real things in life that design should be servicing.

Anna Dyson

Environmental performance concerns in architecture started to diverge completely from artistic and cultural aspirations in the latter part of the twentieth century, especially in North American schools of architecture. This led to a schism within the profession, where you have the so-called performance, or high-tech, architects, and then you have the theoretical architects, known for their aesthetic or cultural practice. Susan does not accept this division, because she's committed to an educational model for architects that fuses industry and academia to create the next generation of environmental systems. Frankly, this approach seems so obvious now, and a lot of people are working that way, but it was not obvious at the time. Susan is basically the only one, among the major design editors, who has unabashedly made her magazine a forum for tackling grand challenges. What she chooses to publish in each issue cross-pollinates across all of the different design criteria—aesthetic, social, environmental—and does not divorce these from performance considerations.

She's taken a jackhammer to the sort of pervasive irony that has infiltrated the design culture of the last several decades—now, it's not embarrassing for an architect to want to take on problems of how to deal with shortages of key resources, for example. She was a huge figure in making these problems sexy again and has been incredibly influential in making sustainability hot. Her role is pivotal because she keeps things light; *Metropolis* magazine is never about the browbeating, holier-than-thou type of environmentalist.

At the same time, Susan refuses to let anybody dumb down an agenda or reduce an ambition; she's constructively critical and, in a sense, becomes a collaborator to the work. I think the best critics are the ones who spur the work forward like this.

(Re)defining the Edge

Patterns are fascinating things. You might be looking at one for some time and see nothing, but all of a sudden you shift your point of view or see a new detail emerge, and the pattern starts taking shape. It might be unfamiliar or even strange for a while, but somehow you know you are looking at something you have known was there all along, yet it is also entirely fresh. Let me tell you what I'm seeing in these first tender years and months and days of the twenty-first century. I see old patterns everywhere—patterns that no longer look and feel as if they could tell the story of who we are, who we have become as individuals, as professionals, as citizens, as members of families and communities, as inhabitants of our small, blue green planet.

Delivered as part of the University of Oklahoma Bruce Goff Chair of Creative Architecture lecture series, Norman, Oklahoma, September 8, 2004

The new pattern that I see emerging is shaped by the growing belief that ethical behavior is paramount to our continuing survival and existence. I began to understand this pattern when, about a half-dozen years ago, I was asked to teach a course on design ethics at Parsons The New School for Design, in New York. Being of adventurous mind and spirit, I accepted the assignment, though I agonized about all that I didn't know or understand about the subject, especially how it relates to design.

As an aside, the important thing to remember in all that you do throughout your long lives—especially when you are given a seemingly impossible challenge—is to say yes. When you say yes to a project that seems unbelievably difficult, you could be opening the door to a whole new way of thinking, to a whole new set of patterns. You are also opening the way to a fuller realization of who you are—and better yet, who you want to become—when you conquer a difficult problem. And when you begin to understand it—and catch a glimpse into the human condition—you realize that you are doing the work of the gods. Now, don't misunderstand this. I am not talking about religion or power. What I am talking about is the adventure of the mind. The divine spark for this grandest of adventures exists in each and every one of us. I am convinced of this.

So there I was, having said yes to teaching ethics and wondering how I would do it. I imagined giving difficult reading assignments to students, many of whom came to design school to escape reading. I had worked with reading lists before. I taught a history course at Parsons (and still do). I knew that few of the students actually read the assignments. Besides, the reading was a technicality anyway. The big question was: How do I approach the subject of ethics? What would be the basis of our inquiry? We could talk about design piracy, unfair bidding for jobs, or any number of topics that fall under the rubric of professional standards. But such discussions always felt empty to me. Though they are important, these topics left out the larger reason for ethical professional behavior.

Then I read the oath that doctors take. The Hippocratic oath says something like, "First, do no harm." I wondered how this do-no-harm rule would apply to designers. There are, by and large, many excellent architects whose buildings support the uses they were designed for. Apparently, they're following the do-no-harm rule. There are wonderful interior designers whose rooms work for the functions they're in. So they do no harm. There are great industrial designers whose products do the job they were intended to do. Neither do they seem to harm us—with the exception of my DVD player, which may cause me to have a heart attack. The responsibility for the public's health, safety, and welfare is written into most professional codes of design ethics. So it felt like I was on to something.

Then, I thought about what we've been doing at *Metropolis* magazine. Could that have had something to do with Parsons asking me to teach ethics? From the start, we felt that design was much more than a styling or form-giving exercise. We always worked under the premise that design is an essential vocation that mirrors culture and operates within our social, economic, and political systems. And because what designers do is so closely tied to the quality of our lives, we have always felt that designers have a set of responsibilities to the public they ultimately serve. This high valuation of the necessity of design is our preferred stance. But many professionals—though they seem to agree with us—run practices that cater, as William Morris said during the second half of the nineteenth century, to the "swinish luxury of the rich." Or as Victor Margolin wrote in the late twentieth century, design is "essentially a middle-class profession that has delivered a comfortable life for middle-class people while indulging the wealthy."

In recent years, we have seen swinish luxury celebrated everywhere, and design hasn't been left out of our consumerist fantasies. Ego-driven—oh, let's be kinder—art-driven projects in architecture are given star treatment by the media as well as the profession. We at *Metropolis* do our own share of this. Though I hope we fawn less than most. So if the do-no-harm rule is applied—if designers are responsible for the public's health, safety, and welfare, and if what they do is essential—then we have the basis of our ethics inquiry. Well, almost.

I turned to an economist, David Korten, to help me get to the next step in understanding how we should think about ethics. He makes a distinction between shareholders and stakeholders, and how the behavior of each shapes our world. Many of your parents, or, in some cases, even you yourselves, have become shareholders in multinational global companies. Middle-class investment in the stock market has grown to unprecedented figures in recent years. As shareholders, your main interest is making a profit. And being Americans, you want that return on your investment to be fast and big.

Now, if making money is your sole interest—and in principle, there's nothing wrong with making money—you will close your eyes to all kinds of nefarious practices. These have included sweatshops, child labor, poisoned aquifers, the formation of brownfields, and the addition of carcinogens to our everyday products. All of these somehow exploit other people, most of them with a fraction of our resources. Stakeholders, on the other hand, behave very differently. They feel themselves to be part of a community that shares its essential resources—food, air, water, and security. Stakeholders are not above making money. They just know that without universal healthcare, without social institutions that support education for everyone, and without a livable wage that accrues to all members of the community, we are birthing a pissed-off underclass that no gated community, no infrared devices, and not even artillery can keep from our backyards. The stakeholder mentality is beginning to redefine the edge.

Talk has increasingly focused on sustainable design. This is a global phenomenon, and it has many interpretations. The British *Sunday Herald*, for instance, recently reported that chain stores are spreading "like weeds in a garden" and turning hometowns into "clone towns." Those who own shares in the chains are doing very well indeed. But just listen to what their financial gain is producing elsewhere. The *Herald* says, "The loss of diversity [which is created by many small, privately owned shops] inevitably leads to a loss of choice for consumers." But there's a bigger price to pay for this stockholder-driven economy. Local livelihoods are decimated. "Profits drain away from smaller areas to 'remote corporate headquarters,'" the newspaper says. Here, you see the social fallout of unsustainable planning practices.

The policies we have in place today favor big multinational companies. In England, for instance, "local shops aren't allowed to apply for any kind of business development grants, whereas manufacturing and service sector businesses are," according to the *Herald*, which concludes that this "is fundamentally unfair." Clearly, the laws we make have a lot to do with the society we live in. But many designers would like to believe that what they do is politically neutral. For instance, whenever we at *Metropolis* write stories like the one about the happy world reflected in the graphics of the Bush Administration's Web site, or about town planning as an instrument of political policy in Israel, we receive a few irate letters from readers. Some even cancel their subscriptions. But these stories must be told if we are to remain faithful to the high value we place on design and design's complex role in society.

In the past dozen or so years, a new pattern has begun to reveal itself for shareholders, who may actually start to see themselves as stakeholders one of these days. A Canadian paper recently reported growing industrial activity in off-the-grid products such as photovoltaics, which will make it possible to light the outdoors without plugging into the local utility. Some companies are harvesting straw for ethanol, which they substitute for polluting fossil fuels. Brownfield reclamation is bound to be big business as we grow to understand the value of waste products of all kinds. Water, and the lack of it, is becoming a survival issue in many parts of the world. Membrane technologies for water filtration are being developed, and ultraviolet-lighting technologies are being used to kill waterborne contaminants as firms search for a substitute for chlorine, a known carcinogen.

Wind power is a reality in many places. It even played a role in selling the reconfigured Freedom Tower on ground zero in Lower Manhattan to politicians and public. New York's governor, George Pataki, has put some pretty good green laws on the books, but can the proposed wind turbines live up to their promise? Will they massacre millions of birds? Will the vibrations from the blades be felt in the building? How much energy will they really supply? How high will the maintenance costs be? And who will end up paying for them? How little we know.

And yet what we do know is that the lost office space will be replicated regardless of whether it will be needed or not, even though the numbers and kinds of jobs that used to occupy the World Trade Center may never again exist. Paul Goldberger writes in his new book, *Up from Zero,* "Perhaps the most disturbing aspect of the entire saga of planning ground zero was the possibility that the Freedom Tower might turn out to be less of a symbol of renewal than of how little had been learned from the troubled history of the original World Trade Center," which destroyed the city grid, created a kind of supersize suburban shopping mall with two humongous towers in the middle, and required all kinds of civic- and art-group interventions to enliven its dead places. All of which points out what happens when the architect's first order of responsibility is to his client. The client wanted 10 million square feet of office space, and so ground zero became just another development site.

While the citizens of New York and the world were looking for transcendent architecture, the architects were giving us rentable space. While the New York architecture community talked endlessly about how the ground zero redevelopment elevated the public discourse on architecture, the reality was that our most powerful architectural firms were in the business of giving shape to a wealthy developer's program. The public's need for beauty, sustainability, and community was a minor annoyance to them both. Such undying respect for the client's needs is often at odds with what the people need. If architecture and design are to truly become part of the public discourse, I suggest that designers become advocates for the people and, by implication, advocates for the environment that gives us air, water, and food.

When I began to understand the reality of the multitiered responsibility architects and designers face, I saw the direction our inquiry on design ethics needed to go. We needed to explore and weigh each designer's responsibility to the self, the client, the community, and the environment. One cannot exist without the others, but this inclusive thinking is very difficult. It confronts the inertia of old thought patterns. Socially and environmentally concerned citizens are dismissed as BMWs—bitchers, moaners, and whiners. People who want to continue on the path of heedless development and consumption—aware that the system isn't working anymore—say things like, "We'd get a lot more accomplished if we didn't have so many BMWs working here." Well, I say to them, we have no choice but to bitch and moan and whine until we are heard.

But maybe we don't need to do that. Maybe if we study history and use its lessons to inspire a fresh new way of thinking, we will be able to make powerful arguments for ethical design. Because I have studied history and have been teaching it for some time now, I decided to base our ethical inquiry on the thoughts, lives, and works of those who came before us. A rule of thumb: always build on what you know. We do, indeed, stand on the shoulders of giants. They lift us up high so that we can see our new horizons.

Who better to teach us about informed, socially responsible, humane design than William Morris? This man of wealth and enormous intellectual curiosity helped create a counterrevolution to the nineteenth century's Industrial Revolution. He taught us that you can enrich human thought, action, and design by looking back—in his case, to medieval times. Though he was idealistic, bombastic, willful, and flawed, Morris nevertheless taught us how rewarding the relationship between maker and user can be. Law has its precedents. Why can't design? Every historic figure we study in ethics class—Morris, Gropius, Dreyfuss, and the Eamses—held high personal standards. They invented lifelong learning before it became a buzz phrase, and they never shirked from sharing their knowledge with their new clients and students.

I can't imagine any one of them would say that they don't explore new materials and processes because their clients don't ask for invention. Who ever asks for invention? You just do it, because you cannot do otherwise. You explore a new material, a new way of building, a new understanding of site and topography because you want to know. And then you share your knowledge—well-founded, solid knowledge—with your clients. Some of them will find your enthusiasm infectious. Some won't. But you cannot let perceived apathy and ignorance stop you.

So, now we have professional behavior, a historic precedent for "do no harm." The missing link in the ethics picture must be environmental sensitivity. I mentioned our blue green planet. It is a twentieth-century image that will inform our thinking about who we are and where we belong for a very long time to come. Through our powerful satellites, we can trace the path of fires in China as smoke chokes distant populations. Web sites brim with useful information if you want to understand the world you are designing in. You can download facts and pictures of everything from melting polar ice caps to polluted rivers to brownfields. These and more are available to us from NASA. We paid for this technology with our tax dollars. It behooves us to use it for the benefit of ourselves, our fellow creatures, and the planet that gives us breath, water, and food—life.

If architecture and design are to truly become part of the public discourse, I suggest that designers become advocates for the people, and by implication advocates for the environment that gives us breath, water and food.

There is something very beautiful and elegant about the thought that we all share one giant breath with each other and every other creature on earth. If you think about that shared breath, you will start to look more carefully at the materials and processes you use. I believe that we are entering a new research and exploration phase. Should you choose to accept the challenge, architects and designers can be at the leading edge of positive change. You are the ones who specify and use a large portion of the planet's resources. Knowing that you can contribute to the welfare—or to the demise—of your fellow creatures obligates you to study your materials carefully and find new ones that do less harm to our environment. This is the ethical thing to do. This is the way of the twenty-first century. Your search is a long-term project. Green is not a fad; it's a means to our survival. All of us have a stake in it and must do the very best we can.

Everyone can come up with a small part of the answer to the humongous problem of how to go from environmental degradation, to remediation, to eventual sustainability. Design and architecture schools can be at the forefront of exploring materials and processes. The studio system is a powerful and potentially dynamic tool—a fertile environment for innovative and intelligent problem-solving. All of you do research, explain your findings, incorporate them in the architecture you make, and test function and performance. Your studios are poised to make essential contributions to redefining the edge. Maybe your teachers are not fully equipped to deal with this new paradigm of interconnectedness, but they know how to navigate the building process, and they understand professional relationships and political bottlenecks.

Many professionals seem to be caught off guard by the growing demand for LEED-certified buildings. We've been talking about this performance-rating system for years. So have the other professional magazines. But it is only now that publications like *Fortune* magazine and the *New York Times* are reporting on the financial merits of energy-efficient healthy buildings, and many architects are asking, what is this thing called LEED? It galls me when I hear that, but then I calm myself down. At least they are asking. Of course, this is after they have lost jobs to better-informed firms. But the most encouraging thing about this growing need to build energy-efficient, healthy buildings is that a new body of knowledge is developing, grounded in historic precedent and technological breakthroughs.

A whole new set of architectural muscles is about to be pumped up. I believe that this new knowledge of designing sustainably will be used differently than current practices would indicate. Collaboration—long lip-serviced by the professions—will need to be learned anew. Working together is hard, but it's extremely rewarding and the results can be stupendous. The edge is being redefined as the province of lean and extremely well informed teams with inspired leaders. Since today's problems are enormous and complex, many specialists are needed to solve them. The jeering across professional lines must give way to mutual respect and trust. It's the only way true collaboration can occur. We'll need some psychologists on these teams, just as we will need people with expert knowledge in life sciences, history, culture, language, and a myriad of other fields. The university ought to be on the leading cusp of collaborative work, but for that to happen, the silos of academia must fall, replaced by a level playing field for every necessary participant.

You—yes, you, me, and all of us—have a stake in leading this change. To do our part, we instituted the *Metropolis* Next Generation Design Prize. We are looking for big ideas that move the profession forward. Sustainability, access, community involvement, material innovation, and systems thinking are what we're asking for and what we're willing to back up with seed money to support the winning idea. I am tired of vanity architecture awards judged from pictures of last year's pickings. I want architects and designers to overcome the low expectations placed on them by other magazines and by their profession's leaders. I want you to strive to propose difficult ideas that need to be tested and developed—ideas that have long-term implications and short-term influences.

The winner of our 2004 Next Generation Prize is a young firm in Cambridge, Massachusetts: Single SPEED Design. They came up with a way to turn garbage from the Big Dig—parts of the federal highway and bridge system that used to choke Boston—as a material for beautiful, accessible housing. An old material used in a new way can come literally from your own backyard, and you don't have to spend money on fossil fuels to ship it thousands of miles. One of the 2004 Next Generation runner-up proposals came from a team working at a research lab at Rensselaer Polytechnic Institute. Students in architecture and engineering, professors, and experts from other institutions have come together to re-invent the photovoltaic cell. Their facade product, which uses fresnel lenses to focus sunlight, is about to be tested. At least one architect in New York City is looking to use it on an academic building. Beautiful, technically sophisticated, and with great potential for energy-efficiency: this is architectural invention. While other architects complain that they have become mere specifiers of standard materials, Anna Dyson—who leads the Rensselaer team—proves that architects can be at the forefront of redefining the edge of building arts and crafts.

Doug Garofalo, Greg Lynn, Winka Dubbeldam, Tom Wiscombe, Hernan Diaz-Alonso, and many others are evolving new forms by using software tools like Maya, Rhino, and CATIA in inventive ways. They work with rapid prototypes, 3D printers, and CNC milling machines to test their ideas and fabricate their buildings. Granted, they're still in the one-off business, and only on rare occasions do they propose ideas for afford-able housing, inner-city schools, and homeless shelters. These remain wide-open fields for architects looking for a special challenge.

Nothing lights your fire of exploration and makes it burn bright more than studying the life and work of people you admire. I came across two people last week worthy of hero status and emulation—both making great contributions to architecture and both exemplars of ethical behavior. They prove that an ethical life can be highly satisfying and even lucrative.

The first is J. Irwin Miller, who died last week in Columbus, Indiana, at the age of 95. He was an industrialist who could have wallowed in greed and spent his life gobbling the wealth of the Fortune 500 firm he ran, the Cummings Engine Company. But this man, who earned a master's degree in classics from Oxford University and played his own Stradivar-ius, had an admirable thirst for knowledge and an unparalleled social conscience. He read Greek and Italian, was the first lay president of the National Council of Churches, was an advocate of civil rights who helped plan the 1963 march on Washington, was a juror for architecture's Pritz-ker Prize for seven years and an unmatched patron of architecture. With the help of Mr. Miller, some 70 buildings by world-class architects were built in Columbus, a town of fewer than 40,000 people. He understood perfectly the immense personal reward of an adventurous mind and an ethical spirit. And he understood the importance of excellent architecture in creating community.

William LeMessurier is a successful engineer whose career and livelihood—along with the lives of thousands of people—could have ended in an instant had he not done the ethical thing. LeMessurier was the engineer of the Citicorp building, completed on New York's Upper East Side in 1977. Shortly thereafter, he got a call from a student who was questioning some of the engineering solutions Mr. LeMessurier had devised for the slant-topped skyscraper. As the story unfolds, you see how important the student's question really was. Upon reexamining his calculations, and after realizing that the contractor skimped on the hardware that holds up the building—and with the hurricane season approaching, unusually high winds being predicted in 1978, and the building not having been tested for certain wind velocities and angles—Mr. LeMessurier saw a potential catastrophe. He could have blamed others—certainly the contractor had contributed to the problem—or he could have kept quiet and hoped the building would not collapse.

Instead, he did the right thing. He did the ethical thing. He alerted the client, the city, the lawyers, the other engineers, the architect, and the Red Cross to the problem. They came up with a solution that would prevent the tower from toppling onto the dense streets below in case the building was weakened by strong winds. The faulty parts were fixed in record time before the winds hit, and Mr. LeMessurier ended up paying a large amount of the cost. He did not lose his insurance though, which would have put an end to his engineering practice. He gained the reputation of being a man of conscience and quick action: an excellent leader.

Everything I have talked about here implies a personal choice made by someone who considered more than his own welfare and his client's needs. As an editor, my job is to ask questions. So the question I ask of you now is this: how will you prepare yourself to make hard choices? And as a follow-up, what can you contribute to making a new pattern which reflects the twenty-first-century ethos of environmental sustainability and social equity? Are you willing to take part in redefining the edge?

Beth Dickstein

What people need to know is that her mind is always working. Constantly working. She is always assessing things. So she does nothing lightly. If she believes in something—if she takes something on—that's it. If you try to oppose her or get in her way, she won't step on you but she will try to convince you. And I guess nine times out of ten she does, because her plan is so well thought out. And I don't know too many people like that.

We have traveled together since 1987—first for business and later, since 1996, for fun and friendship. We've been to Vietnam, Morocco, India, and Peru. And every summer, we go to Italy. With Susan, there is no "no." There is no place I want to go where she won't go. We were in Istanbul, and I wanted to go to Cappadocia, and she said great. Should we fly? No, she said, let's take the bus. It is a 10-hour ride. We were the only non-Turkish people on the bus, stopping in these places where the bathroom is a hole in the ground. And we get there and it is so cold, I can't even tell you. It's December, snow on the ground, and it is a big climb. There were these two young Asian kids who helped us because it was slippery. I was really freezing, and at night, Susan took her coat and she put it on top of me. If you need kindness—or whatever you need in whatever situation—she will provide it. So I always know, no matter what, with her there and how smart she is, that we are going to be OK.

In Morocco, I decided I wanted to ride a camel in the desert. So Rashid, our guide, says, "Oh, I can take you to the Sahara." I think it was $200 or something. And you stay overnight in a tent. The tent is made out of blankets and goat hair. The night before we leave for the desert, I wake up in the middle of the night and scream out, "Suze, they're going to kill us." She turns to me and calmly says, "They are not going to kill us. We are worth more to them alive than dead." OK. So we get into the car the next day, and Rashid drives us to the desert. And he leaves us there with a group of Touaregs. Our tent has just two mattresses on the ground and a candle kind of thing in the middle. And just blankets. And so I think germs. I have all my clothes on, shirt on top of shirt. The desert is very cold at night. It was Christmas Eve, and I was so excited about getting to ride that camel in the morning, to see the sun come up. And all of a sudden, I see this figure. Susan is carrying her mattress away from the door of the tent. I say, "What's the matter?" And she says, "I just got scared. I'm afraid they're going to kill us."

In Hungary, when she was a young girl, they used to kill the chickens for food. Her job was to hold a dish beneath the chicken's neck to collect the blood so they could make something out of it. I was born in Brooklyn. There were no cows, no goats, there was no anything. So we're in the market once in Morocco, and they had a lamb's head right there—cut off, bleeding. I almost fainted. I was like, "OK, Susan, I'm going down." She grabs the back of my head and says, "No you're not. This is the way these people live. This is the way we see it." And I go, "OK." It's always like that. You know, we always bring our childhood with us, and her childhood experience was so different than yours or mine.

Metropolis Magazine Covers

December 1984

December 1988

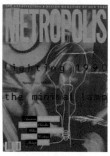

May 1990

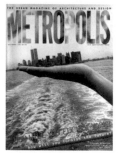

October 1991

November 1992

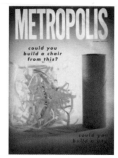

November 1993

October 1994

January 1995

March 1995

September 1995

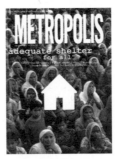

January 1997

November 1999

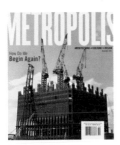

December 2001

July 2003

October 2003

October 2004

January 2005

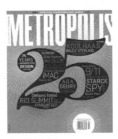

April 2006

July 2006

March 2008

October 2008

May 2009

January 2011

April 2011

June 2011

February 2013

April 2013

December 1984   *Cover designed by Lonnie Heller.* Marking the beginning of the magazine's interest in workplace design, the cover features an archival photo of Steelcase employees standing on the company's sturdy filing cabinets. At the time, when few magazines considered publishing the history of the corporate office, editor Sharon Lee Ryder asked Susan Szenasy, then a free-lance writer, to give context to the rapidly developing field of office furniture design.

December 1988   *Cover designed by Helene Silverman and Jeff Christensen.* To delve into the particulars of sustainability, *Metropolis* photographed New York's Fresh Kills landfill to show what packaging designers were contributing to our solid-waste stream.

May 1990   *Cover designed by Jeff Christensen and Jim Christie.* Thomas Edison's sketch of the incandescent bulb, a symbol of the minimal lamp, is superimposed on a photo of aluminum forms. An enclosed poster showed a century of modern lamps in a postmodern setting.

October 1991   *Cover designed by Carl Lehman-Haupt and Nancy Cohen.* New York City needed fixing, so *Metropolis* asked designers to do it. The logo mimes a liquid crystal formation that changes color as it warms up. The issue contained the Design Explorations: 2001 competition in which the editors asked, "How will we live in 2011?" A new tagline, "The Urban Magazine of Architecture and Design," reflects a more national and international scope.

November 1992   *Cover designed by Carl Lehman-Haupt and Nancy Cohen.* A symbol of ascent to one person can signify an insurmountable physical barrier to another. The computer-stretched photographs of stairways with flat Braille dots spelling out "access" attempt to show the limitations in designing environments and objects, magazines included, that welcome all.

November 1993   *Cover designed by Carl Lehman-Haupt and Nancy Cohen.* Calling attention to paper as a material to study, we showed it shredded and as a toilet paper roll. *Metropolis* was the first American design magazine to run a story on Shigeru Ban's paper architecture.

October 1994   *Cover designed by Carl Lehman-Haupt and Nancy Cohen.* In the early 1990s, an emerging global culture was brought to the attention of the design world. Multiculturalism's impact on the designed environment is an ongoing theme as local cultures assert themselves in a global marketplace.

| January 1995 | *Cover designed by Kristine Larsen, Carl Lehman-Haupt, and Nancy Cohen.* Metropolis has always covered the changing face of technology. The photograph shows a woman eating a computer chip, calling attention to a story on the corporate, scientific, and utopian dreams of an electronic future. |

| March 1995 | *Cover designed by Carl Lehman-Haupt and Nancy Cohen.* Type design becomes a hot topic as graphic designers adapt to technological changes, such as electronic typesetting. The use of Campbell's Alphabet Soup helped *Metropolis* convey this shift. |

| September 1995 | *Cover designed by Carl Lehman-Haupt and William van Roden.* These standard No. 2 pencils represent the quintessential educational tool and the most basic design instrument. The diversity of the course offerings listed on them reflects what was happening in the expanding architecture and design curricula. |

| January 1997 | *Cover designed by Carl Lehman-Haupt and William van Roden.* In November 1996, as hundreds of thousands of Rwandan refugees streamed back into their war-torn country, the world was reminded once more that for a growing number of people, decent shelter is still a dream. |

| November 1999 | *Cover designed by Paula Scher.* Paula Scher, a partner at Pentagram, redesigns *Metropolis.* As the size of the magazine is cut down, the logo gets cropped and the subtitle removed. Inside, the design is cinematic in its approach: the logo moves side to side and up and down, then torques on the last few pages. |

| December 2001 | *Cover designed by Criswell Lappin.* The first cover after September 11, 2001, originally showed a skewed perspective of the World Trade Center towers intact. The image was changed the day before the issue went to press, when we learned another publication planned a similar cover. This archival shot, backed up by an optimistic sky, depicts the towers under construction. We felt it represented the questions surrounding the future of Lower Manhattan. |

| July 2003 | *Cover designed by Criswell Lappin.* Readers have always turned to *Metropolis* for the latest in product design. The unusual image created by the shadow of an inverted Mirra task chair only hints at the chair's form, imparting a sense of mystery. |

October 2003	*Cover designed by DJ Stout and Criswell Lappin.* A new study on global warming found that architecture was a major contributor to pollution. In this issue, *Metropolis* challenged the profession to turn green, and the cover displays blueprints emitting clouds of black smoke—a strong visual call to arms.
October 2004	*Cover designed by DJ Stout and Criswell Lappin.* Collaboration between many design professionals reached a new level of sophistication with the Seattle Public Library. This cover focuses on the teamwork required to complete the project and shows multiple hands working on the same model, dispelling the myth of the imperial architect.
January 2005	*Cover designed by Criswell Lappin and Nancy Nowacek.* The decision to use a bird's-eye view of Lucia Eames in the living room of her father and stepmother's famous house stemmed from a similarly posed photograph of Charles and Ray. The desire to create a unique image while referencing the past was a nod to the importance of preserving modernist architecture.
April 2006	*Cover designed by Criswell Lappin and Nancy Nowacek.* With its silvery sheen, starbursts, bold colors, and colossal "25," this cover celebrated our quarter-century of covering the best in architecture and design. Contained within the numbers are the names of people, places, and objects that appear in the issue.
July 2006	*Cover design by Quick Honey, Criswell Lappin, and Nancy Nowacek.* Workplace design took a leap into the electronic future when Google decided to remake its headquarters to reflect the new ways of the office. The untethered, relaxed work environment included 24/7 food service—perfect for the Geek Shangri-La.
March 2008	*Cover designed by Peter Mendelsund, Criswell Lappin, and Dungjai Pungauthaikan.* With talk about localism in a sustainable world, this special product issue explored everything from Brazil's urban culture influencing furniture design to the first digital database documenting the proportions of Asian heads and faces. The vernacular typefaces underscore the rich variety of design expressions to be found in local flavor.
October 2008	*Cover designed by Chris Ro, Criswell Lappin, and Dungjai Pungauthaikan.* To illustrate how a new generation of design activists is reshaping the world, *Metropolis* focused its attention on the rise of the citizen architect. A caring architect's hand holds up a broken and fragile globe while inspiring projects and ideas spill forth.

May 2009	*Cover designed by Brian Collins, John Fulbrook III, Timothy Goodman, Jason Nuttall, Criswell Lappin, and Dungjai Pungauthaikan.* A French team of architects and engineers won the Next Generation Design Competition in 2009 for adapting existing electrical pylons by adding the windmills they designed. To covey this visionary idea of energy independence, the graphic designers made a cloud-lined pinwheel and showed a hand pinning it to an abstracted pylon, prompting the editors to write, "Pinning Our Hopes on the Wind."
January 2011	*Cover designed by Always With Honors, Dungjai Pungauthaikan, and Ashley Stevens.* Starting with the September 2009 issue, we adjusted the magazine's size once more and reinstituted our full-size logo. To emphasize our legendary multidisciplinary coverage of design, the graphics team created symbols for six areas of "game changing" activities, from redefining civic leadership to transforming architectural practice.
April 2011	*Cover designed by Stephen Doyle, Dungjai Pungauthaikan, and Ashley Stevens.* How to represent 30 years of covering architecture and design? Build "a monumental paper salute," said Doyle. "Using the full spectrum could allude to *Metropolis*'s colorful past. And because the paper model is folded, it's only partially revealed...the twists and turns of the structure and the linear quality were a perfect way to convey a timeline of ideas shared and excellence celebrated."
June 2011	*Cover designed by Bronson Stamp.* The nimble design consultancy IDEO took on the lumbering federal government and created a transparent, online service for the Social Security Administration by mapping Americans' journey to retirement. Our art director, Dungjai Pungauthaikan, designed a festive ribbon to mark the magazine's thirtieth year.
February 2013	*Cover designed by Dungjai Pungauthaikan.* Superstorm Sandy prompted us to ask, "Are we ready for the next one?" In an era of climate change, as human settlements battle extreme storms and rising waters, we explore the idea of resilience, presenting possible solutions by a concerned design community from around globe.
April 2013	*Cover designed by Dungjai Pungauthaikan.* With 3-D printers making everything from guns to human ears, we trace how these computer-driven machines have transformed design. From the scale of buildings to rooms and even shoes, the technology presents new possibilities for how things are made and customized, promising profound repercussions for the industrial system that ruled the last century.

Early Years

First Szenasy
family visit to
New York, with
cousin's husband
in background,
1958

Szenasy Zsuzsanna Zelma (track and field, playwright/director, watercolorist),
wearing the obligatory red kerchief, enters the sixth grade in 1956, a few months
before the Hungarian Revolution breaks out.

First visit to
Statue of Liberty,
1959

First magazine publishing position in New York, 1970s

Professional Years

At the *Metropolis* magazine office

With Michael Murphy, MASS Design Group, and Tim Brown, IDEO, at the first annual Horace Havemeyer III State of Design conference

The *Metropolis* editorial staff, photographed on the occasion of the magazine's thirtieth anniversary on New York's HighLine

@Szenasy

████████████████████

Can we move away from impulsive judgments & start to edit our choices more thoughtfully?

Urban excellence, the 21st century definition: small, committed coalitions make things happen.

Can we #slow down, not embrace the #speed & #efficiency of technology & reclaim delay as a value in art & #design?

Why do we accept the idea of lifetime warranties? Why not consider the need for a warranty after the "life"? #Upcyle

The global trend toward #urbanization—a perfect opportunity to build sustainable cities & create real market change.

#Innovation can happen, as Google knows, when employees are encouraged to give 20% of their time to outside projects.

Designers may want to aspire to David Foster Wallace's words: make our world "passionately moral, and morally passionate."

When #neuroscience research of the design processes becomes an everyday practice, we might get more humane designs.

2012

Designers focus on asking questions. Businesspeople focus on answers. The combination can be powerful.

Our inertia around how our cars define our freedoms is stopping new ideas needed for 21c transportation.

Even if every car is electric, we still have traffic jams. Needed: systems solutions to transportation.

Baby boomers moved us from 3 flavors of ice cream to 100s; don't put them into your mother's nursing home.

There are at least 2 opposing visions for our cities: people vs capital oriented. Which would work? Which do we want?

What kind of world would we have if our maps were drawn to reflect nature, not political & economic boundaries?

It's time we stopped calling the #Olympics an economic catalyst & look closely at the impact they have on communities.

#Architects understand the benefits of #sustainable design, #developers focus on the #financial. How to connect them?

Can #designers attain a state of grace that is rare, brief, and unpredictable, but ever-present in the #natural world?

In a global economy industrial productivity is not enough to single out a business. Innovation, R&D, #design add value.

What if efficiency, conservation, & renewables were not the answers to our problems with our #energy #infrastructure?

If 20th century #architecture belonged to the specialist, the 21st century is the age of the integrator, the connector.

How do you convince a community to become more aware of their daily energy use and the importance of conservation?

We need to design hospitals that encourage a better interface with their surrounding communities.

Quantifying costs & benefits over their life cycle helps us understand how living buildings can be good for business.

As creatures who occupy less than 1% of the Earth, how do we fix the imbalance between our rights & responsibilities?

Why are people with disabilities invisible to so many governments elected to represent everyone?

What happens to public architecture when the right wing releases it attack dogs? Hyperventilation, not civil discourse.

Emerging architects' issues: advancement of the profession, value of design & licensure, economy & change.

As the US urban #bike culture grows, we my want to learn to go with the flow & look out for one another.

Digital native argues for architects to expand their skills + advocates harvesting the wisdom of elders.

2011

The human eye is a complex organ + a window to our soul. Is the quest for light efficiency making us blind?

Have we, in the hype-plagued West, forgotten something that once was key to the human experience: dignity?

Our love affair with the "flash of genius" in architecture has blinded us from focusing on whole systems.

We're just beginning to discover the complexity of integrating buildings with nature. This is a deep dive!

Our built & natural environments deteriorate while our hunger for Charlie Sheen lunacy remains insatiable.

Leadership, Power, and Design

Being asked to speak on gender and leadership—about the opportunities and challenges women have in leadership—brought to mind a great many thoughts, not all of them related to both issues. But as editor of *Metropolis* magazine, pulling together disparate thoughts is what I do.

Sara Little Turnbull is one of my idols. She is well into her 80s and is like a little firecracker with a cherubic face. She teaches design to engineers at Stanford University and is the most amazing person you ever want to meet. One day, she came to a conference we produced and I facilitated; she was wearing a beautiful Japanese robe with a little black hat. She just sort of spun up to me and said, "My dear, you are like Picasso." I said, "What?" She said, "You know the way you pull together everything, like Picasso did in his paintings and made the colors all work and made the patterns all work." And I thought, "Oh my God, it's like that. That is what I do."

That is when I realized that there is value in all the exploration I do. That everything I read and look at and study somehow fits together. That my ethics class at Parsons feeds into my magazine work, which feeds into all the writing that I do, the talking that I do, the conferences that I organize. So everything is part of the same picture, including my civic group, which is working to rebuild downtown (the portion of Lower Manhattan destroyed and damaged in the September 11, 2001, attack). We write well detailed, seriously researched papers to put out there for the rebuilders to use. I can't separate one part of my professional life from another; everything belongs together.

So drawing on everything I know, everything I learn, everything I am involved in is one important quality of leadership. Here are some others:

Collaboration

My father taught me to fly. He taught me to fly intellectually and emotionally. But he was actually a pilot, too. He was trained in the 1930s on some English and German planes in Hungary, where I was born. He loved his life. He was the best pilot around and felt that he was totally independent. So when he married my mother at the age of 29, his commander said to him, "Remember, marriage is like flying in formation. What you do is watch the others' wings. You are in a group of equally skilled people who are trying to create something beautiful together." This story taught me about precision—being precise about how you talk, what you do, what you say, how you explore an idea. It taught me about caring for something and someone other than myself. It taught me about the consideration of some other person's abilities. Collaboration is looking at how you work together, how you make that perfect line of planes, and how you keep them in line.

Adapted from a presentation given at Kendall College of Art and Design, Grand Rapids, Michigan, as part of the lecture and discussion series Gender and Leadership, 2004

I realized that there is value in all the exploration that I do....I can't separate one part of my professional life from another; everything belongs together.

Taking charge

Leadership means taking responsibility—for yourself and others. I was always against hierarchies. I like to imagine that creative people do not want hierarchies, that they do not want someone in charge, and that there is a way to get things done without a hierarchy. But, of course, there isn't; someone has to be in charge. I never fully understood this until I analyzed my life and how it worked. I realized that being in charge came naturally to me. I was a Young Pioneer at the age of six. I was a little Commie, actually, in Hungary, with the red necktie and the whole thing. I was the leader of the troop. I never know why that happened, it just did. In America, I had my first job at 14 working at a baby-clothing factory, where I became the person who was in charge. I was working with people who were packing the clothes, and, all of a sudden, I was keeping the books. But, of course, someone figured out that I was only 14, and I got fired from my first job because I was underage. I was somehow always in charge. I didn't know why this was, but much later, in my career at *Metropolis,* I was still fighting the idea of hierarchy. As my job grew, it became evident that we had to have a layering of responsibilities, so now we have a layering. But I really encouraged everyone to contribute in a big way to the magazine.

Revolutions create opportunities for leadership

If you want a good opportunity for leadership, look for an area that is developing. Developing areas are where you find your own way, because nobody has done it before and that means you can create something.

To me, the area of sustainable design is an incredible opportunity for men and women to begin answering questions to which none of us yet knows the full answers. Whether it is cradle-to-cradle documentation of materials, research on materials, how to use sunlight or energy, what kinds of energy, how to manufacture—the big questions of sustainability touch everything. Sustainable design really remakes our whole social contract. When you start thinking about designing something that goes from concept back into the loop of material use, you are designing things in a totally different way than when you designed products and buildings that end up in the trash after their useful lives are over. I think that is an enormous opportunity for designers, for anybody who wants to be in a leadership position, to figure out certain aspects of sustainability. Right now, it is so big that none of us knows what to do with it, we are nibbling at the edges. But I think that in your field, whatever it is, the best opportunity is in a new area where you have a chance to expand and grow. Your technical knowledge is essential to this new exploration. Technology is very important to sustainable design. Anything that takes you away from the material world into electronic work and helps you document, solve problems, and build models without wasting materials is a big help.

Gender stereotypes: Vive la différence!

We are used to thinking of gender stereotyping as a bad thing, but I think we need to take a broader view. It is easy to get hung up on the wrong things. Think about places in the world that aren't like ours but have some sort of accommodation between the sexes and between the age groups and between people in general. I was on a trip to Morocco recently. That country was very interesting to me, because there we were, my friend and I, two women living in a world of men. No women came in contact with us. Men's lives are lived in public; the women do something else. Now, one might say, "Oh these poor women; these downtrodden abused women!" But they think of it very differently. Moroccan woman are very much in charge of certain areas of society. We saw that there was a definite role division between the sexes that had economic and political reasons for being. That doesn't mean we want to live that way. But the point is that there are accommodations that people make in order to make better lives for themselves, in order to live peacefully in the societies to which they belong.

So I think that women need to consider the idea that we might not want to be men. Instead, women should want to be women but be as powerful as men. I think that is where we are heading. I am tired of seeing female corporate executives who look like the men they work with, dress like men, and act like the worst kind of male that there is. That's not who we are. Let's use our special abilities, such as our natural sense of collaboration; they are needed. We are needed. And when you are needed, then you can achieve what you set out to do, because you become something that people are willing to pay for.

A postwar phenomenon

In my opinion, the source of our current gender stereotypes is a set of economic trends that began after World War II. It became an economic imperative to put American women in suburbia, so they could become consumers of the massive industrial output that emerged during the war. Women adjusted their lives to an economic construct. When you look at women who lived before the war, you see incredible achievement. I was very good friends with Sarah Tomerlin Lee, who was a major interior decorator. Her husband was a decorator before her; when he died, she took over his business. She was a mother, a magazine editor, a writer, a decorator. I think I did the last interview with her before she died at 92. I was always asking her whether it was very difficult for her. She was a vice president at Lord and Taylor in the 1940s. She said, "No, no we did what we did. There were a lot of women like me working in those positions."

So let us not say women were inferior. Women were part of the economic decision that society made in order to produce massive wealth. When my family immigrated to New Jersey, where I grew up, I learned English from Elvis, listening to his records and TV commercials. I always loved watching old movies. What was interesting to me was the power of women like Rosalind Russell, Katharine Hepburn, and Bette Davis in the movies they made before the war, before the rise of suburbia and the radical division of the sexes. These women had great presence. I still watch them. They are like my mentors. There were incredibly strong roles for women. But then, in the 1950s movies you start seeing ridiculous role models, women as airheads and bimbos.

Taking a chance

And yes, having grown up when I did, I have encountered plenty of gender stereotyping, and still see it today. My first jobs were secretarial. It didn't matter what I knew; I was going to be a file clerk. But after my first few magazine jobs, and a master's in modern European history, I landed at *Interiors* magazine. Over the years, I rose from being an editor's assistant to a senior editor. When they divided the magazine into two — *Contract Interiors and Residential Interiors* — initially, we all worked on both. The management decided that everyone who had been working 24 hours a day for a year should get a break. They began hiring high-profile men to run the two publications. Some of these men were doing a horrible job; and by then, I was writing many of the major features in *Residential Interiors*. So with prompting and encouragement from a friend, I sucked up my courage, went into my publisher's office and said, "Look, I am not a star, and I can't bring you name recognition here, but I can edit this magazine. Do you want me to do that? If you want me to do it, I will be your next editor." I got the job. I edited *Residential Interiors* until they closed it after almost three years. It was my first editorship, and it came at a pretty early age. Taking that chance really helped me understand how to be a leader, as well as the editor of a magazine.

More recently, I had another encounter with gender stereotyping. I was invited, as the cofounder of my civic group, to the unveiling of the initial plans for rebuilding Lower Manhattan. In the boardroom at the Lower Manhattan Development Corporation, where the meeting took place, there were three women and 20 men. Of course, the men were all established, middle-aged fellows, comfortably in charge, and there were three of us women, comfortably in charge, in our own ways. As I listened to the presentation, I thought, "Oh my God, what are we looking at here?" Yet everybody was saying to the man in charge, "Great job. You've done a fabulous job."

And as we left, I said to my partner in founding our civic group, "They are calling me from the *Times* to respond to these schemes. I can't say this is a great job. We can't allow them to put this one over." She agreed.

My point is that as women we were shunted into the background, but I got my revenge. I wrote the op-ed piece the *New York Times* had asked me to do. That piece became one of the key factors in turning around the discussion of what should be on the World Trade Center site. The editors gave the article pride of place. It certainly wasn't my op-ed alone that did it, but it played a part. And it happened because the *Times* came to me, as the editor of *Metropolis*. Those men had their power in the boardroom, but I had the power in the *New York Times*.

Hiring for success

I think that power and leadership derive from knowing a lot about many things—from being informed and being willing to be informed. For me, it is also recognizing talent, where talent is, and not being threatened by it. I know of other magazines where editors hire people who aren't exactly mental giants in order to maintain their own power. I am not interested in doing that. I want the people I hire to be better, smarter, and more skilled than I am. In fact, the current editors at *Metropolis* are much better than I ever was or could be.

Design and self-image

One of the revealing experiences in my work as a magazine editor is to see how graphic designers and communications professionals present images of men and women in media.

I was recently looking at ads in *Vanity Fair*. Women were portrayed as victims, whores, anorexics, jokes—stereotypes we do not want to be associated with. This is what young women are fighting today and it is an incredibly difficult thing to fight. Those images have great power.

There was one ad that particularly upset me. I think it was for alligator shoes. This guy's alligator shoes were juxtaposed with a young woman's crotch in a very unfortunate way. This is not right. There are a thousand great ways to do an ad that don't show a woman lying on the floor, being a victim, being abused. This kind of advertising destroys self-image. It deeply divides the sexes. This is what you are fighting today. In 2004, it is still happening, and I think everybody in communication design has to be aware of it. Graphic designers have the ethical responsibility to call attention to it. There are many ways to sell a product, and abuse doesn't have to be one of them.

A philosophy of design

Design is multidisciplinary. It is a culturally significant activity. It shapes our world. It also mirrors our world, and we need to look at it that way. Designers have the capacity to make things more beautiful and to make them better and safer. I sincerely believe that thought applies to all areas of design. Design is more than just creating an object, more than just making a building, more than just drawing a graphic. Design is anything that has an intentional quality, where a skilled person sets out to make a thing beautiful and make it useful. This vision has been maintained through the years at *Metropolis*. We have never veered from it. While other magazines periodically relaunch themselves, I don't believe in re-launching, in remaking a good idea. Improve what you have, yes and always. The world changes, and culture, like design and architecture, is our magazine's focus. Therefore, we need to respond to our world with solid journalism, criticism, and humor. But we do not ever fool with the magazine's DNA. It contains our multidisciplinary vision of the world.

Emily Pilloton

She was this strong female voice. And I looked to her for this. I felt like she was my godmother or a Sherpa. I have constantly struggled with how to be a leader and still be a practitioner, to be a voice and also always be at work, with my hands. There is something about being a female leader—you don't ask for it. And she was there, as a leader who was wholly compassionate and also a warrior. She is maternal, wise, honest, and supportive. But nothing gets past her. She is the most generous person, and at the same time, there is this "I'll kick your ass if I have to" demeanor that she carries. She helped me develop my own balance of love and revolution. She's one of these people who doesn't take crap from anyone, and she does it with love.

Designers Need Heroes

It's early March, and I'm thinking about two events coming at the end of the month. One is an awards ceremony in Manhattan celebrating long and productive lives in design; the other is a talk to University of Nebraska students about how the next generation will shape design. Since I'm always looking for ways to connect those who went before us and those who will come after, the historian in me rejoices in the juxtaposition.

It's no secret that I have a special fondness for interior design and for those who practice it. My attachments were formed early, aided and abetted by Olga Gueft, who hired me as her assistant at *Interiors* magazine some three decades ago. By then, she had been the editor in chief of the magazine for more than 20 years, setting the highest standards for editorial coverage while becoming a tireless advocate for the profession. Her interests went beyond the attractive work she featured; she was intrigued by interior design as a business, as an economic construct. It was this vision of Olga's that helped give the profession its solid footing in the business world and led me to perceive design as much more than a mere styling exercise.

As Olga's assistant, I got to read everything she wrote—and it was a revelation, especially in relation to other writings on interiors. The trade rags were dry and boring; consumers got puff and hype—not much different from today. Olga's language was concise and poetic; she described as well as analyzed design. She showed me that a design-magazine editor can and should be deeply involved in the industry. One of Olga's enduring contributions to the interior design industry is her detailed history of professional organizations, from their formations to their evolutions into more sophisticated and relevant versions of themselves, as with the American Society of Interior Designers and the International Interior Design Association.

Through it all, Olga maintained an almost childlike wonder at the beauty and complexity of the worlds designers create. When she'd call something "beautiful!" it was because it did more than simply catch her eye: she was excited about finding the story behind the gorgeous image. Her abiding enthusiasm, coupled with a boundless intellectual curiosity, made Olga an essential player—a contributor, a mentor, my hero. I hope I can do her justice as I honor her with a National Arts Club Visionary award. It's hard to talk to your hero face-to-face about being a hero.

But as I talk to students, Olga stands firmly behind me. I tell them how much I believe in the contributions they can make; I tell them that I admire both their willingness to tap into the humanist roots of modern design and the ways they take technology seriously. And I remind them of what George Santayana famously said in the early twentieth century: "Those who cannot remember the past are condemned to repeat it." I believe in the importance of history to designers. That's where we find our understanding of our world, as well as our heroes.

Visionary Award: Olga Gueft

There are many stars in the design firmament. They glitter and shine at a cold distance, but down here on earth, it is often hard to discern the qualities that make our stars human. To be truly inspired, we need people who show us empathy, enthusiasm, love of life and life's work, respect for ideas, an endless capacity for learning, and an irrepressible curiosity. These were—and continue to be—qualities abundantly present in the woman we honor tonight as a visionary.

Presented at the National Arts Club, New York City, March 30, 2005

Olga Gueft, as editor in chief of *Interiors* magazine, when the profession of interior design was coming into its own, could have behaved like a star maker, a power broker, a diva. But she did not choose such an obvious path. She chose to practice her considerable skills as a journalist and find the worthwhile stories. She used her love of language and writing skills to discuss interior design as a necessary occupation that adds economic value to a society built on humanistic values. Because she understood history and culture, she insisted that interior design have an indelible history and recognize its evolving culture—that these be recorded and passed on to future generations while inspiring current practitioners. All of this makes Olga a visionary and my hero—our hero.

Heroes inspire us to be better than we are. Their example can guide us through a lifetime. Olga has done that for me. But more than that, she has helped define the path for interior designers.

Now, more than ever, we need the profession to be as generous and constructive as Olga envisioned it to be. Thank you, Olga, for leading the way and for being my hero—for being our hero.

Michael Murphy

██████████████████

I was working on the Butaro Hospital in Rwanda. We had finished the building. But we were in the early stages of conceptualizing, for ourselves, the purpose of architecture in general, and figuring out the direct impact it could have on people's lives. Susan found this interesting, and she really reached out to us. She launched MASS Design Group as one of the "Gamechangers" in *Metropolis* magazine in 2011. Then she paired me in a conversation with Tim Brown in the first annual Horace Havemeyer III State of Design conference, part of the magazine's thirtieth-anniversary programming. Those two decisions were risky—MASS hadn't been around too long at that point. I think she saw a goal that she wanted to help us toward, and I'm eternally grateful to her for being a visionary, for being supportive and guiding us. Susan was really drawing a line in the sand, asking not what design *is,* but what design *does.* She has helped me imagine what's possible if we ask the right question over and over and over again. And that question is: what is the impact architecture can have on people's lives?

The New Generation Gap

If I showed you a 1982 Memphis chair from Italy, you wouldn't identify it "Notes from Metropolis," August 2005 as a product of the Dutch De Stijl movement from 1917, would you? Yet a distressingly large number of 20-year-olds are likely to do just that. In fact, such erroneous readings of designed objects—which speak to us about culture, time, and place through their forms and materials—are becoming the rule, not the exception. This fact made grading design history finals this spring a traumatic experience for me, just as receiving their mediocre grades must have been for the students.

I knew something was wrong at the outset of the semester. Only a few students took notes; most handed in weekly papers that were cut-and-paste jobs from Web sites. Class discussions were nearly impossible because of their shallow grasp of the subject and a general lack of interest in the people and the movements that laid the foundation of our design culture and their future professions.

What was different about this group? My class roster began to reveal the new pattern: a large portion of these 25 students came from the Design and Technology department at Parsons, in New York, and their idea of history seems to be something you Google, not something you study slowly and deliberately. Yet here were some superbright kids, navigating easily and creatively through complex software programs, making sophisticated presentations of information and ideas, but unable to connect with the historic information they were assigned to gather and analyze.

Even as I tried to enforce a more rigorous way of learning history, I came to see that my methods—forged through 17 years of teaching the subject and having a master's degree in it—had stopped working. I remembered the old generation gap we never bridged in the 1960s, but this time, the gap has been made even wider by technology—those who struggle with it (me) and those whose rhythms are completely defined by it (my students). I now see my students as the outriders of our twenty-first-century frontier, pointing the way to what's coming up on the horizon. Yet we try to teach them as if the technical revolution was not raging around us.

No modern profession can survive and thrive without a solid foundation of specialized knowledge—a result of rigorous research that builds on historic precedent while exploring current ideas, methods, and materials.

I trust our outriders' reading of the techno terrain. I consider their skills of great value to those who will follow. And so my faith in the next generation makes me want to find new ways to share my love of history with them, perhaps in a more seamless way than we're doing now. In the

1960s, our picket lines on college campuses shouted for "relevance" in education to the complex midcentury modern lives we were making. Relevance is still a good word.

Liz Ogbu

████████████████████

Metropolis has never been a magazine just for architects or just for graphic designers. It's one of the publications that pushed the design discourse to a higher level by addressing the larger cultural factors that affect design.

When I was in grad school, the sort of work that I did focusing on sustainable architecture was considered alternative practice, not as legit as going to work for Diller Scofidio + Renfro or the Koolhaases of the world. As a teacher, I have so many students who are passionate about using their skills to do something good in the world, and it's pretty powerful for them to know that one of the battles they're not fighting in addition to everything else is the battle for legitimacy, because forums like *Metropolis* have made sustainability OK and acknowledged that it's important and critical to the truth of our lives.

For the longest time, if you did community-based, environmentally sound projects, they were considered as being in a separate category that wouldn't be expected to produce great designs. But for Susan, beauty and quality are high up there regardless of the type of project, and she is an important advocate for sustainable design that is also attractive. There are a lot of architects who talk about building a community center in a low-income part of the world and whose attitude toward the community is basically, Now you have this building, and that's enough. I think it's really important to have voices within the design community to push back and say, No, that's not enough.

New Orleans on Our Minds

September 2, 2005, New York City: A few days ago, the remnants of Hurricane Katrina arrived here as oppressive humidity and ominously gray skies. But today is crisp and clear—much like it was on that September 11 morning in 2001—and we talk of plans for enjoying the last days of summer, complaining about the high cost of filling up the tank for Labor Day trips. But underneath the happy chatter there is a dark realization. We know that hundreds of thousands of our fellow Americans are displaced, and many others are missing or dead. We glean this information by watching the disaster unfold on flat-screen TVs and computers, safe inside our well-cooled rooms.

"Notes from Metropolis," November 2005

Gallons of ink—made from the same fossil fuel that now slicks the toxic, stagnant waters covering most of New Orleans—have been spilled lamenting the demise of this magical city, the place that brought us *A Streetcar Named Desire*, Louis Armstrong, Walker Percy, the colorful tales of Storyville, and the syncopations of the Preservation Hall Jazz Band. For those of us who have spent only a few days there, the loss feels disturbingly personal. For those with deep roots in the city, the tragedy must be unbearable.

If the spirit of a place resides in its historic architecture, streets, and gardens, New Orleans's soul is infinitely more robust than that of most American cities. In the French Quarter alone, some 1,700 buildings are listed on the National Register of Historic Places. But what drew me there was more than the architecture of wealth; it was also that distinctive mix of cultures that made New Orleans what it was—grand, idiosyncratic, and troubled, but absolutely unique.

During its 287-year history, the city has survived fires, floods, and hurricanes, as well as yellow fever and cholera. It weathered gentrification and resisted Disneyfication. It accommodated modernization and its predictable blandness, keeping it a safe distance from the fanciful historic quarters. Now, Disneyland's New Orleans Square may be one of the few reminders to future generations that there was once a flamboyant and eccentric American city with that name.

As thoughts of rebuilding New Orleans and the Gulf region turn to action, some important questions must be raised. At the heart of the matter is finding efficient and humane ways to combine high technology with the area's natural and cultural resources. The design community—with its admiration and respect for the city's creativity and beauty—can play a key role in making the New Orleans region sustainable. Who else will take up the cause of exploiting the area's abundant sun and wind, and the new possibilities these bring for architecture and planning in this hot and humid place whose abundant water is itself a potential energy resource?

Some hopeful signs of this involvement arrive via e-mail; one is from Architecture for Humanity, pleading with designers in the region to come together. But we're waiting for planners to rally around sustainable land use; for engineers to figure out ways to convert defunct oil platforms into wind farms; for LEED-certified architects to contribute their expertise in green building; for landscape architects to enrich our knowledge of the local plant life, soil, and water features; and for interior designers to use their powerful manufacturing connections to demand and develop non-toxic furnishings. All of them together stand to contribute the expertise essential to rebuilding one of America's strategic port cities. In fact, if there ever was a need to form an interdisciplinary coalition, this is the time and New Orleans is the place.

Indelible images of the devastation haunt my mind's eye: young men scavenging for food, a tiny baby finally found by her parents, old people dying by the roadside, thirsty and hungry children wading through murky waters—almost all of them are poor and people of color. These disturbing images serve as reminders that the promise of social justice does not extend to everyone in America.

As climate change brings more cataclysmic storms, each time endangering more people living along shorelines, the role of our building industry becomes increasingly crucial. Planners, architects, and designers—now largely strangers to scientists, physicians, and economists—will need to find ways to collaborate for a greater purpose than each profession alone can envision: to create places that protect the environment and the people it supports.

New Orleans is crying out for help. And it deserves nothing less than a sustainable metropolis—built on the triple bottom line of ecology, social equity, and economy. The new New Orleans must be designed and managed in such a way that it puts an end to the kinds of statistics that should shame every American: as the city was flooded by its long-neglected levees, 38 percent of its children lived in poverty.

Kira Gould

I think Susan did something revolutionary for design. She rescued it, for some of us, from a kind of "design ghetto." She saw that it was important that we all understand that it's not just how design is important to the rest of the world, but how the rest of the world is important to design. That is something that many designers tend to lose sight of, I think. The design communities spend a lot of time trying to convince everyone that design is important, but they have a really hard time trying to integrate other considerations. There is a way to remind designers working at all scales that issues such as ethics, human health, climate change, income disparity, natural disasters, food, and more were important to design and, not only that, critical to design being understood as important to people other than designers. And as a writer documenting these stories, I became increasingly aware that design was not just about being interested in aesthetics or materials, but about being human on this planet. I think reminding designers of this is something that Susan has done masterfully.

Tropical Green

On a bitter winter morning a few years ago, as winds whipped sleet into tiny missiles, I headed to the airport, going south for some sunshine. I was obsessed on this trip to Miami with blue skies, tropical breezes, and sheltering vegetation. Upon checking in to my hotel I imagined opening the windows and falling asleep to the rustle of palms. But this was not to be: I was in a sealed building with a humming air conditioner that ran 24/7, even during those balmy days. In fact, everywhere I went—architects' offices, museums, shops, galleries, and private homes—I bumped into the same steady 70-degree wall of machined air.

"Notes from Metropolis," February 2006

This wasteful reality led me to think of how much more pleasant and beautiful Miami would be if the architects who had designed the buildings there loved and respected the sun, the breezes, and the flora instead of forcing these natural resources into technological straitjackets. That thought buzzed in my brain as I settled into the cool panoramic conference room of architect Bernard Zyscovich. Before long, Bernard and I decided that a conference was needed to bring together the wisdom of tropical builders from other parts with local planners, architects, and city officials. As I was leaving, we promised to find a way to hold a public forum on the unique techniques and poetry of building in the tropics.

But long-distance collaborations are difficult, so the idea languished for a while. When we finally reconnected New York and Miami, first via e-mails and then conference calls, I was still skeptical about the logistics of such long-distance planning. But then I heard the strong and enthusiastic voice of Zyscovich architect Kricket Snow come over the speakerphone, and I became excited about our joint venture.

It took many more of those calls, and even more e-mails, to mobilize the organizing teams at Metropolis and in Miami. At one point, the Floridians e-mailed a dramatic illustration that ran in the Miami Herald of some 100 new buildings about to scrape the city's sky. I discerned no mention of green features in this unprecedented building boom. At a time when the architecture and planning community knows more and more about things like solar collectors and wind turbines, no one in Miami seemed interested in these solutions. All I saw was a lot of modern glass boxes and duded-up postmodern behemoths that could be designed for any city anywhere in the world by architects who still believe that the International Style gives them a license to ignore local climate, resources, and cultures. But this can no longer be the way of architecture.

Putting It Together

The first cover of *Metropolis* called for solar architecture in urban envi- *Metropolis,*
April 2006
ronments. The year was 1981, when those horseback-riding showbiz
ranchers, the Reagans, occupied the White House with their Hollywood
and industrialist friends in tow. The administration, like the country itself,
was happy to be rid of the quaint peanut-farming folk of Plains, Georgia,
the Carters, with their cardigan sweaters and burning social consciousness. Turn down our thermostats to save energy? Wear layers of clothing
indoors? No, that wasn't for Americans—though we had to know, even
then, that our hyperconsumer ways would have to change sooner or later.

In January 2006, the warmest on record, we continued to say "later"
as we bought 1.1 million cars and trucks that month, up 7.5 percent from
last year. Bush the Younger talked of switching from Middle East oil to
homegrown ethanol to fuel our burgeoning fleet of vehicles. But for millions facing chronic traffic jams, it's been clear for some time that our
transportation system is ultimately unworkable. Build more roads, fill them
with more cars, and keep repeating the same expensive and polluting
solution over and over. Is this the way we want to live? An increasing
number of us say no. We know there are more sustainable solutions to
land use and transportation. And now, we have the ability to test our
theories with the aid of software, the new tools of architects, engineers,
planners, and designers. We also have laws to guide us to a human-centered, environmentally clean world.

In the 1970s, we already knew that our modern consumption habits
were wasteful, careless, and even dangerous to our health and well-being.
During that decade, farsighted and comprehensive environmental legislation was written amid oil and gas shortages and in reaction to the degradation of our air, land, and waters. The National Environmental Policy
and Clean Air acts of 1970, the Clean Water and Coastal Zone Management acts of 1972, the Endangered Species Act of 1973, the Safe Drinking
Water Act of 1974, and the National Forest Management and the Resource Conservation and Recovery acts of 1976 were all passed by Congress and—except for the Clean Water Act, which was enacted over
Nixon's veto—signed into law by presidents Nixon and Ford, both Re-
publicans. Environmental regulations were truly a bipartisan initiative.

Although these legal protections for the environment have undergone
six years of assault by an administration determined to undermine them,
they still provide a strong ethical framework. And coupled with our unprecedented access to emerging technology, they continue to offer us
opportunities for progress. Architects and engineers can now document
with greater speed and accuracy such information as a building's heat
gain and wind loads, the movement of sunlight inside rooms, the behaviors of local vegetation, and the geothermal energy of the land that build-

ings occupy, among other things. Numerous Web sites brim with useful facts, available instantly, all helping to bring our natural and designed environments into harmony. Today, there is no excuse to design anything — whether room or cell phone—that does not sustain life and community.

Who would have thought this possible 25 years ago? Only a few NASA scientists, engineers, and industrial designers had an inkling of the ways technology would change us. Now, anyone with access to a computer can find satellite views of a city, a neighborhood, or even a building. For instance, I can examine in graphic detail the disappearing wetlands along our Gulf Coast.

Media outlets across the country publish stories (often read on our computer screens) about smart growth—intelligent uses of energy, technology, and materials. This fall came news from *Building Design & Construction* magazine that the Richard Meier–designed San Jose city hall, a high-rise, uses natural ventilation that takes advantage of the Northern California climate. The *Oregonian* reports that some of the state's public schools are experimenting with architecture that brings in natural light and air, reducing energy bills by as much as half. *National Real Estate Investor* states that in Southern California some buildings are designed with high-mass walls (to insulate their interiors from dramatic temperature variations), as well as screens to bounce light into rooms while keeping its glare out and, incidentally, provide the added health benefit of stimulating production of cancer-fighting vitamin D. According to the *Bergen Record,* a New Jersey hospital has "rooftop meadows" and a school uses rainwater to flush toilets.

Each of these reports represents informed design decisions, with the designer striving to put one small piece of the sustainability puzzle into place. As I read further, I begin to envision the puzzle nearing completion. A bit of news from New York City strengthens my belief for a moment: the newly established Tishman Environment and Design Center at The New School is building an environmental-studies undergraduate curriculum with an emphasis on research. It aims to encourage cross-disciplinary learning at a university where liberal arts, public policy, urban policy, social research, international affairs, design, and architecture are taught in close proximity but never before came together for the benefit of humanity.

But as I go on reading, I realize that the puzzle is still in serious disarray. The *Miami Herald* relays one disturbing fact from South Florida, a region in the midst of an unprecedented building boom: per capita water use is 170 gallons per day (the national average is 100 gallons, already 15 times more than what people in developing countries have access to). And a *New York Times* op-ed reports that by 2009 some 250 million computers will become obsolete, and many of those could end up leaching their mercury and barium into soil and water in China and other underdeveloped countries. In the United States, no workable national recycling program for e-waste exists — though we certainly could use the glass, plastic, lead, copper, and gold embedded in these products. When industrial designers and manufacturers put their considerable creative and financial resources toward solving the problem of e-waste, a large piece of the puzzle will click into place.

As it turns out, we have the technology, information, laws, and growing will to put the sustainability puzzle together. Add to these assets the wisdom of our elders. Like our Nobel Peace Prize–winning former president, Jimmy Carter, they teach us to use our resources wisely. As we learn to look back to history while respecting our laws and employing our technologies, we stand to create new opportunities, solutions, and visions. The growing body of evidence in the new ways of sustainable thinking — appearing daily on my computer screen — leads me to hope, with some confidence, that our designed environment will become fundamentally different in the next 25 years.

Beyond Rhetoric

I'm reading about how architects need to pay special attention to na- "Notes from Metropolis," July 2006 ture—they must learn where wind and sunlight come from, know how their designs relate to water tables and vegetation, and find appropriate materials and building methods to make healthy environments that support life on earth. These thoughts dominate the many design competitions I've been judging, including our own Next Generation prize.

I'm thrilled about what these concerns signal: a new consciousness developing among designers. But when the words don't quite mesh with the design proposals—and this happens too often—I think about how little we actually know and how much preaching we do to cover it up.

Consider, for instance, the Ideas Competition run by two American Institute of Architects (AIA) committees, one on the environment (COTE) and one on design (COD). It called for a scheme that would house an ecologist living in the woods and working on the grounds of the U.S. Fish and Wildlife Service's National Conservation Training Center, in Shepherdstown, West Virginia. The competition organizers hoped for beautiful designs that would take green expression to a high aesthetic level. Indeed, three out of the 79 entries—the winners—met that requirement, almost. They were good-looking, smart, ecoconscious, and succinctly presented. One of them, by Bowen Architecture, was revolutionary; it rethought the program and proposed an entirely fresh idea of building by placing the ecologist in a pod, like a high-tech tree parasite, on the underside of an existing bridge. Only a few entries, however, showed the kind of humane and peaceful room that a tired ecologist might want to retreat to at the end of a long day. But throughout all this judging, a nagging thought kept humming in my brain: will I ever see a time when the design community soars beyond the rhetoric of sustainability and begins to show a deep understanding of such complex concepts as "living lightly on the land"?

Visionary?

████████████████████████

The AC stops working in the middle of an August heat wave. We pull down the shades and switch off the lights in a feeble attempt to manage the deadly temperatures, and sit sweltering in the dark. I feel the incandescent heat from my museum-quality desk lamp, so I shut that off, too. The only light left in the office comes from our computer screens. My co-workers complain, sigh in frustration, and amble out in search of cooler places. It hits 101 degrees Fahrenheit, according to news reports, but on Twenty-third Street—with no protection from overhangs, trees, or any other sunshade—it feels much hotter. Our neighbors down on Twentieth Street, at the new office of Cook + Fox Architects, record temperatures near 180 on a section of their roof that isn't planted with sedum; on the green part, it's about 80 degrees cooler.

Reporting on a similar heat wave in Europe, one TV commentator is moved to ask, Should we be thinking about building our cities differently as we enter a new phase of extreme temperatures? The answer is obvious, according to an increasing number of architects, engineers, and landscape architects. In fact, many are becoming experienced at making roofs sprout with plants, one of the many developing technologies that can help make dense cities livable—and more beautiful.

I find green roofs in the Llewelyn Davies Yeang proposal for revitalizing Istanbul's waterfronts; their project is one of the two winning schemes recently announced by the Greater Istanbul Municipality. The architects put ecology at the center of their development, aiming for equilibrium between the built and natural environments. They studied everything from bird migration to water conditions. In great detail, they show a phased development that considers wetland remediation as important as mass transit. They explore building densities, transportation arterials, parklands, and water features, noting that this might be one of the last opportunities to connect people with nature in the rapidly urbanizing region.

The other winning project is gorgeous, a formal exercise in exploring density and placement of buildings and roads at another Turkish waterfront location. It's a signature project by Zaha Hadid, whose blockbuster 30-year retrospective at the Guggenheim has moved the press to anoint her as a visionary, an artist, a star. She's at once "intuitive" and "brilliant"; her dynamic imagery is between "sci-fi" and "contextual." It's hard to disagree with any of this. I, too, love contemplating her exploding, fragmented, precise drawings; her sensuous furniture forms; and her more subdued buildings.

But given the choice of where to live, I would, without hesitation, choose the Llewelyn Davies Yeang city. Though it's bound to have some artful architecture, it will also have air you can breathe. When heat waves hit, it will have cool places to take refuge from the sun. And when floods come, the wetlands will make the rising waters less severe than they would have been without remediation. I don't see such moments of respite and safety in Hadid's design. And I wonder, Can we honestly call an architect "visionary" if her work ignores the most basic of all connections, the one between people and the earth that gives us life?

Kate Lydon

In 2007, Civil Twilight Collective (Anton Willis, Christina Seely, and I) won the *Metropolis* Next Generation Design Competition for our Lunar Resonant Streetlights. These innovative streetlights dim and brighten in response to available levels of moonlight—to save energy and to reconnect people with the natural rhythms of the moon. Over the course of our research, we discovered that the electrical street grid actually overlights everything—far beyond the levels to which human eyes have evolved. This creates glare, and it's not good on either an ecological level or a citizen experience level. Our Lunar Resonant Streetlights have sensors on top that analyze light levels so that when the moon is full, the streetlights dim, and when the moon is in varying stages of waxing or waning, the street lights generate the correct amount of illumination needed to see.

Susan was completely taken with our idea, and, after we won the Next Generation Award, she featured us in a *Metropolis* documentary on design innovation that she was directing. During filming, we talked about how our work is about "brilliant simplicity"—it seeks a balance between the minimal and the transcendent and explores the relationship between nature and the city. Susan lit up and said, "I think we have the title for our movie right there!"

When Anton and I launched the Oru Kayak, an origami-inspired kayak that folds up for transport, Susan asked us to write about it, saying, "what I would really like is to get at the poetic core notion that's been there since the beginning. What is the through line between the Lunar Resonant Streetlights and the Oru Kayak?" What she was after was the unique, personal narrative about our design and inspiration process—Susan has an incredible way of supporting a singular design vision by sharing the creative journey, not just celebrating the shiny outcome.

I think many other architects and urban thinkers would agree that Susan has inspired us with her insistence that architecture is more than buildings and form; it is about people. She has used her role at *Metropolis* to create a definition of design in keeping with this inclusive, humanistic view. So many great ideas don't have an advocate, and I think one thing that has made her so influential is that she is a voice for the many people working with a really holistic view of design.

Remembering Bill Stumpf

"Notes from Metropolis," October 2006

It's the Friday afternoon before Labor Day, and as the office empties out for the long weekend, bad news arrives: Bill Stumpf is gone. I don't want to believe this, so I contact a couple of trusted sources, hoping that the Web got it wrong. No, word comes back, it is true. He was only 70, young for hardy Midwestern stock. One of his grandfathers lived into his eighties. Frank Lloyd Wright finished the Guggenheim Museum in his nineties. I expected Bill to be around for a long time.

Why should the passing of an industrial designer who lived in a rural Wisconsin town touch me so deeply? We'd met only fleetingly, at some design function or another, and we talked perhaps a few times on the phone. We weren't friends. We were barely acquaintances. But I consider him one of my mentors, a person of lasting value.

I loved—still love—reading his book, *The Ice Palace That Melted Away: Restoring Civility and Other Lost Virtues to Everyday Life,* where he revealed the roots of his deep and abiding humanism as a designer. As a young boy in St. Louis, Bill lived in a house without working locks and roamed the streets without fear. Clearly, he understood the value of trust. The parents who trusted that no evil would come through the front door; the child who trusted that he'd meet only adventure, knowledge, and fun on the city streets. The trust of everyone in the goodwill of the community. I can picture his precise Swiss grandfather, educated as an engineer, who later became a Protestant preacher and emigrated to America in 1910. Through his exemplary stewardship, he taught Bill to respect his possessions: Grandpa's mail-order shoes from Sears lasted for 10 years, his car for 20.

It is no wonder, then, that Bill's ideas about industrial design were much broader than simply serving manufacturing capabilities and marketing trends. When he said that people in his profession were "terminally preoccupied with the quality of life and human artifacts," he was speaking of the best, the most ethical, and the most hopeful of his kind. An environmentalist at heart, this well-read, well-traveled, worldly designer with solid Midwestern roots inspired designers working at every scale. He was truly, as he liked to say of his profession, a "guardian of good experiences."

One of those good experiences—one he wanted us all to have—is eating sweet, freshly picked corn. Though our taste buds have been dulled by the fructose-injected kind, preserved to sit for weeks on supermarket shelves, we yearn for the real. An ear of corn can make us think about how we want to live. Bill asked us to ponder this: "In the crucial pursuit of extending the shelf life of tomatoes or sweet corn, why is chemical technology enlisted as the most immediate and desirable solution, as

An ear of corn can make us think about how we want to live.

opposed to encouraging local agriculture, food distribution systems, and food markets to deliver the real stuff in a fresh, unadulterated state, on time?" Why indeed.

On October 18, when Bill Stumpf's name is called as a recipient of the National Design Award, someone else will have to accept it. But anyone who has found inspiration in his words or comfort in an ergonomic chair will rejoice for him. As I sit here in my Aeron, which he designed with Don Chadwick for Herman Miller, I think of how lucky I am to learn about life and design from an exemplary human being, a man I knew only through the work and values he left behind.

What We Value

Next spring, when the Connecticut countryside turns green again, visitors will take field trips to the Philip Johnson compound in New Canaan. On this formerly private property, accessible only to the architect's 300 or so best friends, they will examine Johnson's iconic Glass House, his neoclassical folly, and his sculptural buildings, as well as a traditional New England shingle-style house. There will be lessons learned about nature as wallpaper, clipped and rearranged to make the best vistas from behind the glass walls. There will be occasion to meander through the late architect's restless, form-making adventures during the second half of the twentieth century as well as examine what he read, find evidence of his glamorous guests in the archives, and, in general, have a pleasant day in the country.

"Notes from Metropolis," November 2006

Another important piece of architecture, in another climate, may not make it to next spring. Paul Rudolph's 48-year-old Riverview High School, in Sarasota, Florida, is scheduled for demolition; a parking lot is to take its place. Though advocates for the Sarasota School of Architecture—a group of modernists who practiced there after the Second World War—are making every effort to save the iconic school, its future seems doubtful. Its breakthrough features, such as an ingenious system of cross-ventilation, concrete sunshades, and daylighting, have been subverted through decades of "modernizing." In fact, the Rudolph design is now barely recognizable. But, the old school's advocates say, the wounds can be healed and the building brought back to teach a vital lesson about connections between people, architecture, and nature.

In 1958, when Riverview was built, "there was a great deal of interest in natural ventilation, which is what the design is predicated on," Bert Brosmith told HeraldTribune.com earlier this year. "The elevated areas over the walkways permitted air to come down through the glass in the walkways and through the glass in the outside wall. That was the idea. In those days it seemed to work," added the architect, who worked in Rudolph's Florida office at the time. These days, the precedents established at Riverview, as well as other regional modern buildings in the county, offer helpful lessons to current practitioners who are challenged to find new ways to save energy and realign their buildings with the natural world. Rudolph's experimental architecture can pass on what he learned about observing climate (subtropical), terrain (the building was sited to blend in with the surrounding pines), and culture (progressive modern buildings represented the aspirations of the county as a center for the arts).

Johnson reinterpreted socially conscious European modernism as the International Style, which could fit into any climate and many cultures. Glass buildings work very well in Connecticut and in the subtropics when the AC can blast 24/7 and you forget about the rich variations of seasonal shifts in temperature and humidity. Rudolph's work teaches us to pay attention to these things and learn how to use them well. It looks like Johnson's legacy will endure. Can we afford to lose Rudolph's legacy?

Two Lives in Design

How does it happen that an heir to America's sugar king ends up working with a homeless immigrant from Eastern Europe? Horace and I seldom discuss the good fortune of our collaboration, but we each recognize how lucky we are to work on a magazine we both love, focused on a subject that fascinates both of us, incessantly (you'll notice the word "love" comes up a great deal in this talk).

Delivered at the Art Center College of Design, upon the conferral of honorary doctorates to Susan S. Szenasy and Metropolis magazine publisher Horace Havemeyer III, Pasadena, California, December 16, 2006

I admired the Metropolis Horace started even before he hired me 20 years ago as his second editor in chief (it's pretty unusual for a magazine to have had only two editors in chief in a quarter of a century). His magazine, with its social consciousness, was such a unique idea that after 25 years, it's still the only publication on design that makes a detailed study of all design disciplines and puts them into a cultural context.

So why did these two very different people end up with a lifelong curiosity about design, though neither of us is trained in it? I can only offer some possible answers here. Horace grew up with Impressionist paintings in the parlor, in houses designed by important architects. He lived among beautiful objects in households with strong female voices. Both his environment and the strong women must have made lasting impressions on him.

My story could not be more different. In elementary school in Communist Hungary, my watercolors always ended up in class displays. I wrote, produced, and acted in plays that glorified the Red Army as Hungary's "liberators." Though my parents told me the real story of oppression that the Red Army represented to them, in rebellion I produced communist-themed theatrical events at the age of eight or nine. A few years later, someone gave me a little notebook and some colored pencils in one of the refugee camps my family ended up in after we escaped when the Hungarian Revolution was crushed by that same Red Army. By the way, when I say "escaped," we literally did that—there was gunfire involved that evening in November 1956.

And so in this little notebook I wrote the narrative of our travails through refugee camps in Austria, Germany, and, later and finally, in New Jersey. I also illustrated what I saw: architecture, rooms, objects, cars, and the very first orange I ever ate. That notebook was lost, but my love of words and images remained and grew with the years. I hope you can see evidence of that love in Metropolis. For me, this magic of words and images is reaffirmed each month as we produce the magazine.

In fact, I never fully internalize the significance of a story—no matter how well it is written, and we are known for our emphasis on good writing—until I see the art that goes with the text. I am truly happy when I can finally look at the layouts each month and discover how our designers pulled together their multilayered presentations of narrative text, sidebars, factoids, information graphics, quotes, heads, credits, and images, including some illustrations in cases when photographs aren't enough to communicate a difficult idea.

Our layered graphics are no accident. They are the result of our constant search for ways to show—to make transparent—the complex nature of what designers do. We strive to reveal the inner workings of the design process—be this focused on the making of ergonomic chairs designed for disassembly or green roofs built to reduce heat islands in dense urban neighborhoods.

Horace and I have agreed from the very beginning that design is an essential human activity—that it, indeed, is a humanist vocation. I use the word "vocation" to imply a "calling." And therefore, we who report on the activities of designers owe it to them, to ourselves, and to society to find stories of ethical creativity as well as responsible professional behavior. We are interested in more than just the fulfillment of the design brief. We want to know how the user, the earth, and the client are served by the design. We want to know what the design says about us as a people.

The people we hire catch on early that they must demand of themselves the same excellence as writers, editors, and art directors as they demand of their subjects. Each person who works with us feels an ownership in the magazine—and we're happy that they do. After all, they're responsible for producing it.

I spent yesterday here at Art Center and came away exhilarated by what I saw and heard. Horace, I would like to tell you, here and now, that we have some great material coming our way in the next few years! I can guarantee you that.

I saw real-world, feet-on-the-ground visionary work. I heard articulate and poised young people describing memorable work that can range from socially connected zines to sustainable shoes to critical texts expertly laid out. I learned, for instance, that Americans can recognize 10 species of plants while they know 1,000 logos. This is dramatic information about our culture. Such facts—memorably presented—can have a huge impact on our desensitized consumer society.

Big ideas—of which we need plenty today—can only be communicated by designers who do their homework. Homework, by the way, is forever. Horace and I study every day and so do our editors and art directors.

As one of your teachers told me, you leave this beautiful place today with "creative survival skills." That you are proficient in design is clear to me. What you will need to keep a steady eye on is your engagement with humanity and the earth that gives us life.

Just think of the lasting appeal of the Eames work, 50 to 60 years; the Aalto work, 70-plus years. This is something to strive for—to know the human condition well enough to be able to design things that talk to us through the years—not some trend that's here today and in the landfill tomorrow. We can no longer afford this kind of wasteful design. Now, more than ever, we need designers who can create the future classics, things that will be recycled and loved by many different generations.

You are trained to do work that is noble and rewarding. You are form-givers and communicators who have the ability to create a new, humane, and sustainable vision of the world. You can make useful things beautiful and meaningful and lasting.

So what do I leave you with today? What one small nugget of inspiration can I give you that will help you think about your own life in design? I'd like you to envision the mighty California redwood, which we all look at in awe. That redwood found an environment it can thrive in and help support whole ecosystems in the process. If you are lucky enough to recognize such a supportive environment—the way I did at *Metropolis*—put down your roots and watch yourself grow. It's exhilarating!

If you love design, nurture that love, not just by observing other designers' work but by learning about the culture, the people, the environment that design supports. If you don't love design, use the great education you got here and experiment until you find what you love. Life is too short to spend it bored, discontented, and disconnected.

And, finally, I'd like to tell you that we are coming to a time when design is becoming necessary once again as an essential contributor to our health, safety, and well-being. You have inherited a poisoned earth plagued with enormous inequities in resources (and remember, the design community is a major specifier of materials); just think of the difference between what you have here in Pasadena, and then think of the pictures from Darfur or, closer to home, New Orleans.

You're in good shape to meet these challenges. You have learned the ways of creative thinking. Your ability to build models based on research makes your contribution a highly valued skill. But more than that, you can communicate complex ideas clearly, elegantly, beautifully. Whether you enter a boardroom, a consultancy, or your own office, you arrive with the confidence of a well-trained specialist whose contribution is sought out by others in different specialties other than your own. Respect those other specialties and learn from them. Incorporate what you learn into your design work, then come to *Metropolis* and tell us about it so we can tell the world. Remember, we're all in this together: telling stories about design is as important as the design itself.

That you are proficient in design is clear to me. What you will need to keep a steady eye on is your engagement with humanity and the earth that gives us life.

If you love design, nurture that love, not just by observing other designers' work but by learning about the culture, the people, the environment that design supports.

And, I hope, when you stand where I am standing now, you can say with confidence, as I do now: My work in design is my life. And I love both my life and my work. It can't get any better than that!

Space-Age Wisdom

On Christmas Eve 1968, we watched as the Apollo 8 spacecraft beamed those first astounding images of earth into our living rooms. As the glistening blue planet—the color of water and vapor, which scientists call a "perfect shield"—was revealed to us that day nearly 40 years ago, the first postindustrial environmental movement was on its way. Though it has waxed and waned in the ensuing decades, just as the first hot excitement of the space program has cooled, work being done in places like Houston's Johnson Space Center retains its culture-shaping power. Previous innovations had already made possible our now famous connectivity: where would Google Earth and cell phones be if not for the most ambitious publicly funded exploration in the history of humankind?

All this rushes into my consciousness at the "After Taste" symposium, organized by Parsons' AIDL (Architecture, Interior Design, and Lighting) department in late March, as I listen to the architect Constance Adams. She is known for her work on TransHab, the inflatable habitat that is part of the International Space Station.

What does the space program have to do with the future of interior design, the topic of the conference? A lot, according to the promotional piece that preceded the event, as "a new agenda for the study of interior design" unfolds. The swank flyer also revealed that the symposium was supported by two well-known decorators, Jamie Drake and Kitty Hawks, whose success is often attributed to their "taste" and "style."

"Who we are as humans is less about notions of taste and style, but more about our fundamental biological being," Adams noted, basing her argument on documented observations of people's behavior in extreme environments, where their relationships with enclosed spaces are revealed dramatically. In fact, we seem to become more human when we leave the earth's gravity, carrying with us our ingrained concepts of shelter and place.

Adams reminded us that we have a fixed sense of up and down (weightlessness wipes away the sensation, yet our minds are organized according to the cardinal directions); that we are creatures engaged with gravity ("in a constant dance with the earth," and without gravity the fluids in our body shift, our senses of smell and taste alter, our muscles atrophy); that we need to face one another whenever important topics are discussed (with the ambient noise of the spacecraft, astronauts can't hear each other if they're not face to face); that we need to connect to the earth's natural cycles (with 16 sunrises in a 24-hour orbit, space travelers must be reengaged with the circadian rhythms humans are born into); that sensory deprivation "breaks down our feeling of wholeness" (attention to color, pattern, texture, signage, and lighting are as important in deep space as on earth); that ergonomics as designers practice it on earth is a primitive science compared to the complex need to interface people with technology and interiors in space. People, she concluded, require a sense of time, place, and wellness.

What if our interior designers connected with what Adams and her crew are learning about habitation and human interaction in space? What if every designer took the lessons of our space travels to heart?

Choices

There's a mechanical buzz inside the architecture office on Seattle's Pier 56. I hate this sound. In the summertime, it makes opening my windows at home, back in Manhattan, a bad idea. What with all those cooling systems running in my dense condo complex, even on balmy nights, there's no escape from the racket. No way to take a breath of fresh air without hearing the persistent noise, no way to drift into an uninterrupted sleep. Heading to work in the mornings, I run into the same wall of sound on Eighth Street. And when I travel, as I do so much these days, each time I check into a hotel room, I face the same din. Turning off the AC doesn't help; I continue to hear the building's system humming.

"Notes from Metropolis," September 2007

But things are not always what they seem. I discover this as I tour the former dockside storage shed, home to the integrated-design firm Mithun, and I suddenly realize that the building is not air-conditioned. The sound I hear is not from the structure's mechanical systems, but from the traffic on the nearby viaduct. Inside this cavernous space, with its operable clerestories and windows, and large glass doors opening onto the dock, I feel waterfront breezes and hear seagull cries and the occasional blast of a ship's horn.

Later, in another corner of Seattle at NBBJ, in a recently redeveloped area with an old church and community garden nearby, I hear exterior louvers close with a whoosh as the sun starts to heat up the curtain wall. As I step into the shady side of this large open office, I notice a green light. It's there to alert workers to the cool temperatures outside; some opt to open a nearby window to let the breeze in. I feel the air move, and with it my spirits rising.

The next day, in the enormous concrete-walled central atrium of the Busby Perkins + Will offices in Vancouver, British Columbia, I notice that the warm air is wafting upward and out of the building. Here, we're gathered around a long conference table, from where we can observe the sidewalk and hear its errant sounds. On this warm July afternoon, my hosts wear lightweight summer casuals as they talk about shedding and adding clothing in response to the constantly varying temperatures in the building. Some grouse, but most like it this way. One woman says she hasn't had a cold since she started working here. A man mentions how he looks forward each morning to hearing the chatter of kindergartners pass by.

My visit to the Pacific Northwest reaffirms my belief that our buildings can put us in contact with the earth and its creatures as well as each other. Indeed, I come away thinking that we have many choices about how we want to experience our world. Working behind sealed glass windows, in steady settings of 70 degrees and 50 foot-candles of light, may not be as universally desired as we've been led to believe.

Educating the Next Wave

Once again, all eyes were on the built environment when, earlier this year, the catastrophic collapse of a Minneapolis bridge and a steam-pipe explosion in midtown Manhattan brought back the nightmares of 9/11. But soon, the headlines returned to Hollywood starlets and their sordid rehab sagas. And one of the biggest questions of the twenty-first century — how can we maintain and rebuild our aging infrastructure? — remained unasked. True, some engineers and architects were initially consulted by reporters. But their ideas, opinions, and solutions were not sought out later; their unique knowledge has not become the foundation for our long-overdue national discussion on the built environment. I know literally dozens of concerned citizens in the design community who are willing to participate in such a debate and offer smart ways to save and make safe our buildings, bridges, schools, hospitals, and transportation systems. How come they can't get airtime?

"Notes from Metropolis," November 2007

This thought was buzzing in my head on an early autumn evening as I settled in to listen to the third-annual Deans Roundtable at the Center for Architecture, in New York City. I wondered: what will I hear from those responsible for educating our next generation of citizen designers? After all, this group of students is part of the most globally connected, tech-savvy, environmentally and culturally aware generation our schools have ever seen. What are the deans doing to reach them, to teach them the expected intellectual rigor while helping them connect with their heartfelt social and environmental concerns?

The 16 deans from regional architecture and interior-design schools agreed in general that the education they offer is inefficient, too expensive, and "committed to teaching students to design the equivalent of a Hummer," as one said — basically a luxury profession for middle-class kids. Aside from scholarship programs, what are they doing to recruit from the most needy neighborhoods and backgrounds? How do the schools tap into this new human energy? No one asked. Instead, the deans were concerned that the current buzz phrase, "Design for the other 90 percent," presents an incorrect number, given the narrow influence architects have in the United States today.

Much was made of the frustration with school accreditation, which, as the group agreed, is "stuck in the box." This concern was defused by news that the American Institute of Architects (AIA) and the Association of Collegiate Schools of Architecture are working to bring curriculum evaluations into the twenty-first century. With the AIA's public adoption of Ed Mazria's 2030 Challenge, which calls for the elimination of fossil fuels from building operations within the next 23 years, we can expect new standards to push for the elimination of carbon emissions from buildings. Will the deans wait for this shift, or are they already gearing up for it? Some have programs in the works. But from what I heard that evening, most seem mired in ambivalence.

When asked about Mazria's wildly successful event "2010 Global Emergency Teach-In," through which the Santa Fe architect aimed to give a boost to the environmental knowledge of architecture and design students and teachers, the gathered deans said that "it had no traction" in their schools. Though a quarter-million people tuned into the Webcast, most of these deans didn't deem the event important enough to encourage their students to participate. I see this as an ethical lapse on the deans' part. They know of their students' commitment to green design and how eager they are to delve into the complexities of a sustainable world. In light of this, making room for the teach-in during a busy school day should have been each dean's priority and considered a unique opportunity for learning.

There were very few students in the room that night at the center. Perhaps their absence signals the kids' frustration with their remote, disconnected, and seemingly clueless deans. Though the deans like to talk about educating citizen designers, it feels empty to me, and apparently to the students, too. Which leads to some painful questions: Can this socially conscious generation get an education that connects them to their fellow creatures' needs and concerns? Do the schools know how to educate a new generation of civic leaders? Who will inspire fledgling designers to dedicate themselves to upgrading and rebuilding our crumbling infrastructure while protecting our environment?

Connecting

Just about now, you may be thinking of grabbing your iPhone or Black-berry or some other digital tool you own and sending off a quick message to a friend seated behind you, or to your mom or dad somewhere in this room, or to someone who could not be here to share this important day with you. I think it's great that you care so much to be in touch with so many, so often—sharing all the minutiae that add up to the sum of your life. Your phenomenal ability to be in touch, to connect, is something I'd like to talk to you about today.

Delivered at Pacific Northwest College of Art upon receiving an honorary doctorate, Portland, Oregon, May 25, 2008

This unprecedented connectivity is now helping us write the story of the twenty-first century. And I would like to remind you that every age writes its own, unique story. Call it a myth, a fable, or culture—this story is of a central belief, a widespread understanding that helps humanity organize its thoughts and focus on its destiny. For instance, the early-twentieth-century story was about the machine and what it could produce for the benefit of humanity. America's late-twentieth-century story was about hyperconsumerism and the happiness that would come with material accumulation.

Today and in the near future, all of us together are writing the story, the organizing thought, of the twenty-first century. Surely our web of con-nections, with their worldwide reach, and our ability to share personal information supported by instantly available data, will be a major part of our own story. But this connectivity is too important to leave in the bits-and-bytes world of electronics. This new hyperconnectivity must enter our phys-ical world, the world of all our senses. So let's experience what this phys-ical connectivity might feel like. Let us, all of us in this room, inhale now, exhale, inhale again. What just happened? We did more than clear our sinuses. The moment we experienced together has a much larger, more profound meaning. We just shared a breath together. No, this is not a gross thing. It's a beautiful, poetic sign of our inescapable connectivity.

What is more fundamental to our newfound connectivity than the air we breathe? Indeed, the story of the twenty-first century has to center on protecting and restoring the fundamental things that make life on earth possible, pleasant, and healthy. Clean air and clean water are among these basic necessities for everyone alive on earth.

In a world defined by connectivity, it's hard to ignore news from elsewhere. Today, 3 billion people live on less than two dollars a day. Just to get some perspective on this number, last year, the U.S. population hit the 300 million mark. How do we process these facts? How do we make them real? How do we communicate such vital information in a connected world?

We elect public officials who promise to spread democracy all over the world. Yet our own knowledge of democracy has eroded to sheer idiocy. How do we re-engage with democracy? How do we communicate democracy's time-tested processes? How do we use this communication to connect us here and connect us to others elsewhere—the 300 million of us to the 3 billion of them?

Graphic communication, art, and design have never been so important! Your skills can be applied to show the essence of an idea, to organize complex data. Simple and beautiful communications are needed at all scales, everywhere, in every language of the world.

As artists, you are learning to see what's around you. Some may be comfortable with the tight focus or the local; some may want to take on the world. Whatever your focus, we need your skills of analysis, interpretation and, above all, your ability to evoke emotion—in order to help us write the story of humanity in a world of scarcity.

Your role as visual communicators and provocateurs is key in our search for new ways of inhabiting the earth. Now that we can examine human settlement patterns, ice caps, forests, and all signs of habitation at the click of a mouse, our connections can be read in great graphic detail. Anyone with a computer can get Google Earth and the NASA Web site. And let us remember that once, in the 1960s, we had the political and societal vision to create the National Aeronautics and Space Administration for the exploration of the universe, which, in turn brought us GPS, computers, photovoltaics, and a whole array of technologies that we now take for granted. The political and social will that it took to create the space program is once again needed, this time to create a new era of exploration of benign, nontoxic materials and new processes necessary for building a sustainable world.

As artists and communication designers, you can choose to be the outriders of society. Like the scouts in the old Western films, you can be in the position of surveying the horizon and alerting the rest of us to the dangers and surprises ahead. But I worry about you. I worry that while you have evolved the use of your thumbs to work at phenomenal speeds, you are not as interested in developing the habits you need to accumulate knowledge, knowledge that can inform your vision as artists. I mean knowledge of the world—science, literature, and history—knowledge of the great contributions others are making or have made to our rich understanding of humanity and the earth, our home.

It is not enough to find information instantly and use it opportunistically to support your argument. To be able to analyze and synthesize you need to delve deeply into a subject, build up your understanding incrementally, and own that knowledge. Own it, so you can call it up when you need it, without turning to your PDA, and use your amazing brain-power to interpret what you know when critical analysis is needed. What I'm asking of you is what I have always asked of myself: to be endlessly curious about everything, to search for facts when you need them, but more important, to search for ideas and meaning. Read a book, look at a building or a landscape, drink it all in—make it your own.

This kind of broad-based knowledge will make you a valued collaborator. Yes, connectivity is also about collaborations. Today, more than in recent memory, teams of people with many different skills are forming around complex problems like designing buildings that breathe and make their own energy; designing gardens and large-scale landscapes that clean up brownfields and filter rainwater and help replenish aquifers; designing communities near transit systems and with all necessary services, including schools, within walking distance; and always, always thinking of how human energy and clean, alternative energies can be used instead of fossil fuels.

In the new world hungry for new ideas and proposals at many scales, the creative community must become a key contributor. So what do you bring to the decision-making table? As I see it, you bring critical thinking, your ability to create beauty and poetry, and your skills in making things. Do not underestimate the power of the contribution you can make. Just look around in any city or any highway to see how aesthetically impoverished and inhumane some sites are. If you think that no human being should be asked to pass through a place, let alone live and work in it, you will immediately understand how necessary your chosen profession is.

To be a valued contributor in these vital collaborations, every member of the team needs to be a good communicator. No arrogant, know-it-all language, please. Every participant needs to speak in clear and concise sentences, with passion and conviction—passion and conviction not just for your art but for how it can contribute to make life better, more pleasant, and more beautiful for those living today and those who come after us. What a grand concept! Designing and making art for today and for the future can be an inspiring and motivating occupation.

The best news of all is that you are an environmentally conscious and socially concerned generation. You know intuitively as well as rationally that the twenty-first century is yours to shape. And what a great opportunity you have! To do meaningful and necessary work—that is the secret dream of every human being. And you get to do it. What a story you will write!

So I challenge you to use your existing skills and expand them. I challenge you to use your famous ability to connect with others and share information about big, world-changing ideas. I challenge you to form creative collaborations that reach further and deeper than we've seen before.

With your technical proficiency and a growing understanding of nature and its processes, you stand to give voice to a connected world. Just remember the breath we took together. And now, exhale, get your diplomas, and party—before you take on the twenty-first century.

Sam Aquillano

At a certain point when my business partner and I were running the Boston chapter of the Industrial Designers Society of America, we realized, Oh man, there's so much more out there than just product design, and no one's talking to the public about it. And we wondered, how can we break down these barriers between the different design disciplines and organizations to engage the public in a more meaningful way? At Design Museum Boston, we show people how design thinking can help tackle and solve every set of problems, going beyond markets or products and into social and environmental issues. *Metropolis*'s humanistic approach of using the design process for social good has had a tremendous impact on my work in that we're not so concerned with the supersmart designer or the individual superstar project. In the years that I've been reading the magazine, its very clear, overall message has been the importance of the integrated experience that designers are creating, so that the result is not just architecture or design but also how these things weave together. There are so many designers who are all about self-promotion and their own brands, but Susan is so down-to-earth, all about content and ideas. That's inspiring, because design is not about us as individuals but as a collective whole. She really embodies that.

Wanted: People's Architects

In 1973, 60 percent of American kids walked to school; today, that num- ber is down to 13 percent. In 1980, 61 percent of households were com- posed of a married couple with children; today, this group is a minority. A typical suburban house uses three times more BTUs than an urban apartment does. The two largest segments of the U.S. population (baby boomers, at 77 million, and millennials, at about 76 million) are choos- ing to live in cities, and many of these households are made up of one or two people.

These were just some of the figures that circulated in the lecture rooms at the 2008 American Institute of Architects (AIA) Convention, in May, when more than 20,000 architects landed in Boston. The message behind all the numbers was that our needs have changed dramatically, as have our expectations. Consequently, the built environment requires a massive overhaul, and it could use an infusion of creative ideas. Housing—and all the supportive services that add richness to life, including schools, cultural institutions, parks, stores, and transit—calls for many imaginative proposals for the many different ways we want to live. Dense urban high- rise neighborhoods, tightly planned row houses with access to nature, and small single-family houses without water-guzzling lawns—schemes that serve households headed by single men (7 percent), single women (18 percent), and couples who are not married (25 percent)—need to take into consideration our many cultures and ethnicities and the various ways we build social networks.

"We the People," the convention's theme, elicited a lot of talk about finding ways to serve this diverse public. As I listened, I wondered what the world would look like if the design professions were seen by the public as trusted and skilled contributors to healthy, safe, and environ- mentally sensitive places where everyone could thrive. This, in turn, re- minded me of another statistic I heard: by the end of third grade, one out of six kids in the United States has attended at least three schools. Blame this gross instability, one speaker said, on unhealthy and dangerous hous- ing that forces people to move too often for their own good. Could decent housing change these nomadic lives for the better? Why do we even need to ask this question?

Mulling over what I heard, I settled in to listen to a panel of Afri- can-American women talk about their struggles and triumphs, mostly in minority architecture practices. I heard them discussing the kinds of work they could get (urban preservation, not a lot of new construction), identi- fying their mentors (the name Marshall Purnell, AIA president, came up), choosing mentees, and writing the history of African-American women for a profession in which women's history is largely missing. As I surveyed the room, I wondered what happened to the conference's message of diversity. Here were a couple of white men and several white women in a basically black audience.

Later, I talked about this segregated experience with an enlightened and practical friend, who asked, "You mean all those architects weren't looking to hire these accomplished women?" Judging by the few who showed up, they were not apparently looking to hire, nor were they looking to learn firsthand about the diversity they heard about in the abstract for three whole days. Which makes me wonder, how do we—the people—convince architects that we need them, and that they need us?

Out of Reach?

I'm at Duane Reade in Manhattan's Port Authority bus terminal, the hub for New Jersey–New York commuter traffic. It's Christmas Eve, and the place is buzzing with last-minute travelers and shoppers. Pushing my way past those gathered around cosmetics, baby stuff, and paper products, I arrive at my destination—the painkiller aisle. I scan the boxes placed at eye level, looking for my brand. No luck.

"Notes from Metropolis," February 2009

Finally, I find it on the bottom shelf. As I reach down to retrieve the container with its bold, colorful logo and tiny instructional typeface, a man with a cane approaches me. "Miss, would you mind getting those pills for me, right there?" he asks, pointing to where my hand is now. And again, pointing with his cane to the opposite shelf, "Could you grab that foot powder, too?" Both of these items are displayed on the lowest rung of a tall shelf, difficult to find and clearly out of reach for the man with the cane.

As I do my neighborly duty and hand him the boxes, I wonder if the store's manager has heard of universal design, design for the aging, transgenerational design, or any of the other phrases that have been bandied about since the Americans with Disabilities Act was signed into law, by Bush the Elder, nearly two decades ago. A lot of care seems to have been expended to find just the right eye-level spot for lip gloss, but those in pain, those who can't bend down to retrieve things, and those who would benefit from considerate product placement seem to have been ignored or simply forgotten.

I'm especially sensitive to issues of accessibility at this time of year. My birthday is coming up, and, inevitably, my consumer profile is looking like that of the leading edge of 78 million baby boomers, who are experiencing, even if not admitting to, new pains and aches as well as other physical challenges. I wonder if the generation that invented the sexual revolution, plus consumerism and political protest as we know them, has enough steam left to call attention to a poorly designed, carelessly managed physical environment. Awkward ramps, small print, hard-to-open packaging, bad lighting, and insensitive and discriminatory store displays are just a few of the many things that need fixing—made accessible to teens as well as aging boomers and populations with other unique needs.

Then, I remember that we're in the midst of a design revolution, ignited by an environment in distress and an economic system in peril. In the process, we're learning how to be more connected to one another. And I think that as we become truly interconnected, we may find ourselves members of a movement Paul Hawken identifies in *Blessed Unrest* as "coherent, organic, self-organized congregations involving tens of millions of people dedicated to change." Activists, some boomers among them, are pushing new boundaries in environmental and social justice. But in this big push toward major change, no one can forget the importance of the small detail.

It does matter that the painkiller is at least as accessible as (if not more so than) lip gloss. It does matter that health-related information, in addition to the glossy logo, is delivered in readable type. Design at all scales needs to acknowledge the complex needs of a complex society. The drugstore shelf is just the beginning. We can change its configuration immediately. A talk with the store manager can lead to some accommodation. Many people talking to that same manager will lead to dramatic change. We're all advocates for design change.

Reinventing Invention

I'm having a wabi-sabi moment. Thoughts of simplicity, tranquility, and balance envelop my senses even as I feel a lively intelligence hovering around me. I've escaped into Tadao Ando's Suntory Museum, on Osaka's carnivalesque waterfront, and I'm strolling through white interiors, looking at an array of familiar objects. They tell a story about how inventive forms, in conjunction with material and technical innovation, can result in an iconic family of industrial designs. These products—from a breakthrough 1956 phonograph with a clear acrylic cover to an elegant shelving system that was recently updated with thin, strong materials—are part of the traveling exhibition *Less and More: The Design Ethos of Dieter Rams*. An accompanying film illuminates this work's strong moral underpinnings. Rams, a mid-twentieth-century heir to the Bauhaus, was ingrained with the ethos of specifying minimum resources in the service of maximum performance, while never forgetting the elusive concept of beauty. What he made, and what he can teach us, needs our full attention as we reevaluate our own design culture. And while his past is our prologue, we face unique problems that call for a new era of invention—invention with an ethical underpinning.

Watching the film—a chorus of German and English voices extolling Rams's importance to what used to be called "good design"—and contemplating the prudent use of resources in times of global scarcity, I recall a prescient conversation from two years ago. I was teaching ethics at New York's Parsons The New School for Design, hoping to provoke a discussion around the morality of using environmentally safe materials in new product design, when a young man challenged my premise. "What makes you think that we would design a product at all?" asked my student, who saw his role as much more than a creator of new stuff. "Maybe what the manufacturer really needs is an evaluation of available resources, a study of capabilities, a look at a new client base, or even a system of communication—and then, perhaps, a product design." He was not convinced that another toaster, TV, cell phone, or chair was what was actually needed.

Here was a future designer arguing for an expanded role for the field. He saw himself as a knowledgeable collaborator who could exceed his clients' expectations; he was familiar with the kind of research we've come to expect of firms like IDEO, which began life as a product-design consultancy and is now a source of useful information about how people behave and what they need to be happy and healthy in classrooms, hospitals, and other spaces. Yes, he was deeply interested in the ethical issues he'd be facing, and he foresaw himself facing these challenges through action and skill.

While I'm immersed in Rams's century, I remember my student's eager face and forceful argument, and feel that what's brewing now will be as important as the contributions of those who went before us. And so here is our wish list for the design ethos of the twenty-first century: we need objects that are not only beautiful, affordable, enduring, functional, ergonomic, accessible, sustainable, and well made but also emotionally resonant and socially beneficial. If we can figure this out, we'll indeed enter a new era of creativity that may, once again, yield the good design we all crave—as well as satisfy that young man who made me think.

A Tale of Two Campuses

I'm visiting the General Motors Tech Center, in Warren, Michigan. It's a "Notes from Metropolis," May 2009 few days before CEO Rick Wagoner is asked to resign by the Obama Administration. But today, on this luminous, early-spring afternoon, the large artificial lake glistens in the sun, the stainless-steel water tower shines like new, and the glazed bricks—burnt orange, paprika red, and bright blue—shimmer on the windowless sides of low, rectangular buildings, looking like huge pieces of modern art that punctuate the gray campus with its glass, steel, and aluminum details. The architecture, as Eero Saarinen and his client saw it, expressed American optimism, innovation, technology, and design excellence—the cornerstones of our auto industry between 1946 and 1955, when the campus took shape. This progressive center of technology and design gave definition to an industry that reshaped the American landscape. It also put in place a complex business that helped create the wealth of nations in the twentieth century.

Later that week, I'm in Charlottesville, Virginia, walking toward Thomas Jefferson's Academical Village on a gray Saturday morning, the Blue Ridge Mountains barely visible in the mist. As I leave behind the sprawling campus of the University of Virginia (UVA) and come upon the great lawn, edged by parallel colonnades that organize rows of small student rooms and gracious pavilions (each of them a unique design), I'm again struck by the power of place. With its red brick, white woodwork, and classical order, assembled to echo our national belief in unity and independence, the Jefferson campus is also an expression of its architect's restless intellect. His dramatic rotunda (based on the Pantheon, in Rome) opened its grand windows to views of untamed nature beyond the well-tended lawn. Inside, when the university opened in 1825, were books on architecture, astronomy, botany, philosophy, and political science. This library, built to take the place of the church that dominated other nineteenth-century campuses, went a long way toward defining liberal education in the United States.

On this weekend, the UVA campus is alive with students, parents, and tourists. Groups of them gather on the lawn examining everything in sight. I overhear earnest discussions of Jefferson, democracy, history, and architecture. Nearly 200 years later, they're still coming "to drink the cup of knowledge," as Jefferson predicted. They all seem to know, intuitively, that the architecture around them embodies a big idea that needs tending.

Though the GM campus was also based on a big idea—the efficient production and distribution of a technologically sophisticated product—it now conjures a very different mood. But I want to remember the original spirit of the Warren campus, so I imagine what it must have been like when the place was abuzz with the best and the brightest in design, engineering, materials science, and manufacturing know-how. That was when the Calder fountain still worked, when the Bertoia sculpture in the dining room wasn't competing with the garish Quiznos signs, when the elegant furniture in the reception areas was upholstered in the bright reds and blues of the campus rather than the dull black of today. I marvel at architecture that still feels innovative after more than 50 years, and I note the results of Saarinen's meticulous research: neoprene weather sealant, a luminous ceiling that incorporates air-conditioning, and the eggshell-thin aluminum covering the dome that houses new cars.

In trying to understand what happened here, I keep asking questions that Wagoner and other CEOs might have asked themselves: When did GM's managers stop seeing what Saarinen gave them? How does an institution lose its appreciation for such a major, and visible, asset? How different would things be today if GM had committed itself, long-term, to the research and innovation its architecture so eloquently symbolized?

Ghost Architecture

Students who graduated long ago from Riverview High School were roaming the building's decrepit halls late in May. The dark, moldy passageways were once bathed in Sarasota, Florida's subtropical sunshine and shaded expertly from its brutal heat. The crowds came to bid farewell to their much-loved school, the locus of their progressive education, now destined to become a parking lot. They saw for themselves what years of disrepair, neglect, and ham-fisted "modernization" did to Paul Rudolph's 1958 design. This modern structure harmonized with the region's unique climate, terrain, and culture of outdoor living. The original skylights and ventilation stacks that kept the building cool and added to the quality of light; the huge plate-glass windows that opened to bring the outdoors in; and the clerestories that added their own light to the interior were now only a memory. Heavy-handed installations of air-conditioning, pipes, conduits, and paint all worked to subvert and disguise every brilliant detail.

Though some of the visitors envisioned a newly climate-sensitive structure, a technologically upgraded version of Rudolph's original design that could grow from the building's excellent bones, they could not save their school. They did briefly halt the swing of the wrecking ball and, in the process, called attention to Riverview's importance to the community's architectural legacy. But their arguments seemed meek and quixotic as "progress," represented by a new school designed for 3,000, rose nearby. And so the ball is poised to swing at the fragile-looking glass, steel, and brick structure that was meant to house a small fraction of today's student population.

When news of Riverview's imminent demise landed on my computer screen, I was reminded of the similar fate that befell Frank Lloyd Wright's Larkin Building, in Buffalo, New York, in 1950, just three years after Rudolph got his architecture degree from Harvard. The Larkin, too, represented progressive thinking—in business rather than education—and architecture. The hulking 1906 structure, which fronted a sprawling campus of warehouse buildings, was designed to move multiplying reams of paper that recorded a burgeoning mail-order business. Its young architect practiced what turned out to be his lifelong respect for nature, flooding the central atrium with sunlight through skylights. And he installed air-conditioning, among the first of the modern systems that would change the way Americans make their buildings. But by the time it was demolished, the Larkin was a depressing remnant of its former optimistic self. Along with the company motto inscribed on the facade, "Honest Labor Needs No Master," the massive structure was beaten into a pile of rubble, also making way for a parking lot. The stories of one pending ghost and another real one add up to a cautionary tale that repeats itself all too often. We build greatness, then we neglect, abuse, and misuse it, and eventually, we lament its demise.

As we learn about the embodied energy of buildings and the cultural value of our modern patrimony, we must ask ourselves: How do we maintain great architecture? Is it enough to learn about the great buildings from old books, films, magazines, and Web sites? How many ghost buildings are you willing to live with?

Twenty Years and Counting

Somewhere, there's a black-and-white photo of me shaking hands with a smiling Dan Quayle. It marks the moment when the former vice president took his victory lap around the country, landing briefly on the island of Manhattan, to celebrate the passage of the Americans with Disabilities Act (ADA) on July 26, 1990. (The resounding bipartisan vote, 91 to 6, seems like a distant dream today.) He came to thank the many special-interest groups—ministers, politicians, educators, community leaders, media, and other advocates—for helping to push forward the ADA, which was signed into law by the first President Bush. The ADA was in many ways similar to the Civil Rights Act of 1964. It extended legal access to the good life: the American Dream would now be available to everyone from wheelchair users to the sight-impaired—people with any disability, temporary or permanent.

My moment in the spotlight with the vice president came around the same time that our November 1992 issue gave a full account of the first universal design conference, produced by Pratt Institute's Center for Advanced Design Research, in New York. We built the issue around the idea of access for daily living, starting with the dismal reality of millions of Americans who struggled to work, shop, and live like other human beings. We were convinced that the law would lay the groundwork for inclusion and pinned our hopes on designers' storied abilities to solve difficult problems beautifully. Words of encouragement came from Quayle's special assistant for U.S. disability policies, George Covington, himself sight-impaired, who said, "The first barrier to universal design is the human mind. If we could put a ramp into the mind, the first thing down the ramp would be the understanding that all barriers are the result of narrow thinking."

Has that ramp of the mind worked? Yes and no. While some fixes are now common—no city street gets paved without curb cuts, bathrooms in hotels and homes often have grab bars, and some kitchen cabinets are designed for people of many different heights—our built environment remains inaccessible for many. Blame this on our moral lassitude, our litigious society, or simply the snail's pace at which change takes root. I blame the slow progress on our inability to think about whole-system fixes rather than piecemeal designs. What if, for instance, a restaurant designer thought about how a man with a walker moves from the street to the front door, how he finds a comfortable seat, and if he can read the menu without a flashlight? How would a whole system of interrelated design solutions create a pleasant place for everyone who came to dinner?

In 2010, we're redefining design as a socially and environmentally sustainable activity. But green design, its critics claim, is not widely accepted because we don't have a green policy. Yet we've had an accessibility policy for two decades now. So let's decide to bring the two experiences together and admit that all design today must be about people, planet, and profit—and that this requires holistic or, as Bucky Fuller might say, systems thinking.

Embracing Science

They were once bankers, teachers, and social scientists. One of them was a doctor. Now, they're all grad students in their late twenties and early thirties, studying for their master's at the New York School of Interior Design's newly opened graduate outpost on Park Avenue South. I sat in one of the attractive, minimalist meeting spaces with Chris Cyphers, the school's dynamic president, who is brimming with the optimism of someone with a clear vision: interior design in the twenty-first century is grounded in social and environmental consciousness. This vision is apparently what led 220 prospective students to apply for the new program's 32 seats.

"Notes from Metropolis," November 2010

There were teachable moments all around us. Daylighting and how it helps shape a space and determines material, color, and texture choices; the constant and transparent monitoring of everything from air quality to energy use—these are among the many things the space teaches its occupants. There were no telltale odors of that familiar (and, we now know, unhealthy) new-building chemistry here. The interior was as fresh as Park Avenue can be on a clear, crisp, blue-sky day. In addition to being pleased with the building's design (by Gensler), the president is proud of the state-of-the-art computing, design, and model-making technology.

While all this has come to define an excellent design education, I kept thinking about another resource here: the students themselves. I also imagined the richness of the conversations—and the design solutions they will come up with—when the doctor brings up issues of health, the social scientist introduces new findings on human behavior, and the banker analyzes the bottom line while safeguarding the well-being of people and environment. Then, I imagined even greater possibilities.

What if every designer had a deep understanding of science or at least knew what to ask of a biologist, a sociologist, an anthropologist, a psychologist, a material scientist, and a banker? After all, each of these experts holds part of the intricate knowledge system that defines humanity. What if we combined a designer's razor-sharp intuition and creativity with the scientist's rational and analytical approach? Charles and Ray Eames clearly envisioned this connection in their classic 1968 film *Powers of Ten*. Are we finally ready to become our design heroes' true heirs?

What if every designer had a deep understanding of science or at least knew what to ask of a biologist, a sociologist, an anthropologist, a psychologist, a material scientist, and a banker?

Susan Lyons

Having a conversation with Susan is like going on a great vacation, because she takes an expansive, almost poetic worldview. You get to go from place to place and tag along with her nimble mind and all these surprising connections that she makes. She seamlessly toggles between the micro and macro aspects of design and sees that everything is organically linked in some way. Her purview has always been to look at the larger reality and identify complicated design problems that we should be solving. For example, rather than doing an issue of *Metropolis* devoted to health care, Susan will do an issue on general wellness. She'll take that big topic and look at it through all possible lenses, throw down the gauntlet, and say OK, what does the idea of wellness really mean in terms of product design and architecture and the environment? The point is always that design isn't just about surface or simple aesthetics—it is really about three-dimensional or even five- or six-dimensional experience, and it includes smell and touch and taste. A lot of what you'll see in other design magazines is all about what's cool now and what it looks like, not what it means in the long view.

Big-Picture Thinking

The Acela glided through the Eastern Seaboard's autumnal landscape, whisking me from Baltimore to New York. Among the bright yellow, red, orange, and green foliage, I saw the Great American Sprawl. Though in some spots there were new, dense developments of clustered or row houses, none of them—whether single-family or attached—seemed to be located within walking distance of a school, an office, shopping, or any other service. The only visible transportation to all these destinations was the car. Though the scenery that slipped by told many tales, I'd like to concentrate here on what it said about our piecemeal treatment of the built environment.

"Notes from Metropolis," December 2010

I have been observing the same sights for years, but this year's trip was different. It came after my moment of truth at the Baltimore Convention Center while attending NeoCon East in October. My thoughts began to roil during a panel discussion, "The State of the Market." The stage and the audience were filled by members of the Design Leadership Council, a Washington, D.C., group that apparently likes to party in furnishings showrooms. These were the movers and shakers of interior architecture and design, representing organizations such as Gensler and AECOM. They told a now-familiar story: how we survived the recession.

They also talked about how the down market pushed them to diversify their firms' services, all performed under tight deadlines, with fewer people and for less money. They mentioned how quickly their young staffs are given serious responsibilities these days (much faster than their own generation was) and the need to use social media—all good but piecemeal solutions. It became clear that none of them made an attempt to apply design thinking to recalibrate their firms for a sustainable future.

None of their actions seemed to recognize that a sustainable economy requires a rethinking of the ways and means of planning and designing offices. Call this shift in the ethos and the marketplace "nexus planning," or use Bucky's term: "systems thinking." Whatever name you give it, we're talking about a renewed focus on people and our shared resources. The new scenario goes like this: When a community is built or an old one is adapted, at its nexus or center may be the school, the library, the farmers' market, or any other natural gathering place. All necessary services should be reachable by walking, biking, public transit, or other low-impact means.

This kind of systemic planning and design requires all specialists to be at the top of their games, at the table from the outset, breathing the air with members of the community. It's also becoming clear that designers who hope to be at the center of the discourse need new skills: an ability to talk in easily understood ways, a curiosity to learn about land use, policy, biology, materials, science, and the myriad other issues that are redefining what used to be called "liberal arts." All of these, of course, are in addition to sharp design thinking and a capacity to visualize scenarios that others at the table are not trained to see. "The state of the market" is beginning to call for such an interdisciplinary approach. It promises to bring unprecedented opportunities that will broaden designers' influence. But piecemeal tweaks won't get us there.

Turn, Turn, Turn

Time and again, some song or another hums in my brain, but none as often as Pete Seeger's "To Everything There Is a Season." His lyrics (borrowed from Ecclesiastes) pop up at the most fortuitous moments, as they do now while I'm trying to encapsulate my 25 years at *Metropolis*. The phrase that keeps singing in my head—"a time to gather stones together"—helps me say what I've been thinking about the design movements that have defined the 30 years of our publishing adventure. Modernism has deep historic roots, beginning with the founding ethos of the new, industrially sophisticated twentieth century, but by 1981, all we had left of it was an eviscerated philosophy, turned into a style and divested of its social mission.

With this corruption of modern design came a long, dark season of Style Wars. But we believed in the design community's humanist impulses and tried to keep its larger mission alive. So when postmodernism came along, I was hopeful. Seeing architects search for historic inspiration with great tomes of exquisite architectural details open on their desks, I thought, this is good. Surely they will also find the time-tested secrets of building siting, daylighting, natural ventilation, and using water and plants to bring nature into action and into view—the sum total of human understanding of how to build on the land. That didn't happen, of course. We kept suffering from that storied modern illness, amnesia, and ended up with Italianate palazzos and Greek temples, facades tacked onto sealed buildings with energy-guzzling cooling and heating systems.

As minimalism gained strength, with its impulse to do more with less, in the service of creating beauty that functioned perfectly for its intended purpose, I grew hopeful once more. Surely, we would start debating our reckless use of materials and spaces. But that didn't happen either. Minimalism, too, turned into a high style without much talk about environmental and social underpinnings.

When lawmakers discovered that nearly half of Americans were victims of these Style Wars, they passed a momentous piece of civil-rights legislation, the Americans with Disabilities Act. The mandate of the law—that everything in the built environment should be designed to enable people of all sizes and with varying abilities—was met by truculent compliance by the design community. Sure, a lot of things have improved in the past two decades, but I have yet to see systems thinking embedded in the design process. What if, for instance, wayfinding began on the city streets and was carried into the smallest nook of the home or office?

We now know that the piecemeal fixes of the past decades represent an outdated approach. As natural disasters flash across our screens with increasing frequency, we understand that it's time to address the complex problems we face. We're learning about systems thinking, which is about the connectivity we must find between every design project and the sum total of human knowledge that's embedded in our technical inventions, the sciences, our cultures, and beliefs. As I see it, this is our season "to gather stones together."

Bill Valentine

We've been sort of a tag team to see if we can't find a way to make some sort of sense out of things. That's because most architects are out designing very expensive museums and libraries and things that are all well and good but not really helping the plight of common men and women around the world. You can find somebody interested in innovation, you can find somebody interested in the basic side of things, but when you get the two together, that's where the magic happens.

I'm working now with some HOK folks designing the jail for San Mateo County, just south of San Francisco. The interesting part about the jail is there can be nothing extra. It's really playing chess instead of checkers. You actually have to use all the basic things that are at your disposal and none of the frivolous things. There can't be a series of curved glass walls with little spires and random windows and all the clichés that pop up all around. It's got to be much more monastery-like.

It gets design down to its most basic level, because you can't waste. What does money do? Apart from occasionally buying expensive talent, money buys steel, concrete, aluminum, glass, paint, drywall, and stuff. So, if you can get a project to actually cost less and still be a value, now that's sustainable all on its own. Susan is really on top of trying to discover people who are out doing good, simple things related to helping humanity. She's a humanitarian first and foremost, I think.

Reflections on Sustainable Design

I came to understand sustainability long before I ever heard the word. *Journal of Interior Design,* November 2011 Long before, in fact, I spoke a word of English. As a child growing up in cold war Hungary, I learned to use our meager resources respectfully. When, for instance, there was pumpkin on the menu, we did not throw the seeds away but gave them to the chickens, or if we had the good fortune to own a large source of protein, such as a pig, the pumpkin seeds, the rind, and the skin got mixed into her dinner. Sometimes my mother would make the seeds into a delicious clear soup, or dried the seeds and the rind to make a tasty snack. Every bit of our food supply sustained someone or something. Very little of it was thrown away, and when it was destined for the trash heap, the birds and small animals feasted on it.

When the first oil crisis hit, in 1972, and large, gas-guzzling cars lined up for blocks around filling stations, we had an inkling that our resources, even in America, might be limited. Until then, it seemed that everything on earth was made for us, including the seemingly bottomless barrels of crude shipped in from the Middle East. By that time, I was in grad school at Rutgers University, in New Jersey, where the campus often erupted with civil-rights protests.

During the first Earth Day, I was in our college cafeteria just as a large crowd headed down the street, carrying placards printed with slogans about saving the earth. As I surveyed the now nearly empty room, I was astonished to see the enormous amounts of garbage the students left behind. Food remnants, plastic, and paper packaging littered the tables and the floor. It would take a long time, and even for this activist generation, to understand that saving the earth also means cleaning up our own mess, conserving our resources, designing more compact and biodegradable packaging, among other things that have since become the hallmarks of what we came to call sustainability.

When I arrived at *Metropolis* 25 years ago, the magazine had already shown an interest in covering things like using solar power in densely developed cities; photovoltaic panels tended to appear mostly on suburban rooftops. By then, I was a die-hard New Yorker, a committed urbanite who had what later came to be called a small carbon footprint. I didn't drive a car. I used public transportation or walked everywhere. I lived in a small apartment (my apartment today is even smaller, down to 400 square feet). I bought fresh foods whenever that was possible, to avoid preservatives as well as bulky packaging.

One of the first stories we ran under my watch as the magazine's new editor told how Patricia Moore, then a young industrial designer, dressed up as an 85-year-old woman in a complex outfit she made of balsa wood and bandages that wrapped around her joints, gels under her contact lenses, weights that distorted her youthful spine, and heavy wrappings everywhere to slow down her movement. She grew to sympathize with the needs of the aged as she navigated urban streets and spaces, eventually getting her Ph.D. in gerontology and continuing her good works on behalf of people with all kinds of disabilities. This was before Congress passed the Americans with Disabilities Act (ADA); it was before anyone heard of universal design, before the idea of social sustainability was born.

Our small editorial staff, avid readers all, was always on the lookout for big societal changes that would change the ways and means of design. Thus began our season of reading and research. Some of the seminal books of our time were on our growing list. For instance, we dove into Neil Postman's *Amusing Ourselves to Death: Public Discourse in the Age of Show Business* (1985) and *Technopoly: The Surrender of Culture to Technology* (1993). Postman talked about the dangers facing a society that blindly embraces technology. "The milieu in which Technopoly [which he located in the United States at the time] flourishes is one in which the tie between information and human purpose is severed, that is, information appears indiscriminately, directed at no one in particular, in enormous volume and high speeds, and disconnected from theory, meaning, or purpose." These were fighting words. And we took up the good fight. Our editorial mission embraced the thought that big ideas shape times, so they must be integrated into design thinking. And so we set out to give our readers information on topics that they would not find in other design magazines—which were, and still are to this day—mostly geared to covering style, mired in the beauty shot, and telling stories that recognized nothing of the ideas that make our world turn.

We went on to read Bill McKibben's 1993 book, *The Age of Missing Information,* seeking to learn more about things like sustainable and green design. McKibben's words resonated with us: "We…live in a moment of deep ignorance, when vital knowledge that humans have always possessed about who we are and where we live seems beyond our reach." Yes, this made sense to us. We knew that we had to expand our coverage to include a broader range of human knowledge, context, as we like to call it, for every story told. We asked ourselves, how can we concentrate on what's new without also showing what continues to work from times past?

We observed as architects struggled to shift their thinking from a purely formal approach to design, working hard to switch from building sealed-glass boxes with frozen air inside to a more environmentally connected practice. We found examples of green buildings in Germany and Scandinavia and told stories about industrial designers working on products that could be disassembled easily and quickly, and the postindustrial materials that remained and could be put back into the material stream, rather than cluttering up landfills.

While we felt it important to talk about these new, environmentally sensitive approaches to design, we were also frustrated. Where were the American examples? Not until the formation of the U.S. Green Building Council, a collaboration between manufacturers, architects, designers, and policy makers (not, as some think, a government agency) was formed in 1993, and its LEED rating program was introduced a year later, did we begin to see some action on the American front. Remember, 1993 was also the year when Paul Hawken's influential book *The Ecology of Commerce* was published. In it, Hawken, a successful businessman turned writer and environmental advocate, brought business into the growing discourse on sustainability.

"The promise of business," he wrote, "is to increase the general well-being of humankind through service, creative invention, and ethical philosophy. Making money is, on its own terms, totally meaningless, an insufficient pursuit for the complex and decaying world we live in." In fact, one industrialist did come forward, and it was someone whose business was closely connected to the architecture and interior design communities. Ray Anderson, recently deceased, then chairman of Interface, became an agent of change for the notoriously dirty carpet industry, eventually earning him a reputation as the greenest CEO in America. He appeared at design conferences, keynoting conventions like the American Society of Interior Designers annual meeting, preaching sustainability, showing how everything from manufacturing-plant design to product design can work to reduce (and eventually eliminate) the use of virgin fossil fuels. We followed his many speeches and read his 1988 book, *Mid-Course Collection: Toward a Sustainable Enterprise, The Interface Story* and later, his *Confessions of a Radical Industrialist: Profits, People, Purpose—Doing Business by Respecting the Earth* (2009). It was Ray who introduced us to Daniel Quinn's novel *Ishmael* (1992), a riveting and totally credible account of a captive gorilla who asks, "Is it man's destiny to rule the world? Or is a higher destiny possible for him—one more wonderful than man has ever imagined for himself?" Today I feel that designers may be, if they choose to fully embrace the challenge, at the forefront of creating that "higher destiny."

I say "if," because too many architects and interior designers are all too happy to check off LEED points and forget that for design to be truly sustainable—that means keeping its carbon footprint to the barest minimum—requires some serious design thinking, not just a convenient checklist that may or may not produce real results. Increasingly, we must ask ourselves, how many LEED buildings actually perform according to their promise? The jury is out on this question. Thorough and unbiased postoccupancy studies are almost nonexistent, and we do not have a system whereby owners and designers work together to achieve what Hawken called "creative invention and ethical philosophy." And yet, that's what's needed for sustainable design to grow into a productive, everyday practice that we will one day be proud to call "good design," or just "design," without needing to label it "green" or "sustainable" or "accessible" or "universal" or any other add-on qualifier. Design, as we have grown to know it during the industrial age, falls short of meeting human and environmental needs and is unsustainable.

Increasingly, we hear that Building Information Modeling (BIM) software is helping interdisciplinary teams—essential for complex projects that require the unique expertise of every design specialist—as well as their consultants in engineering, biology, hydrology, and many other specialties. Yet most designers are working with missing information and cannot claim to have deep knowledge of their subject. Interior designers, for instance, seem content with leaving the exposition of furnishing toxicity data to third-party examiners. Yet there are over a dozen such programs—including Cradle to Cradle and Green Guard—for-profit services located around the world, each providing a somewhat different analysis of material performance and toxicity. Choosing one that works in New York may not be sufficient in California, where environmental laws are strict, let alone in other countries around the globe (as even small, young firms are now building in places like China).

My highly personal story recounting the evolution of sustainable design in the United States would be incomplete without a mention of Ed Mazria, architect and longtime advocate of solar design who reconfigured the energy consumption pie chart, finding that the building sector is responsible for contributing at least 48 percent of U.S. energy consumption. This was actually good news to those of us who believe in the inherent humanism and creative genius of the design professions.

But a large portion of the architecture profession did not have a similar faith in itself and seemed unprepared to rise to the challenge. When the October 2003 cover of *Metropolis*, boldly said, "Architects Pollute," we were greeted with hostility. But when Mazria and I went on the road with our "Lowering the Global Thermostat" symposium, audiences responded to our positive message: we have a big problem, but the design community possesses the talent, the drive, and the ethics to create the necessary solutions. In the ensuing year, Mazria announced his 2030 challenge to make major reductions to our carbon footprint during the next few decades. Subsequently, the American Institute of

Architects embraced that challenge, as have individual firms, cities, and neighborhoods—everyone who wants to fix our degraded environment through thoughtful design. Now, we have a new definition of excellence to live up to, a steep learning curve to be surmounted.

And what does environmental sustainability have to do with social sustainability? Think of that cold-war child who hadn't seen an orange or a banana until she arrived, homeless, in a U.S. military-run German displaced persons' camp after escaping from Hungary through the Iron Curtain. Poor, yes. Undernourished, yes. Nevertheless, she was given an equal opportunity to learn, along with her well-off American classmates, and to prove her worth. It is this same opportunity that every human being—regardless of ability or disability, economic or social strata—needs and deserves. After all, social equity is one leg of the three-legged sustainability stool; the other two legs are ecology and economy. Without its third leg, the stool topples.

Lessons of Place

Your eight-year-old son runs into the kitchen holding a tomato he just picked from the plot you and the kids have been working this summer in the nearby neighborhood garden. As he gives the luscious red fruit to you, you can still feel the sunshine warming your hands. Your 10-year-old daughter likes to spend time at the nearby creek, observing the aquatic life while dreaming of becoming a marine biologist. And you are about to walk over to the community center to discuss climate change with your neighbors. No, this is not some utopian dream or a saner version of *The Truman Show*; people actually live this way in Oregon's Willamette Valley, in a place called Pringle Creek Community.

I came across the Pringle Creek story last month at Greenbuild in Toronto; this was the first time that the U.S. Green Building Council held its conference and trade show, now in its tenth year, outside the United States. As expected, the 23,000 attendees learned about the many ways that Americans, Chinese, and others around the world are opting to live sustainable lives, with the aid of architects, landscape architects, designers, planners, policy makers, manufacturers, and developers. From using software that provides feedback on our personal and local energy consumption, to the next generation of economic development that's expected to focus on abundant natural resources like the Great Lakes region's fresh water supply, there were many hopeful stories.

Perhaps because I've been railing against the old-style New Jersey suburb where I own one of those ticky-tacky Frank Lloyd Wright–imitation houses with a chemical-dependent lawn (that I let go to seed, much to my neighbors' chagrin), Pringle Creek had the most resonance for me. Unlike my subdivision and thousands like it, with names like Lakefront Drive and Piney Woods Court—guilty memories of dead lakes and decimated woodlands—there is an actual creek in Pringle Creek.

And that's the point of this story, told by the community's architect, James Meyer of Opsis Architecture. The development is in a region known for its benign climate, long growing season, and abundant rains. Recognizing these resources is key to the design of Pringle Creek. In addition to "passive" open spaces, as Meyer called the undisturbed wetlands around the creek, there's "active" open space created for community gatherings. In a highly detailed report, the architect talked about making sure there were "opportunities for spontaneous hellos." He emphasized features that usually aren't part of our current cost-accounting system: watching sunrises and sunsets, listening to birds singing in old-growth trees and on green roofs, rainwater disappearing under porous pavements and replenishing the aquifers, streets designed to calm traffic, and homes where the occupants can "age in place."

This is not the age-segregated, sanitized world we've made for ourselves, where fruits and vegetables taste like the cardboard they were shipped in. Pringle Creek is designed to teach kids and their parents that nature needs time to grow things, that cultivation is a fruitful human occupation, and that life is an endless cycle—lessons we all need to learn.

Niels Diffrient

Commerce has corrupted the whole activity of magazine publishing lately, and it takes someone with a strong inner compass to stay on track. Susan is among a very small handful of people I would trust to do it honestly. What you hear from her is the undecorated, unembellished truth.

There are very few magazines where you can find intelligent interpretations of the language of design. An awful lot of publications treat it as a decorative art or use "design" as a buzzword, but for Susan and her team at *Metropolis*, design is a fundamental and far-reaching activity. The magazine is a place readers know they can go to for really intelligent discourse about design and discussion about urbanism and architecture with a little weight to it.

Susan has never lost sight of her standards and always assumed that readers were interested in the technological and intellectual aspects of design. Susan is real. She's not playing games; she's not creating an image or facade. I have found some foreign magazines, particularly from Germany, that still take design and architecture seriously. But there aren't many of those publications in the world, and in this country, *Metropolis* stands alone.

An Appreciation: Eva Zeisel

As a young adult in search of a stronger identity than that provided by a bland New Jersey public education and an equally whitewashed neighborhood, I went on a reading rampage. Among the many titles that I devoured was Arthur Koestler's *Darkness at Noon*. In it, he describes prison life in the Soviet Union during Stalin's most paranoid phase. Koestler helped me understand the brutality that crushed the Hungarian Revolution of 1956, an event that landed my family on the Eastern Seaboard of the United States. He made me realize that my parents' decision to leave home, a decision I challenged growing up, was made for reasons of survival. This insight gave me peace. It also gave me an abiding appreciation for our adopted country.

At the time, I wondered how Koestler knew the details of such excruciating incarceration, and the constant fear of death that went with it. I did not know until recently that the horrors were experienced by a person I would meet later and grow to admire. Koestler's Deep Throat, his source for those harrowing details, was the designer Eva Zeisel. This, and many other details of her life, became public with the news of her death at the age of 105. Though the length of her life is cause alone for celebration, it's her eight decades of unrelenting work as a designer for industry that touched millions. Her graceful and fluid forms asked to be touched, admired, and used. Reaching across generations, Eva's vases, teapots, saltshakers, and every other item needed to create beautiful and functional tabletops came to symbolize convivial and satisfying meals.

When I asked her about these very organic but modern forms, so different in spirit from the angular shapes favored by the Bauhaus—the design movement that dominated an Eastern Europe where she, too, was considered avant-garde—she explained with a gesture unique to someone committed to the tactile. She lifted her generous and expressive hands and outlined a square in the air. Then she asked me, "Have you ever seen nature create this shape?"

Aside from softening sharp edges, Eva was also known for studying history, something anathema to the modernists bent on inventing a new world. To her, this wholesale denial of the past was nonsense. So she set out to learn everything about the ceramic works that employed her. Her interest was not in craft but in industrialization, and in that she could claim a kinship to the Bauhaus. But more than any of its designers, Eva's work was mass-produced and sold to a wide audience.

Eva's legacy reaches far beyond her many designs. Her daughter, Jean Richards, has been her tireless advocate. Her son, John Zeisel, a Ph.D. trained in architecture and sociology, is widely known for his Alzheimer's research. And true to the progressive spirit with which she imbued everyone who came in contact with her, an iBook (with photos, maps, audio, and video accounts), *Eva Zeisel: A Soviet Prison Memoir*, is about to be released. I am looking forward to seeing what Koestler left out.

Connected

It's one of those days when patterns start forming in rapid succession. Many of them are invisible, and they're about to change how our cities work, how we learn, and how we collaborate. I no longer wonder if the patterns I see are a coincidence. They're not. They signal a confluence of skills, ideas, innovations, and the will to change things for the better in a rapidly changing world. Here's how my day begins:

I'm on a conference call with Tony Douglas, who works in mobility services at BMW in Munich. He's describing the company's BMWi program, which is about to change how we think of urban transportation. These electric cars (with carbon-fiber chassis) will be deployed on the West Coast by late summer and on the East Coast by the end of the year. The services they offer are a direct outgrowth of our familiar smartphone technology. Through these small, handheld devices you'll be able to reserve a car and find a parking space and a charging station. But the connectivity goes beyond the automotive; in fact, even people like me who don't drive will be able to take advantage of this multimodal system. We'll connect to all available transportation options—in New York, that means finding out about the next bus, train, and plane schedules, and bike-sharing locations.

After hearing about this efficient information system, I realize I cannot go on working at my desk today. The paper pileup next to my keyboard is hiding the command keys. As I dig through the pile, my notes appear from a panel I moderated this past winter on the digital architecture studio, held in Boston by the Association of Collegiate Schools of Architecture. The four schools presenting included a graduate program from the Boston Architecture College, where a class of 15 students is scattered around the world. They bond through common problem-solving in their digital studio. They get their instructional materials through an open-source wiki and, eventually, an intense face-to-face experience. By the time these students get together, they know all about each other through their social networks as well as the problem-solving skills they've exhibited online.

Another pattern of connectivity preoccupies me today. I'm about to fly to Chicago to attend NeoCon, the annual contract-furnishings trade show. And I'm worrying about how to frame my talk to the ASID and IIDA Fellows at their unprecedented joint meeting there. These two interior design organizations are setting on a new and potentially groundbreaking course. They're asking: how do we present a united front to the public as well as to the diverse profession? In previous years, the word "merger" would have been bandied about. But today, in our connected world, such potentially homogenizing approaches feel out of touch. The idea is to enrich the profession's knowledge base through the information that resides in each group.

As new patterns form in transportation, education, and collaboration, I finally understand the game-changing meaning of the familiar but narrowly interpreted term "World Wide Web" to be an intense and fruitful connection between information, places, and people.

Visual Fixation

"Notes from Metropolis," September 2012

Every time I open my bag, the scent of lavender fills the air. It brings back, in vivid detail, the many sense memories I collected on an olive farm in the Umbrian hills: from the clear blue sky with thunderheads gathering in the distance, to the spectacular blood orange and indigo blue sunsets; from the tawny stone facade of the house, with its rustic tiles on the roof and cool rust-colored tiles underfoot, to the cooling breezes wafting through the rooms on even the hottest day; and from the garden shaded by ancient cypresses and other generous trees to the sunflowers in bloom to the lavender bushes edging the shimmering azure pool. More than that, each of my visual and olfactory memories came with its own aural imprint: the cicadas' staccato buzzing in the trees, the bees humming around the blossoms, and the birds singing on the fence.

I was hoping to share these multisensory memories with an interior designer, a leader in her field, as we lunched together recently. But as I rhapsodized about the lavender scent my bag exudes, I made the mistake of pulling out the little plaid bag itself. Admittedly, it's not a sleek, well-designed object but an unpretentious little sack that contains all my summer memories. My designer friend did not stop to smell the lavender. Instead, she began describing the designs of memorable sachets that she had encountered.

This seemingly benign exchange made me think of an issue that crops up, time and again, in conversations with designers. If design is truly a humanist activity, which I believe it must be, then why is the profession, and every one of its specialties, so fixated on only one aspect of our complex species?

Dwelling on the visual has turned design into an image-driven, superficial practice that provides sleek buildings, rooms, and objects of consumption. But we're not as one-dimensional as that. Our species also collects information through touch, smell, taste, and hearing. It behooves us to create a constructive design discourse about the needs of the whole human being.

Let's all ask ourselves how we can make our cities, buildings, interiors, and objects serve the multisensory creatures that we are. And let's begin by smelling the lavender, even if it comes in a homemade bag.

Sandy Hits Home

As Hurricane Sandy bears down on Manhattan, my tiny downtown loft goes dark and silent. The small points of light from the microwave, the modem, the TV, the laptop, the radio, and the cell phone have gone out; the fridge's hum is stilled. The candles, already flaming in front of the cupboard, are my only source of light. I look toward a neighboring building with unshaded windows that usually glow with their reassuring light and visible human activity; it, too, is dark under a strange, gray-lit sky.

The hundreds of books and CDs that line my shelves are of no use now. I cannot read E. O. Wilson by the flickering flames, watch Bette Davis, or listen to Rod Stewart. I've been transported to a preindustrial century, without the necessary survival skills. The only tool I have is my giant flashlight; it will be my steady companion for the next five days. It lights my way as I head to the front door. The hallway is pitch black and eerily quiet.

But I'm prepared: water in pitchers, cooked meals still cooling in the fridge, canned foods in the cupboard, a small transistor radio at the ready. I dial up the public radio station and follow a steady stream of storm information, trivia, and commentary. The utter peacefulness inside, as the winds tear at my windows and the rain pelts them with frightful force, induces the kind of deep sleep I haven't experienced for years. When daylight comes, it has a faint glow and the wind and rain seem less threatening.

I go about life in my tiny universe. By the third day of this making do, frustrated by information I cannot use—the radio repeatedly details Web sites to check and phone numbers to call—I venture down the dark staircase and walk uptown, where I hear there is power. Sure enough, my phone starts working around Twenty-third Street where the *Metropolis* offices are locked up, just like every other business in the neighborhood. A friend on the Upper East Side, grateful to hear I'm not dead, invites me to use her shower and share some hot food. I walk as far as my legs will carry me, then I find a cab. There are no buses or subways.

Each day, I return home to listen to Governor Cuomo, Senator Schumer, and Mayor Bloomberg talk about the need to update and redesign our systems. Smart grids, defensive buildings, and district energy become part of the daily chatter. Someone mentions that New York University, the campus that's just a block away from where I sit in the dark, has had district energy since 2010. What kept the lights burning and hot water flowing in many of its buildings is a cogeneration plant under Mercer Street, just a few steps away from me. This neighborhood power and water plant will surely be studied as the city makes its plans to enter the twenty-first century.

While the massive redesign of the built environment will need to enlist some brilliant, collaborative design thinkers, I wonder how we can redesign our connectivity to each other. This basic human need becomes clear as the outcry of abandonment is heard from New York's devastated neighborhoods that had no way to dial in, turn on, or tune in. Going forward, we'll need to figure out how to connect to each other when none of our sexy electronic devices work. Or even when they do.

Role Model: Ada Louise Huxtable

I don't remember the date or the award Ada Louise Huxtable received on "Notes from Metropolis," February 2013 that soft spring evening. I do recall that we were gathered in the wood-paneled living room of a brownstone on New York City's Fifth Avenue, where I said to the person about to introduce the legendary architecture critic of the *New York Times*: "I want to be Ada Louise Huxtable." This was wishful thinking on my part. Nobody could be Ada Louise Huxtable: not in her long and productive lifetime, nor after her death.

At the time, I was a young design editor in search of a role model. Naturally, I became an avid reader of her columns. Powerfully argued, fearlessly precise, and surprisingly humorous, her writings had the kind of intelligent humanity that began to appeal to me when I reached the age of reason. So I eagerly absorbed her passionate yet coolheaded arguments for excellence, her ability to connect architecture to the urban form and the politics that shaped both, and her admiration for the most excellent modern buildings (even as she condemned the mediocre facsimiles that grew to dominate our cities). Contrary to the modernist dogma hovering over the land during her tenure at the *Times* in the 1960s and 1970s, the Pulitzer Prize–winning critic had the courage to break ranks and admire historic buildings. She understood the necessity of preserving the best designs of bygone times.

It seemed right, then, that we were gathered that day at the Salmagundi Club. One of the oldest art organizations in the United States, it was founded in 1871 as a place to teach, exhibit, and auction art. With its membership roster reading like the story of excellence in nineteenth-century New York City—Louis Comfort Tiffany and Childe Hassam among them—and its landmark status, the old house itself was celebrating the woman who was a catalyst behind the city's preservation laws. As she waited patiently for the awkward ceremonies to start, the elegant, trim, small woman with big hair did not look like the most powerful voice in architecture. Her soft speech and seemingly shy demeanor seemed to be in contradiction with her public image. But she was much more than she appeared at that moment. Her skillful critiques of our built world have been making me think for decades. And now that she's gone, I still keep her books near. I met Ada Louise Huxtable that day only to be introduced as the young woman who wanted to be her. I still do.

Personality Test

Each time I visit a global metropolis, I take a rather unscientific survey: Is this city humane or inhumane? Soulful or soul-sapping? Textured or bland? Then I go on to ask: Do I feel secure here? Is the rhythm of movement pleasingly brisk? Does the city connect to the chunk of earth it occupies?

"Notes from Metropolis," March 2013

My hometown of New York City (population 8,244,910) is made up of a peninsula and islands, one slim with a disciplined grid and a grand park in the middle. From my historically textured downtown neighborhood, I can walk to the newly revived waterfront or sit in a park and listen to impromptu musical performances. Humane, soulful, textured: this fast-paced city began as a financial deal and grew up with this ethos of trade.

Before a recent visit to São Paulo, the financial center of Brazil, I studied photos of its array of modern high-rises; thousands of them crowd the skyline of this city of 11,244,367. Though I felt a wave of alienation, I was determined to come face-to-face with the architecture of Oscar Niemeyer, Lina Bo Bardi, and Ruy Ohtake.

For years, I had marveled at Niemeyer's 38-story condo, the Copan, with its dramatic, undulating facade. But when I entered the massive concrete building's ground floor, I found a dank interior with questionable detailing, cluttered with cut-rate businesses, reaffirming my long-held belief that a city can be truly experienced only on its streets and inside its buildings. Starchitecture has nothing to do with effective place-making.

When I walked the wealthy Jardins District, with its purveyors of high-end brands and eateries, I noticed men wearing white shirts and black suits, cleaving close to the fancy addresses fronted by double gates, creating wrought-iron cages—presumably to capture thieves. (The Los Angeles Times reported that more than 4,100 people were killed in São Paulo in 2012.)

As I watched the well-dressed with their branded shopping bags being buzzed into their safe havens, I wondered if they indeed felt secure, if their security men in black really did deter the desperate poor from wresting some of that well-guarded wealth. Humane? A place that tolerates such dramatic income diversity cannot be humane. Soulful? A settlement carved out of the jungle by Portuguese, German, and Japanese immigrants and African slaves who, together, created distinct music and food is definitely soulful. But a chunk of São Paulo's soul is missing in its modernist buildings. Any city will become a fearful and bland habitation without the texture created by a diversity of people and a variety of architectural expressions.

Powers of Five

In 1972, Apollo 17 sent high-resolution images of the earth from space. These visuals of a fragile green, blue, and white sphere, uniquely designed for life to thrive, began to open up a new way of thinking.

We're all connected on this small and beautiful planet. We share one giant breath with each other as well as with other creatures that inhabit our ecosystems. We share the earth's resources, including clean air and water and materials of all kinds. We live in a global economy, where money and goods flow around the world, while many of our customs remain local.

All of this reminds me of the importance of Bucky Fuller's "systems thinking," a concept that considers our connectedness to natural systems, including the planet, our shared resources, and each other—people who were once out of sight and out of mind, but who now face us every night on the evening news or anytime on our iPhones, iPads, and other conveyors of instant information.

This view of the earth is also symbolic of our ever-growing technological sophistication. If it wasn't for our computing technology, programmed with a constantly evolving software system, this picture would not have been possible. Without the technology of high-resolution photography and massive computing power, we would still be guessing what space and the earth look like.

Now that it runs almost every transaction we make, nearly everything we touch, software— specially written code—is at the core of every design practice. Today, we talk about generative software, meaning that code is written to update itself constantly, making itself smarter, without any human interference along the way. This, of course, turns out to be a mixed blessing.

You know about cloud computing. "The cloud" simply gives us access to information from a network of remote servers; indeed, we have much more information than we could have imagined even a few years ago. Information anywhere, anytime—this development is changing everything from how we work, live, and play, to where we do all of these things.

As a result of this tech dominance, we have more questions than answers today. Technology has altered our interactions with one another, with data, with distant lands. What are the design responses to these changes?

Charles and Ray Eameses' 1977 film *Powers of Ten* gave me an idea. I came up with the Cycle of Responsibility—my own Powers of Five. Responsibility starts with yourself, then extends to your profession, your client, your community, your planet. Like Fuller's systems thinking, these five layers form a system, too. If you remove any of the layers, your

Excerpt, "Ethical Design: What Does It Look Like?" a continuing-education presentation delivered to the Orlando Chapter of the American Society of Interior Designers, part of the ASID Distinguished Speaker program, September 28, 2013 responsible behavior collapses. But when one layer supports another, and that one the next layer, and so on, then you have a system of human accountability that is broad and sustaining.

**"A design idea remains just that—
a thought, a dream, a projection—
until it materializes."
Susan S. Szenasy**

Biographical Notes

Susan S. Szenasy is deputy publisher/editor in chief of *Metropolis*, the award-winning New York City–based magazine of architecture and design. Since 1985, she has led the magazine in landmark design journalism, achieving international recognition. A respected authority on sustainability and design, she served two terms on the boards of the Council for Interior Design Accreditation and the Landscape Architecture Foundation, as well as on the FIT Interior Design board and the NYC Center for Architecture advisory board. She has received two IIDA Presidential Commendations, is an honorary member of the ASLA and AIA NYC, and the 2008 recipient of the ASID Patron's Prize and Presidential Commendation. Along with *Metropolis* magazine publisher Horace Havemeyer III, Szenasy received the 2007 Civitas August Heckscher Award for Community Service and Excellence. She holds an M.A. from Rutgers University and honorary doctorates from the Art Center College of Design, Kendall College of Art and Design, the New York School of Interior Design, and the Pacific Northwest College of Art.

Akiko Busch is the author of *Geography of Home, The Uncommon Life of Common Objects,* *Nine Ways to Cross a River,* and, most recently, *The Incidental Steward,* a collection of essays about citizen science and stewardship. She was a contributing editor at *Metropolis* magazine for 20 years, and has written about design, culture, and nature for numerous national magazines, newspapers, and exhibition catalogues. Her work has been recognized by grants from the Furthermore Foundation and the New York Foundation for the Arts. She is on the faculty of the MFA program in design criticism at the School of Visual Arts.

Ann S. Hudner is a strategist specializing in communications, cultural and community engagement, and media relations. For the past 30 years, she has been active in developing strategic platforms, collaborative initiatives and complex partnerships working with artists, designers, socially progressive businesses, nonprofits, institutions of higher education, and the media. She led the external relations department at Rhode Island School of Design for 13 years and served as the vice president for communications and public programs at Pacific Northwest College of Art. She is the principal of Hudner Strategies and serves on the board of Design Museum Boston.

Angela Riechers is an award-winning art director and writer whose work focuses on design and visual culture. She is a recipient of an AOL Artists 25 for 25 grant for Sites of Memory, a map-based digital memorial project. Her design work includes *Harper's* magazine and iPad apps for *O, the Oprah Magazine*, and she has written for such publications and organizations as *Print, Wallpaper, Metropolis* magazine, *Design Observer, GRID, AIGA*, the *Atlantic, Architect's Newspaper*, and the Cooper-Hewitt, National Design Museum. She is a lecturer in the School of Visual Arts design criticism program.

Sam Aquillano is co-founder and executive director of Design Museum Boston. An industrial designer by training, he teaches design and entrepreneurship at Babson College, one of the world's top-ranked business schools.

Ralph Caplan is a writer and communications design consultant. His books include *By Design, Cracking the Whip, The Design of Herman Miller*, and *Say Yes!* He is on the design criticism faculty of the School of Visual Arts and has been writer-in-residence at the Haystack School of Crafts. An AIGA Medalist, Caplan also received the 2010 Design Mind award from the Cooper-Hewitt, National Design Museum.

Beth Dickstein is the founder of bde, a public relations and marketing firm in New York City, and a lifelong friend of Susan Szenasy.

Niels Diffrient was an industrial designer for more than 50 years. He launched his own practice in 1980, having worked for 25 years with Henry Dreyfuss. His explorations of human factors and ergonomics helped reconfigure the workplace, most notably with the Freedom and Liberty chairs, manufactured by Humanscale. He acquired nearly 50 patents in furniture design and received dozens of awards, including the Chrysler Award for Innovation, a Cooper-Hewitt National Design Award, and the Legend Award from *Contract* magazine. Niels died in 2013.

Anna Dyson is the director of the Center for Architecture, Science, and Ecology at Rensselaer Polytechnic Institute, and a professor of design, technology, and theory. Her collaborative work brings together researchers from the sciences, arts, architecture, and engineering. She is a co-founder of Materialab, an interdisciplinary research group at RPI that integrates advances within the arts and sciences to develop new ways to reinvent the built environment.

Jean Gardner is an activist, writer, teacher, and consultant on sustainable and resilient design issues. She is an associate professor of social-ecological history and design in the School for Constructed Environments at Parsons The New School for Design. Jean is the author of *Urban Wilderness: Nature in New York City*, and, with Brian McGrath, *Cinemetrics: Architecture Drawing Today*.

Kira Gould is the co-author of *Women in Green: Voices of Sustainable Design* and director of communications for architect William McDonough. A former managing editor at *Metropolis* magazine, she currently writes about sustainability and design for a number of publications. She served as chair of the American Institute of Architects National Committee on the Environment.

John Hockenberry, journalist and author, is a four-time Emmy Award winner and three-time Peabody Award winner. He has written for publications including the *New York Times*, the *Washington Post*, the *New Yorker*, and *Wired*. Since 2008, he has been host of *The Takeaway*, a morning news program co-produced by PRI and WNYC Radio. His books include *Moving Violations: War Zones, Wheelchairs, and Declarations of Independence* and *A River Out of Eden*.

Karrie Jacobs is a contributing editor for *Metropolis* magazine, for which she has written since 1987. She is the founding editor in chief of *Dwell* magazine, the founding executive editor of *Colors,* and the author of *The Perfect $100,000 House.* She is on the faculty of the School of Visual Arts master's program in design criticism.

Hilary Jay is the first director of Philadelphia's Center for Architecture. In 2005, she co-founded DesignPhiladelphia, an annual citywide festival of design exhibitions, lectures, workshops, and tours. Previously, she was director of the Design Center at Philadelphia University, where she created nationally acclaimed exhibitions and programs championing multiple design disciplines.

Jack Lenor Larsen is a textile designer, author, and collector who is celebrated as one of the world's foremost advocates of traditional and contemporary crafts. He founded his eponymous firm in 1952 and since then it has grown into a dominant resource for signature fabrics. Recognized worldwide as an innovator, Larsen has won numerous awards and is one of four Americans to be honored with an exhibition in the Palais du Louvre. LongHouse, his home in East Hampton, New York, was inspired by the Japanese shrine at Ise and built as a case study to exemplify a creative approach to contemporary life.

Kate Lydon is an architectural designer at IDEO and a partner in Civil Twilight, a design-build studio focused on sustainable design. She received the *Metropolis* Next Generation Award for her lunar resonant streetlights and was included in the *Metropolis* film *Brilliant Simplicity* and in the 2010 *ID Design Annual* for her origami-fold Oru Kayak.

Susan Lyons is the president of Designtex, a design company that develops textiles and materials for the built environment. Previously, she was the creative director for materials for Herman Miller. A pioneer in sustainable-product development, Lyons sits on the board of the Green Blue Institute.

Roger Mandle was president of Rhode Island School of Design for more than 15 years. He has served as senior advisor to the chair of the board of the Qatar Museums Authority and was executive director and chief museum officer for the QMA. He was deputy director of the National Gallery of Art and director of the Toledo Museum of Art. He currently advises universities and museums around the world on issues of sustainability, institutional design, and not-for-profit leadership.

Edward Mazria is an internationally recognized architect and educator. He founded Architecture 2030, a research organization focused on protecting our global environment. His numerous publications include the influential *Passive Solar Energy Book*. He speaks internationally about climate change and architecture and serves as a senior analyst for the Southwest Climate Council. Mazria has been honored with awards from the American Institute of Architects, the American Planning Association, the Department of Energy, and the National Wildlife Federation.

Patricia Moore is an internationally renowned gerontologist and designer, and a leading authority on consumer lifespan behaviors and requirements. She was named by *ID* magazine as one of the world's 40 Most Socially Conscious Designers and ABC World News featured her as one of 50 Americans Defining the New Millennium. Syracuse University awarded Moore an honorary doctorate in 2012 for serving as a "guiding force for a more humane and livable world, blazing a path for inclusiveness, as a true leader in the movement of Universal Design."

Michael Murphy is CEO and co-founder, with Alan Ricks, of MASS Design Group. He has taught design for infection control at Harvard University's School of Public Health and serves on the Clinton Global Initiative Annual Meeting Advisory Board. In 2012, *Contract* magazine named MASS Designer of the Year and the Curry Stone Foundation awarded the firm its Design Prize. MASS was chosen as one of the Architectural League of New York's Emerging Voices in 2013, and its Umubano School project was recently shortlisted for the Aga Khan Award for Architecture.

Liz Ogbu is a designer who focuses on sustainability and spatial innovation in challenged urban environments. She runs her own multidisciplinary consulting practice and is on the faculty at California College of the Arts, UC-Berkeley, and Stanford University's d.school. Previously, Liz was on the staff at Public Architecture

and was a Global Fellow at IDEO.org. She is also a Senior Fellow of the Design Futures Council.

Sylvia Plachy is an internationally recognized photojournalist. Her books include *Unguided Tour*, which won the International Center for Photography's Infinity Award as best publication in 1990, and *Signs & Relics*, a collection of her photo-essays published in *Metropolis* magazine. She teaches, lectures, and has had many exhibitions. Her honors include a Guggenheim Fellowship and the Dr. Erich Salomon Prize from the German Society for Photography for lifetime achievement.

Emily Pilloton is founder and executive director of Project H Design, which teaches design, applied arts and sciences, and vocational building skills to enable young people to make long-lasting change in their lives and their communities. Trained in architecture at UC-Berkeley and product design at the School of the Art Institute of Chicago, she believes design is an honest process of building and activism for community benefit.

Von Robinson is a principal designer at Steelcase. He lectures at design conferences and schools and has written about design for a number of magazines. He created the course Poetics of Design for Parsons The New School for Design, in New York City. His furniture has been produced by Philippe Starck and Teruo Kurosaki, and was featured in an exhibition with the work of Marc Newson and Karim Rashid during Tokyo Designers Week.

Bill Valentine is chairman emeritus at HOK, the global design, architecture, engineering, and planning firm where he worked for 50 years. As a sustainable design pioneer, Valentine led HOK's adoption of sustainability as a core value in the 1990s. He served as the firm's president from 2000 to 2007 and its chairman from 2007 to 2012. He is a Fellow of the American Institute of Architects.

Beverly Willis is an architect, artist, author, social activist, and philanthropist, and a founding trustee of the National Building Museum. Now retired, she was principal of her architecture firm, Willis and Associates. Her best-known project is the San Francisco Ballet Building in the City Civic Center. She has received numerous design awards, including an AIA Award of Merit, and her work has been exhibited at the Cooper-Hewitt, National Design Museum. She is president of the Beverly Willis Architecture Foundation, which promotes equality for women in the building industry.

Index

Energy Analysis

Every effort was made to produce this book sustainably. The trim size was chosen to minimize waste; the paper—13,550 lbs. of Cascades Rolland Enviro 100 Print—is made from 100% post-consumer waste fiber; and the book was manufactured by Oliver Printing, which is leading the way in integrating sustainable practices into its production processes as well as its daily operations. And by printing in the U.S.A., fuel consumed in shipping was reduced. Compared to paper made with 100% virgin fiber, just the paper alone saved:

115 trees,
an area nearly equal to
8 tennis courts

37,346 lbs. of CO_2,
the emissions that 6 compact cars produce in 1 year

111,106 gallons of water,
the amount that 1 American uses in 1,207 days

96 MMBTU,
enough to power 467,393 60-watt bulbs for 1 hour

11,367 lbs. of waste,
enough to fill 119 ½ 95-gallon containers

48 lbs. of NO_x,
the emissions that 1 18-wheel truck produces in 67 days

For further information on the sources for these statistics, see
http://www.cascades.com/en/sustainable-development/commitment/environmental-calculator.

Project director: Diana Murphy
Design and production: Paula Scher and Jeff Close, Pentagram
Editor: Anne Thompson
Separations and printing: Oliver Printing Co., Twinsburg, Ohio, U.S.A

Typeset in a custom version of Futura and printed on Cascades Rolland Enviro 100

Metropolis Books
ARTBOOK | D.A.P.
155 Sixth Avenue, 2nd floor
New York, N.Y. 10013
tel 212 627 1999
fax 212 627 9484
www.artbook.com
www.metropolisbooks.com